OCR HISTORY A

The USA and the Cold War in Asia 1945–75

Sheila Randall | Series Editors: Nick Fellows and Mike Wells

www.heinemann.co.uk
✓ Free online support
✓ Useful weblinks
✓ 24 hour online ordering

0845 630 33 33

Heinemann

Part of Pearson

Heinemann is an imprint of Pearson Education Limited, a company incorporated in England and Wales, having its registered office at Edinburgh Gate, Harlow, Essex, CM20 2JE. Registered company number: 872828

www.heinemann.co.uk

Heinemann is a registered trademark of Pearson Education Limited

Text © Sheila Randall, 2010

First published 2010

13

10 9 8 7 6 5 4 3 2

British Library Cataloguing in Publication Data is available from the Britsh Library on request

ISBN 978-0435312 305

Copyright notice

Designed by Pearson
Typeset by Jerry Udall
Original illustrations © Tek-Art, Crawley Down, West Sussex.
Cover design by Bigtop Design Ltd
Picture research by Kath Kollberg
Cover photo: 1950s propaganda poster: Support the Resistance to the USA With All Your Strength and Aid the Volunteer Army (in Korea) © The Bridgeman Art Library/The Chambers Gallery, London
Printed and bound by CPI Group (UK) Ltd, Croydon, CR0 4YY

Acknowledgements

The author and publisher would like to thank the following for permission to reproduce photographs/written sources:

Photos and Images

Figure 1.2: National Archive; Figure 1.3: Alamy/INTERFOTO; Page 24, Figures 4.6, 5.5: Corbis/Bateman; Figures 2.2, 2.4, 2.6, 3.5, 3.11, 4.7, 5.3, 5.6, Page 119: University of Kent Cartoons; Figure 2.3, Page 146: Getty/Time Life Images; Figure 2.5: Topfoto/Roger-Viollet; Page 46, Figures 4.5, 5.2: AP/Empics; Figures 3.1, 3.8: Alamy/North Korea Picture Library; Figures 3.6, 3.9, 4.2, page 152: Corbis; Figure 3.7: Collection International Institute of Social History, Amsterdam; Figure 4.4: Getty; Page 125: Tribune Media Services/David Horsey; Figure 5.7: The Buffalo News/Bruce McKinley Shanks.

Written sources

p8, p10 Source A, p13 *The USA and the Cold War, 1945–63*, O Edwards, Hodder & Stoughton; p16, p17 Source B, p25 Source C, p27 Source B, p28, p29, p45 Source A p71 Source A, p97 Source C, p129 Source B, p131 Source B, p138 Source B *Cold War: A History in Documents and Eyewitness Accounts* ed Hanhimaki & Westad, reproduced by permission of Oxford University Press; p17 Reproduced with permission of Curtis Brown Ltd, London on behalf of the Estate of Sir Winston Churchill. Text Copyright © The Estate of Sir Winston Churchill; p.22, p25 Source A *America's Strategy in Southeast Asia: From Cold War to Terror War*, J Tyner reproduced by permission of Rowman & Littlefield Publishers; p27 Source B *Japan in War and Peace*, J Dower reproduced by permission of Harper Collins Publishers Ltd; p.30 *New York Times*, p31, p32 Source B *Embracing Defeat: Japan in the Aftermath of World War II*, J W Dower (Allen Lane The Penguin Press, 1999) Copyright © John W Dower, 1999; p32 Source A *Dear General MacArthur: Letters from the Japanese during the American Occupation*, R Sodei, reproduced by permission of Rowman & Littlefield Publishers; p36 *General MacArthur: Speeches and Reports 1908–1964*, Edward T Imparato; p41, p43, p47 Source A *The Cold War: History at Source*, E G Rayner reproduced by permission of John Murray Publishers Ltd; p44 *The Age of McCarthyism*, ed Ellen Schrecker reproduced with permission of Palgrave Macmillan; p58 *The Coldest Winter: America and the Korean War*, D Halberstam, reproduced by permission of Pan Macmillan; p60 Source A, p61 Source B, p81 *The Korean War* by Sir M Hastings, reproduced by permission of Pan Macmillan; p61 Source C, p65 Source A, p68 Sources A–D, p75; p65 Source B, p71 Source C *Present at the Creation: My Years in the State Department*, D Acheson, copyright © 1969 by Dean Acheson used by permission of W W Norton & Company Inc.; p68 Source E *Khrushchev Remembers,*

Nikita Khrushchev / Edward Crankshaw, reprinted by permission of Andre Deutsch Publishers; p71 Source D used by permission of the author; p77 *Firefight at Yechon: Courage and Racism in the Korean War*, C M Bussey, reproduced by permission of Potomac Books, Inc.; p97 Sources A and B, p99 Sources A–D, p103 Source A, p103 Source E, p105 Source B, p111 Source A, p112 Source C–E, p116 Source B, p133 Source B, p143 Source B, C, p144, p149 Source B, p160 *The Vietnam War*, K Ruane, Manchester University Press; p110 Source B, *The Making of a Quagmire*, D Halberstam, published by Rowman and Littlefield Publishing Group; p111 Source B *Viet Cong the Organization & Techniques*, D Pike, reproduced by permission of MIT Press; p124 Source B *Mao: The Unknown Story*, J Chang, J Halliday, published by Jonathan Cape, reprinted by permission of Random House Group Ltd; p129 *It Doesn't Take a Hero*, General N Schwarzkopf, reprinted by permission of Bantam Dell Publishing Group; p130 Reprinted by arrangement with The Heirs to the Estate of Martin Luther King Jr., c/o Writers House as agent for the proprietor New York, NY, Copyright 1967 Dr Martin Luther King Jr; copyright renewed 1991 Coretta Scott King; p131 Source A *New York Times*; p142, p147 Source A, p156 *The Vietnam War*, M K Hall reprinted by permission of Pearson Educational Ltd; p143 Source A *The Bad War* ed K Willenson, reproduced with permission of Penguin Group (USA) Inc; p147 Source B Used by permission of the Landon Lectures at Kansas State University; p148 Source A bbc.co.uk/news; p150 *In Our Own Words: Extraordinary Speeches of the American Century*, A Carroll; p157 The Times, 24 January 1973, reproduced by permission of N.I. Syndications

Every effort has been made to contact copyright holders of material reproduced in this book. Any omissions will be rectified in subsequent printings if notice is given to the publishers.

Contents

How to use this book

Notes for teachers

This book, *The USA and the Cold War in Asia 1945–1975*, is designed to support OCR's History A specification. The chapters are closely linked to the Key Issues in Unit F964B, and focus on one type of historical skill required: Enquiries (Unit F964B).

Enquiries

The approach of this book is to analyse the evidence and interpretations of policies, strategies and events, integrating primary, and occasionally secondary, source material into the text to build up the skills of source analysis and evaluation to answer specific questions. Exercises will offer practice in linking and comparing the content and provenances of sources, grouping sources by view and treating them as a set for evaluation of an interpretation. Each chapter begins with key questions, which form the structure of the text, and ends with a final review of key issues covered. The final synthesis integrates sources and evidence to evaluate synoptic issues across the whole period.

Many of the sources have been abridged and adapted to make them more accessible to OCR students.

Exam support

There is detailed exam preparation and support in the *Exam Café* on pages 174–190.

Exam Café focuses on the type of questions assessed in the exam in Enquiries. It is divided into three areas:

- ■ **Relax and prepare** is an area for sharing revision tips.
- ■ **Refresh your memory** is an area for revising content.
- ■ **Get the result** includes exam advice, plus sample questions and student answers with examiner comments and tips on how to achieve a higher level answer.

The USA and the Cold War in Asia 1945–1975 has been written specifically to provide teachers and students with a taught course that exactly reflects the key issues and skills in the specification topics. Chapters 2–5 begin with key questions on a key issue which are then discussed in sequence, with supporting activities.

Additionally, chapters 1–5 include a timeline that gives an overview of the chapter's chronology and a review of skills learned appears at the end of each chapter.

Methods of assessment

F964B is a document studies (Enquiries) papers. Four or five unseen sources are set for each exercise. The question paper contains a two-part document study question for each study topic. Candidates answer one question from the study topic they have studied. Question (a) is worth 30 marks and question (b) is worth 70 marks. Each paper is 1.5 hours long and is 50% of the total AS GCE marks.

Notes for students

This book has been written to support you through the OCR A AS GCE History course. *The USA and the Cold War in Asia 1945–1975* will help you to understand the facts and concepts that underlie the topic you are studying. It can be used as a reference throughout your course. You should refer back to this book during your revision. The *Exam Café* section at the end of the book will be helpful as you prepare for your exam.

The book makes use of the following features:

Key questions: Each chapter opens with some key questions. The content of the chapter will help you to find answers to these.

Sources: We have included sources throughout the book to allow you to practise your historical skills. Note: the sources tend to be longer than they would be in the exam.

Activities: The activities have been designed to help you understand the specification content and develop your historical skills.

Information: You should be thinking like an historian throughout your history course. These highlight content to provide extra detail to the main questions in the chapter.

Biographies: Biographies provide useful background information about key people.

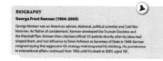

Case studies: Case studies are used to further illustrate the main questions. Most of the examples can be applied in some way to the topic you are studying for your AS exam.

Definitions: Definitions of new words can be found in the margin next to where the word appears in the text to help put the word in context.

Analysis: This is an analysis of the situation in each chapter. It stimulates ideas on how to approach lines of enquiry.

Stretch and challenge: These activities pull together the work done in each chapter giving you practice in the skills needed for your final exam.

Examiner's advice: These give advice on how to tackle the accompanying activities.

Exam support

In our unique *Exam Café* on pages 174–190 you'll find ideas to help you prepare for your exams. You can **Relax** because there's handy revision advice from fellow students, **Refresh your memory** with a checklist of the key issues you need to revise and **Get the result** through practising exam-style questions, accompanied by tips on getting the best grades.

Websites

There are links to relevant websites in this book. In order to ensure that the links are up to date, that the links work, and that the sites are not inadvertently linked to sites that could be considered offensive, we have made the links available on the Heinemann website at www.heinemann.co.uk/hotlinks. When you access the site, the express code is 2305P.

This book will examine the changing role, policies and strategies of the USA in the Cold War in **South-EastAsia**, and form judgements on its varying degrees of success. However, like any period in history, 1945–75 cannot be understood without establishing its background context (see the timeline, opposite). This introduction aims to establish that context, and show how two superpowers emerged from a wartime alliance to become Cold War enemies in Europe and Asia.

South-East Asia

A geographical region lying south of China, east of India and north of Australia along the volcanic rim of the Pacific Ocean. It includes the mainland countries of Cambodia, Laos, Thailand, Vietnam, Singapore, Burma and Malaysia, island arcs such as Indonesia, and offshore islands such as the Philippines. Some definitions include Taiwan to the north. The dominant religion of the area is Buddhism, followed by Islam, and Christianity.

Cold War

Where tensions do not result in fighting.

Hot war

Where tensions result in fighting.

Dollar imperialism

A term used by Soviet Foreign Minister Molotov to describe the Marshall Plan (see page 17), which he saw as the USA using economic aid to buy itself an empire or 'sphere of influence'.

Proxy wars

Where a client state fights a conventional war on behalf of a superpower.

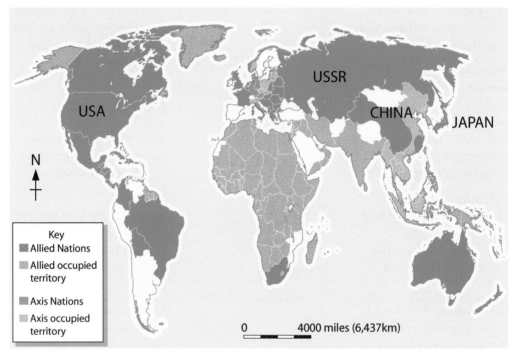

Key
- Allied Nations
- Allied occupied territory
- Axis Nations
- Axis occupied territory

0   4000 miles (6,437km)

Figure 1.1   The Grand Alliance of American, Russian and British Empire allies at the beginning of 1945. The Allied Nations had fought against Germany, Italy and Japan in the Second World War. This map shows the area of Asia still occupied by Japan (countries shaded orange in the east) and the area of Europe still occupied by Germany (countries shaded orange in Europe) on 1 January 1945.

What was the Cold War?

Cold War is the term used to describe the period of persistent hostility from 1945 to 1989 between the democratic powers of the West, dominated by the USA, and the Communist bloc of the East, dominated by the USSR. The American journalist Walter Lippmann popularised the term in 1947 to describe the head-to-head contest for global power between the United States and Soviet Russia. This hostility never resulted in open armed confrontation between them in a **hot war**, but was characterised by:

- propaganda
- **dollar imperialism**
- espionage
- the frightening spectre of nuclear obliteration of the world.

- a space race
- arms race
- **proxy wars**

Timeline 1945–1975

1945
6 August ———— USA dropped atom bombs on Hiroshima (6 August)
9 August and Nagasaki (9 August).
15 August ———— • Emperor Hirohito announced surrender of Japan.
• MacArthur became Supreme Commander of US occupation forces in Japan.

1946
February ———— Kennan's Long Telegram.
June ———— Civil war resumed in China.
1947
February ———— The Truman Doctrine
March ———— Churchill's 'Iron Curtain' speech
1948
August ———— Syngman Rhee elected President of the Republic of South Korea.
September ———— People's Democratic Republic of North Korea set up under Kim II Sung.
1949
August ———— USSR successfully tested its own atomic bomb.
October ———— • Communist Mao Zedong established the People's Republic of China.
• Truman administration announced a 'Defensive Perimeter Strategy'.
• Huk rebellion began in the Philippines (ended 1951).

1950
February ———— Mao signed treaty of friendship with Stalin.
June ———— Korean War began: Communist North invaded across the 38th parallel.
1951
September ———— Independence of Japan agreed by the *San Francisco Treaty*.
1953 ———— End of Korean War.
1954
May ———— • French defeated at the *Battle of Dien Bien Phu*.
• USA gave increasing amounts of aid to anti-communist South Vietnam.
July ———— Geneva Accords divided North and South Vietnam.

1963
November ———— Assassinations of Ngo Dinh Diem and John F. Kennedy.
1964 ———— Gulf of Tonkin Incident and resolution.
1965 ———— Johnson authorised operation *Rolling Thunder*.
1968 ———— Tet Offensive by North Vietnamese forces: 535,000 US troops in Vietnam.
1969 ———— Nixon secretly bombed Cambodia.
1970 ———— Large-scale anti-war protest in the USA.
1971 ———— Nixon bombed Hanoi and Haiphong.
1973 ———— *Paris Peace Accord* ended US involvement in the Vietnam War.
1975 ———— Vietnam united under a communist government.

Total war

Where countries fight until total victory is achieved.

Liberal democracy

Form of government where individual rights and free elections, freedom of the press and free speech are guaranteed by a constitution.

Free world

Countries which respect human rights and individual freedom.

Axis

The name given to the Second World War military alliance between Germany, Italy and Japan.

Superpower

A state which is an international leader with the ability to influence events in its own interests and project power on a worldwide scale to protect those interests; having a greater status than 'a great power'.

'Window on the west'

This phrase described the effect of the building of St. Petersburg by Tsar Peter the Great in 1712. It faced onto the Baltic Sea and gave Russia its first links to Europe, rather than just to Asia.

As a return to **total war** was unthinkable, the Cold War was sometimes characterised by limited, local wars, such as those in Korea and Vietnam (1950–53 and 1954–75). Some of these are termed proxy wars, where the client states of the USA or USSR fought a conventional war in their interests. National independence movements, such as those in Korea and Vietnam, were sometimes inspired or aided by a superpower. At times these were misunderstood as veiled imperialism by the USA or the USSR, who sometimes fought in them, or supplied resources, for political and economic reasons under a cloak of 'Cold War' ideology.

The fundamental basis of hostility was the political clash between Western **liberal democracy** on one side, and a Soviet one-party state that suppressed individual liberties on the other. The **free world** encouraged private ownership, free market capitalism and free speech, whereas the 'Communist bloc' imposed state ownership of property and censorship of the press in 'police states'. But Communism was also an attractive option for many people struggling in a post-colonial world. It offered welfare and security for all in a classless society.

Over the period that this book discusses, the Cold War in Asia was central to the American policy of Containment (see also pages 17–18).

What was the situation in 1945?

In April 1945, Hitler foresaw in his 'Testament' that when Germany was defeated:

> '...there will remain in the world only two great powers capable of confronting each other – the United States and Soviet Russia. The laws of history and geography will force these powers into a trial of strength, which may be military, economic or ideological.'

In August 1945, the world was dominated by these two rival superpowers. Nearly six years of total war had changed the world order, loosening the grip of the old European colonial powers on their empires and giving rise to new national movements. The **Axis** around which the world rotated at the outset of the Second World War, Berlin and Tokyo, had shifted to Washington and Moscow. It was a 'bi-polar' world, where governments and populations fell under one or other **superpower** influence and few were neutral. Decisions in the USA and USSR shaped the fate of countries struggling to recover from devastating warfare.

The superpowers

Superpower status arose partly from the size of a country's territory and population. By this time both the USA and USSR were modern powers, following the rapid and successful Soviet industrialisation under Stalin. America's fertile land and more clement climate gave it an advantage over the USSR, whose frozen wastes and vast swathes of unproductive land posed problems for food production, communications and resources. Both countries were made up of many different states and a varied ethnic mix of peoples, gathered together over centuries of expansion and conquest.

America had vast prairies, productive oilfields, modern industries and technology. Across the Atlantic was Britain, its original mother country and a dependant and dependable ally. Conquest of its untamed western states gave it a window on the Pacific. There it controlled Alaska, the Hawaiian Islands and the Philippines.

Russia covered a vast expanse of land stretching from the Pacific Ocean to the Baltic Sea, with borders touching countries from Mongolia to Poland. Its original peoples had moved westwards from Asia, and its old capital faced Europe through its '**window on the west**'. Russia's European and Asiatic lands gained some unity by the building of the Trans-Siberian railway to link the two continents. It touched the Baltic Sea in the West and the Pacific Ocean at Vladivostok, near the Korean border.

What were the origins of the Cold War?

Superpower status also arose from the strength of a political system. European democracies had long mistrusted the ambition of the all-powerful Russian Tsars (now comparable to the dictatorial role of the Communist Party Chairman, such as Stalin). The Bolshevik Revolution in 1917 intensified this mistrust. The Union of Soviet Socialist Republics (USSR), set up by Lenin, was based on a one-party communist system, censorship of the press and a state-controlled economy. This inherent threat to US capitalism, based as it was on liberty of speech, free enterprise and democratic elections, had bubbled into open conflict during the Russian Civil War in 1918–21. Lenin's desire for a worldwide communist revolution and his seizure of capitalist assets in Russia led some Western democrats (especially Churchill), ultimately unsuccessfully, to support the 'Whites' against the 'Reds' to try to destroy the USSR before it could be established. Therefore, relations between Russia and the West remained cool during the inter-war years.

At the outbreak of the Second World War, the USSR found itself allied to Nazi Germany in the Hitler–Stalin Pact. Ideological differences had prevented the possibility of an alliance with Britain and France, and Stalin blamed Chamberlain's weak appeasement policy for encouraging Hitler's aggression. To protect against Nazi ambitions for 'living space' in the east, Stalin had entered into a 'shotgun marriage' with Hitler. Both sought the opportunity to carve up Poland, though Stalin realised that it was merely a matter of time before this unlikely Fascist–Communist alliance would collapse. It did so in June 1941, with ***Operation Barbarossa*** which launched Hitler's invasion of the USSR. Stalin now needed a 'marriage of convenience' with anti-Nazi countries.

Attitudes which later held sway were forged at this time – in the early stages of the Second World War. The USA developed an enduring opinion of French weakness after France's shameful surrender and collaboration with the Nazis in 1940. This was to reap consequences later in Indochina. Britain became isolated in Europe, dependent on American Lend-Lease materials (see page 38). This stimulated the US economy, allowing it to prosper by producing war supplies, giving wealthy US industrialists an interest in foreign policy after years of **isolationism**. The USA began to frown on the British Empire as hypocritical in the light of British opposition to Nazism. US public opinion was shaped by propaganda, media interests and the views of prominent journalists. But the wartime Grand Alliance of the USA, USSR and Great Britain was not born until 1941 when the Japanese advanced through Asia and dominated the Pacific.

Operation Barbarossa

The name given to the Nazi invasion of the USSR in June 1941.

Isolationism

The foreign policy adopted by the Americans between 1919 and 1941, which isolated the USA from involvement in overseas affairs and stopped it from joining the League of Nations.

Stop this monster that stops at nothing... PRODUCE to the limit!

This is YOUR war!

Figure 1.2 US propaganda during the Second World War urging Americans to increase production to defeat the 'two-headed monster' of the Nazis and Japanese imperialists.

League of Nations

An international peace-keeping force set up at Versailles in 1919, after the First World War. It was led by Britain and France, who followed a policy of appeasement – i.e. giving in to an aggressor in the hope he would be satisfied and end further demands. The League failed to stop aggressors and keep world peace in the 1930s, as it had no backing from the USA, limited membership and no military capability.

Why did Japan and the USA enter the Second World War in 1941?

The USA had denied Japan trading areas in South-East Asia, driving it to expand and seize the raw materials it lacked. Under a military government with an authoritarian Emperor, Japan allied with Germany and Italy in the Anti-Comintern Pact of 1936. Japanese troops drove through Asia, sweeping aside the objections of a weak, appeasing **League of Nations** under French and British leadership. The USA reacted to the Japanese attack on Pearl Harbor in December 1941 by entering the war on the side of Britain.

US public opinion was softened towards the Soviet Communists, as they faced the 'two-headed' monster of Japanese and Nazi military tyranny represented in wartime propaganda (see Figure 1.2). On the other hand, the Russian was portrayed in the USA as a friend, and Stalin as 'Uncle Joe' (Source A). The administrations of Roosevelt and Truman maintained the Grand Alliance by conciliating Stalin when his demands clashed with their political principles. But their concessions were to sow the seeds of the Cold War.

Source

A After a visit to Russia in 1943, a team of US reporters wrote in an American magazine.

Like the USA, the USSR is a huge melting pot. It contains 175 nationalities speaking about 150 languages and dialects. ...The race of Great Russians brought all these people together. Three hundred years ago they crossed Siberia and reached the Pacific. They were one hell of a people long before the revolution. To a remarkable degree they look like Americans, dress like Americans and think like Americans. ...Today the USSR ranks among the top three or four nations in industrial power. It has improved health, built libraries, raised literacy to about 80 per cent of the population and trained one of the most formidable armies on earth. If the Soviet leaders tell us that control of information was necessary to get this job done, we can afford to take their word for it for the time being.

(See: www.heinemann.co.uk/hotlinks)

ACTIVITY

What can we learn from this source about US relations with the USSR during 1943?

Note: read the Analysis also.

ANALYSIS

These details of historical context might be used to explain why Americans were willing to overlook the negative actions of their Russian allies:

- The Russian victory at Stalingrad in 1943 was the first major turning point in the Second World War.

- The USA had followed a policy of isolationism between the wars.

- The American people were much less well-informed about international affairs or even real life in the Soviet Union than their counterparts in Europe. They relied on publications like *Life* magazine, which specialised in photojournalism, to give them an insight into other cultures. (*Life* sold 13.5 million copies at its peak. Truman, MacArthur and Churchill all serialised their memoirs in it.)

The State Department assumed that '*men everywhere are basically just like ourselves, with the same hopes and aspirations*'. Americans had enormous confidence in their country's values of private enterprise and liberal democracy as a basis for future world peace. However, despite Roosevelt covering up ideological differences, tensions within the Grand Alliance had already begun to show. Nowhere was this clearer than during the set up of the United Nations.

What were the aims of the United Nations organisation?

Churchill and Roosevelt founded the United Nations organisation by signing the *Atlantic Charter* in August 1941, laying out their goals for the post-war world. They agreed:

- not to expand their spheres of influence
- to uphold territorial boundaries
- to support the right of peoples to choose their own governments
- to restore self-government to countries which had lost this right
- to grant free access to raw materials and trade to all countries
- to seek economic collaboration between all countries
- to strive together for peace and freedom from fear and want
- to work towards disarmament.

The United Nations organisation was intended to be an effective peace-keeping power with military capability. By 1945, 50 members had signed the *United Nations Charter* formulated by representatives of the main Security Council:

- China;
- the USSR;
- Great Britain;
- the USA.

However, from the start, there was a contradiction between the idea of self-determination and the authoritarian one-party state created by Stalin inside the USSR. His repressive purges, forced requisitioning and destruction of the well-off peasant 'kulaks', were cloaked by communist propaganda and the cult of his personality. Stalin's Five Year Plans allowed the USSR to withstand the Nazi onslaught and win the 'Great Patriotic War'. However, this victory was at the cost of nearly 20 million Russian lives, as the USSR bore the brunt of fighting the Nazis in Europe until 1944. Tensions between the Allies increased as the USA and Britain delayed the opening of a second front, which Stalin sought in order to take pressure off the USSR.

As the Nazis retreated, Stalin's troops advanced through Eastern Europe, occupying the Baltic States, Poland, Hungary, Czechoslovakia, Eastern Germany and much of the Balkans.

Figure 1.3 Winston Churchill (left), US President Truman (centre), and Josef Stalin (right) shake hands at the Potsdam conference in 1945. The wartime conference decided the fates of liberated countries.

The Conferences at Yalta and Potsdam in 1945 gave the outward appearance of solidarity (Figure 1.3), but behind the scenes, enmities within the Grand Alliance were intensifying.

Stalin set up communist governments throughout Eastern Europe, in defiance of the Atlantic Charter. He prevented the Soviet 'buffer' of satellite states from accepting offers of US economic aid. The only communist government independent of Soviet domination was that of Marshall Tito in Yugoslavia. The defeat of their common enemy, Nazism, loosened the ties binding the Grand Alliance. In central Europe, American and Soviet troops faced each other along the line of furthest military advance. To obtain Soviet support in the war against Japan, the US recognised Mongolian independence, and Soviet interests in Mongolian railways and Port Arthur. This was done without consulting China.

Harry Hopkins, a close adviser of Roosevelt, who attended the Yalta conference was recorded to have said:

> 'I think we have the most important business in the world, to do everything within our diplomatic power to foster and encourage democratic government throughout the world. We should not be timid about blazoning to the world our desire for the right of all peoples to have genuine civil liberty. We believe our dynamic democracy is the best in the world.'

As early as September 1944, **George Kennan**, a leading US adviser in Moscow and critic of Stalin, had pointed out in a memo to Washington that the USSR was intending to establish spheres of influence in Eastern Europe and parts of Asia. He suggested a 'thorough-going exploration of Soviet intentions with regard to the future of the remainder of Europe'.

Containment

Containment was a US foreign policy which used military, economic and diplomatic strategies to contain any further spread of communism in the world after the Second World War, with the goal of enhancing America's security and influence abroad.

BIOGRAPHY

George Frost Kennan (1904–2005)

George Kennan was an American adviser, diplomat, political scientist and Cold War historian. As 'father of containment', Kennan developed the Truman Doctrine and the Marshall Plan. Kennan then criticised official US policies shortly after his ideas had shaped them, and lost influence to Dean Acheson as Secretary of State in 1949. Kennan resigned saying that aggressive US strategy misinterpreted his thinking. His prominence in international affairs continued from 1956 until his death in 2005, aged 101.

Kennan also advised the USA not to allow Soviet influence to go unchallenged. This was the basis of **containment** policy. His suggestion hardened State Department attitudes, sowing seeds of later 'Defensive Perimeter Strategy' (see pages 47–48). Washington ignored Kennan's comments at the time. The USSR saw the US advance in Europe and Asia as military imperialism.

Information box head

The Yalta conference took place in February 1945. The conference was attended by Joseph Stalin, Winston Churchill and Franklin Roosevelt. Its objective was to discuss the post war organisation of Europe and the Pacific War with Japan. Key agreements:

- Stalin would commit Russian troops to the Pacific War with Japan in return for influence in the Manchuria region
- Establishment of the United Nations
- Stalin agreed to free elections in Poland once the war in Europe was over

- Stalin secured an agreement that the Soviet/Polish border would be the Curzon Line and the Polish/German border would be the Oder-Neisse Line

Key to the negotiations was Stalin's agreement to enter the war against Japan. At the time Roosevelt and Churchill felt that victory in Japan was impossible without Soviet intervention. By the time of the Potsdam conference in July 1945 distrust between the US and USSR had grown. Britain and the US believed Stalin had broken his promise to hold free elections in Poland and had become increasingly concerned about Russia's occupation of Central and Eastern Europe.

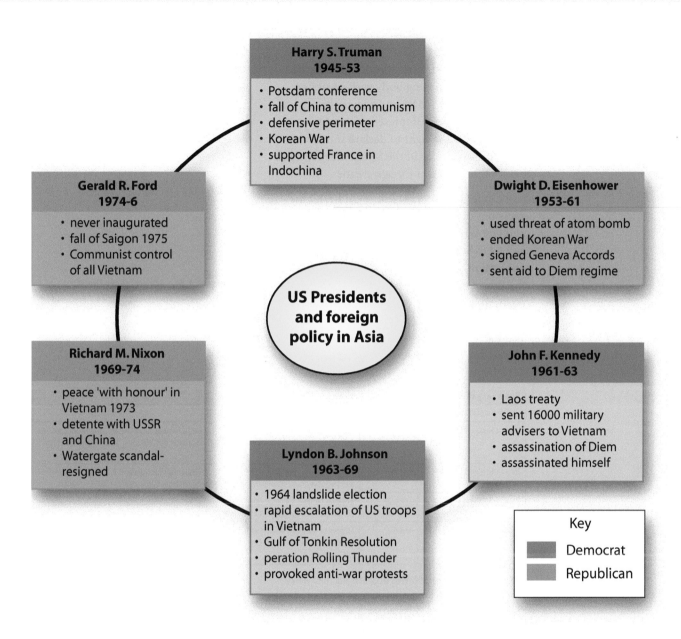

Figure 1.5 US presidents and their foreign policy in Asia 1945–74.

Where did the power lie in US foreign policy?

The American President chose a small group of trusted advisers to inform his decisions. The Secretary of State was particularly important as Head of the State Department, the equivalent of Britain's Foreign Office. The inner circle of advisers included: the Defense Secretary; the Director of Central Intelligence (Head of the CIA) and the leaders of the armed forces, known as the Joint Chiefs of Staff. Beyond these lay the outer ring consisting of: the State Department; the CIA (Central Intelligence Agency); the National Security Council and the Defense Department (see Figure 1.6).

The outer circle gathered information, gave advice and implemented decisions made by the inner circle.

What was the role of the US Congress?

Congress also had powers over foreign policy laid down in the US constitution. It was the American law-making body with an upper house called the Senate and a lower house called the House of Representatives. Only Congress had the right to declare war, and a two-thirds majority in the Senate was required before the signing of foreign treaties.

Sometimes a **Democrat** President found his decisions blocked by a **Republican** Congress and *vice versa* (see information opposite), so he had to be very persuasive to win over the opposition. The Senate also had to approve all the President's appointees to foreign policy posts. In practice, of course, the Supreme Commander of US armed forces in the field also had enormous day-to-day power, as MacArthur later showed.

Figure 1.6   Advisers to the President.

Secretary of State	President	Views
George Marshall 1947–49	Truman	Containment – Marshall Aid, Truman Doctrine
Dean Acheson 1949–53		Sought détente with USSR, designed NATO; saw loss of China as inevitable; McCarthyists claimed he was appeaser; Republicans called him to resign, became one of 'Wise Men' who supported Vietnam War then opposed it
John Foster Dulles 1953–59	Eisenhower	Supported French in Indochina; refused to shake Zhou Enlai's hand at Geneva, 1954, built up NATO and SEATO; very anti-communist; retaliation policy; brinkmanship; escalated Cold War tensions
Dean Rusk 1961–69	Kennedy Johnson	Began as cautious diplomat; didn't work well with Kennedy; advocated anti-communist military action; became strongly pro-Vietnam War and target of anti-War protests
William Rogers 1969–73 Henry Kissinger 1973–77	Nixon	Eclipsed by Kissinger; détente with USSR and China; SALT treaty; Vietnamisation, peace mediator; key role in secret bombing of Cambodia which brought Pol Pot to power; unpopular with anti-war left

Figure 1.7   Main **Secretaries of State** and their views

Secretary of Defense	President	Views
George Marshall 1950–51	Truman	Rearmed for the Korean War
Robert Lovett 1951–53		Rearmament; proposed reorganisation of National Security
Charles Wilson 1953–57	Eisenhower	Cut defense budget
Neil McElroy 1957–59		Prioritised space race over missiles
Thomas Gates 1959–61		U2 spy plane; NSTO; met with JCS; closed the 'missile gap'; massive retaliation policy
Robert McNamara 1961–68	Kennedy Johnson	Flexible response policy; limited non-nuclear war policy; Cuban Missile Crisis; Green Berets; counter insurgency; strategic bombing; MAD (Mutually Assured Destruction); escalation of US forces in Vietnam; resigned disillusioned
Clark Clifford 1968–69	Johnson	Vietnam self-determination; ended bombing; disagreed with escalation in Vietnam; SALT
Melvin Laird 1969–73	Nixon	De-centralised planning to JCS; cut conventional forces, nuclear priority; SALT treaty; Cambodia, Laos; Vietnamisation; disagreed on lengthy withdrawal from Vietnam; aided Paris agreement; suspended Draft; avoided Watergate scandal
James Schlesinger 1973–75		Prioritised conventional forces; partial counterforce policy – ICBM missiles

Figure 1.8   Main **Secretaries of Defense** and their views

The Democrat and Republican parties

The Democratic Party

- voters: Deep South, industrial cities of North-East (Catholics)
- supports a liberal and/or centre-left platform of equal opportunities
- favours farmers, labourers, labour unions, religious and ethnic minorities, especially Jews
- opposes unregulated business and finance
- favours progressive income taxes
- supports welfare spending programs targeted at the poor
- as a government should play a role in alleviating poverty and social injustice

- is internationalist (including interventionist) in its foreign policy.

The Republican Party

- voters: Southern conservatives and 'Bible belt' moderates in New England; typically White, families, Hispanic and Asian American
- is for a free market pro-business economy
- has a strong anti-communist stance
- is strong on national defence
- favours a non-interventionist foreign policy
- favours or promotes democratisation of foreign countries.

The need for re-election was also continually a factor. Stalin could not understand the influence of US public opinion on foreign policy, as in the USSR there was no such freedom of expression. The American media had considerable influence, especially journalists such as Walter Lippmann, who saw his job as 'intelligence work', and Walter Cronkite, who was CBS News 'anchor man' from 1950. Some American businessmen followed foreign affairs as they were keen to maintain overseas markets after wartime prosperity. However, many US immigrants remained isolationist and were happy to acquiesce to presidential decisions. Public opinion became much more influential in the 1960s.

Why is George Kennan known as the 'father of containment'?

In August 1945, the USA showed its devastating strength by dropping atomic bombs on the Japanese cities of Hiroshima and Nagasaki to end the war in the Far East. After the defeat of Germany and Japan in 1945, the USA stockpiled 50 atomic weapons. As the only nuclear power, its foreign policy was backed by the threat of strategic bombing of the USSR. This allowed conventional US armed forces to be gradually reduced to about one-tenth of their wartime level: from approximately 12 million in 1945 to a low of 1.4 million in 1947. This military downsizing alarmed George Kennan, the leader of the US mission in Moscow. A State Department request for routine research gave him the opportunity to investigate the whole basis of Soviet foreign policy. He sent his findings in an 8,000-word telegram.

George Kennan's 'Long Telegram', February 1946

Kennan suggested that Soviet leaders assumed:

- they were surrounded by capitalist enemies they would inevitably have to fight
- disagreements amongst these capitalist enemies could be exploited
- that to defend the USSR they had to fight 'a patient but deadly struggle for the total destruction of rivals'.

Kennan sowed seeds of anti-communism by the alarming tone of his telegram:

> *'The USSR is a political force with fanatical commitment to the belief that there can be no permanent coexistence with the United States. To secure Soviet power, Moscow feels it must disrupt the internal harmony of our society, destroy our traditional way of life and break the international authority of our state. This threat is undoubtedly the greatest challenge which we will ever have to face.'*

(see: www,heinemann.co.uk/hotlinks)

Kennan had not intended a provocative or forward anti-communist policy to be embarked upon and would have preferred Roosevelt's more conciliatory approach. He said that sections of his telegram were taken out of context, distancing himself from blame for escalating Cold War tensions.

Kennan's recommendations were to:

- focus US military strategies on just one threat: the USSR
- defend three areas: the Atlantic community; the Mediterranean; and the Western Pacific, including Japan and the Philippines
- restore economic health and political self-confidence to Britain, France, Germany and, later, Japan
- fill power vacuums in Germany and Japan for stability
- educate the American public in the realities of the situation
- act as chief defender of freedom, and present a positive, constructive picture of the world the USA would like to see.

The telegram had a great impact within the State Department. Kennan was recalled to Washington, and Truman gave him a major role in drawing up the Marshall Plan (see pages 17–18).

What was the effect of Churchill's 'Iron Curtain' speech?

In 1946, Churchill was no longer the British Prime Minister, but his 'Iron Curtain' speech in the presence of President Truman at Fulton, Missouri had a profound impact in turning US public opinion against the USSR. Churchill's sharp criticism of Soviet policy in Eastern Europe hit the headlines, exposing the Soviet threat to democracy, but his more subtle message was lost. Churchill hoped that the Anglo-American 'special relationship' might pave the way for world peace and strengthen Europe as a barrier against Soviet advance. He had also intended to emphasise the work of the United Nations organisation 'in fraternal association' as the basis for peace (Sources A and B opposite).

The Truman Doctrine

Economies throughout Europe were shattered by war, allowing communism to gain inroads in many countries. Marshal Tito had established communism in Yugoslavia; there was civil war in Greece and unrest in Turkey. When, in January 1947, Britain was forced to withdraw its military support for these countries for financial reasons, the USA had to step in to defend the area from communism. Harry S. Truman, then President of the United States, showed he was ready to send out a more confrontational message to the USSR. Congress agreed.

The Truman Doctrine is expressed in the President's address to Congress requesting support for a $25 million aid package for Greece. His messages about 'survival' and 'freedom' made it a landmark in Cold War history:

'At the present moment in world history nearly every nation must choose between alternative ways of life. One way of life is based on the will of the majority, and is marked by free institutions, representative government, free elections, guarantees of individual liberty, freedom of speech and religion, and freedom from political oppression. The second way of life is based upon the will of a minority forcibly imposed upon the majority. It relies on terror and oppression, a controlled press and radio, fixed elections, and the suppression of personal freedoms.

I believe that it must be the policy of the United States to support free peoples who are resisting attempted subjugation by armed minorities or by outside pressures. I believe that we must assist free peoples to work out their own destinies in their own way. I believe that our help should be mainly through economic and financial aid which is essential to economic stability and orderly political process.'

(from a speech by President Harry Truman, February 1947.)

ACTIVITY

What does a comparison of Sources A and B reveal about the origins of the Cold War?

Sources

A An extract from Churchill's 'Iron Curtain' speech given at Fulton, Missouri in the presence of President Truman, who was fully aware of its contents.

From Stettin in the Baltic to Trieste in the Adriatic, an iron curtain has descended across the Continent. Behind that line lie all the capitals of all the ancient states of Central and Eastern Europe. Warsaw, Berlin, Prague, Vienna, Budapest, Belgrade, Bucharest and Sofia, all these famous cities and the population around them lie in what I must call the Soviet sphere. All are subject to an increasing measure of control from Moscow. The Communist parties, which were previously very small, have been raised to power beyond their numbers and are seeking everywhere to obtain **totalitarian** control.

I do not believe that Soviet Russia desires war. What they desire is the fruits of war and the indefinite expansion of their power and doctrines. If the Western Democracies stand together in strict adherence to the principles of the United Nations Charter their influence in furthering freedom and democracy will be immense. If they become divided or falter in their duty, then indeed catastrophe may overwhelm us all.

From: Churchill's 'Iron Curtain' speech, 6 March 1946

B From an interview Stalin gave to a Soviet daily paper, in which he criticised the former British Prime Minister's tough reaction to events unfolding in Eastern Europe.

In substance, Mr Churchill now stands in the position of a firebrand of war. And Mr Churchill is not alone. He has friends not only in England but also in the USA. The Soviet Union has lost in men several times more than Britain and the United States together. It may be that some people are trying to wipe from our memory these sacrifices of the Soviet people, which ensured the liberation of Europe from Hitler's control. What can be surprising in the fact that the Soviet Union, in a desire to ensure its security for the future, tries to enable these countries to have governments loyal to the USSR? How can any reasonable person see these peaceful aspirations of the Soviet Union as 'expansionist tendencies' of our government? The influence of the Communists grew because they showed themselves to be reliable, daring and self-sacrificing fighters against fascist regimes for the liberty of the people.

Stalin, quoted in *Pravda*, 16 March 1946

Marshall Aid

The Marshall Plan was named after General George Marshall, who was entrusted with the task of overseeing the use of $400 million of economic aid to reconstruct Europe and make it prosperous in order to contain Soviet-inspired communist expansion. A similar approach was later adopted in South-East Asia.

Totalitarian

A political system through which the state regulates every aspect of public and private life.

Source

An eminent US Republican historian reflects on the thinking behind the Marshall Plan of June 1947. He is known for his right-wing view that Stalin's personality and strategies were the main reason for the Cold War.

Several premises shaped the Marshall Plan:

1. *that the gravest threat to western interests in Europe was not the prospect of Soviet military intervention, but rather the risk that hunger, poverty, and despair might cause Europeans to vote their own communists into office, who would then obediently serve Moscow's wishes*

2. *that American economic assistance would produce immediate psychological benefits and later material ones that would reverse this trend*

3. *that the Soviet Union would not itself accept this aid or allow its satellites to, thereby straining its relationship with them*

4. *that the United States could then seize both the geographical and the moral initiative in the emerging Cold War.*

Stalin fell into the trap laid for him, which was to get him to build the wall that would divide Europe.

John Lewis Gaddis, *The Cold War*, 2005

ACTIVITY

Use your own knowledge to assess how far the above Source supports the interpretation that the main aim of the Marshall Plan was to defend Europe against communism. (See Bibliography on this page for information on Stalin's other motives.)

Conclusion

The Truman Doctrine of 1947 expressed the change of US foreign policy to one of containment as a global ambition to support free peoples. But while America was distracted with the reconstruction of Europe and Japan, China successfully established a communist regime under Mao Zedong in 1949. Faced so soon with unexpected failures and domestic criticism, America became even more determined to actively prevent states falling to communism. With the post-war crisis of European empires in the Far East seeking independence, and the start of British decolonisation in India, it seemed that Asia was to be the new sphere of communist expansion.

Bibliography

Bell, P. M. H. (2005). *The World Since 1945: An International History*. London: Bloomsbury.

Edwards, O. (2002). *The USA and the Cold War, 1945–63 (Access to History)*. London: Hodder Education.

Gaddis, J. L. (2005). *The Cold War*. London: Penguin.

Gaddis, J. L. (1989). *The Long Peace: Inquiries into the History of the Cold War*. Oxford: OUP.

Gaddis, J. L. (1983). *Strategies of Containment: A Critical Appraisal of Postwar American National Security Policy*. New York: Oxford University Press.

Higgins, H. (1993). *The Cold War (Studies in Modern History)* 2nd ed. Oxford: Heinemann.

McCauley, M. (2008). *The Origins of the Cold War, 1941–1949*. Harlow: Longman.

Rayner, E. G. (1992). *The Cold War: History at Source*. London: Hodder Murray.

Sewell, M. (2002). *The Cold War (Cambridge Perspectives in History)*. Cambridge: Cambridge University Press.

Vadney, T. E. *The World Since 1945: A Complete History of Global Change from 1945 to the Present* 2nd ed. London: Penguin.

Websites

See www.heinemann.co.uk/hotlinks

In this chapter we will look at America's part in the reconstruction of Japan; US failure to prevent the 'fall' of China to communism in 1949 and the consequences of this failure. We will also explore US involvement in South Korea, the Defensive Perimeter Strategy and the effect of NSC 68 (a foreign policy document produced in 1950).

You will also have the chance to practise analysing and evaluating primary and secondary sources.

Key questions:

The main elements of the specification content dealt with in this chapter relate to the key issue of 'How successfully did the USA seek to contain communism in Asia?' Key questions for study include:

- How was the US policy of containment applied to Asia and where did this succeed and fail?
- What was the strategy of 'model states'?
- What part did America play in the reconstruction of Japan, 1945–51?
- Why did the USA fail to prevent a communist victory in China in 1949?
- What was the 'Defensive Perimeter Strategy' of 1949 and why did the USA adopt it?
- Why and how did the USA support South Korea, 1945–50?
- How far did NSC 68 represent a change or a continuity of policy?

Japanese expansion in Asia

European colonial powers such as the British, French and Dutch had established control of Asian markets over centuries, exploiting resources and dominating trade in the area. The Japanese, with limited resources of their own, had been squeezed out. So, while European powers were distracted by the outbreak of the Second World War, Japan took the opportunity to seize these markets. The attack on Pearl Harbor not only brought the USA into the Second World War, but it focused public opinion on trade in South-East Asia. Japan tried to create a 'Great East-Asia Co-Prosperity Sphere' by establishing a self-sufficient bloc of Asian countries under Japanese control, with economies free from Western influence. Though its purpose was to serve the interests of an aggressive Japanese empire, it was presented in propaganda as 'Asia for the Asians'.

At the height of Japan's expansion (see Figure 2.1), it dominated the Pacific. Korea, Manchuria, Inner Mongolia, Taiwan, French Indochina, Burma, Thailand, Malaya, Borneo, the Dutch East Indies, the Philippines and parts of China all came under its control.

Japan expelled the European imperial powers, such as Britain, France and the Dutch, from their colonies. Japanese subjects were treated brutally. When the war turned against Japan, its troops stripped these countries bare of resources, and left behind devastated economies and strong national feeling. Poverty and devastation made these countries vulnerable to communist expansion. The Japanese left behind a dangerous power vacuum.

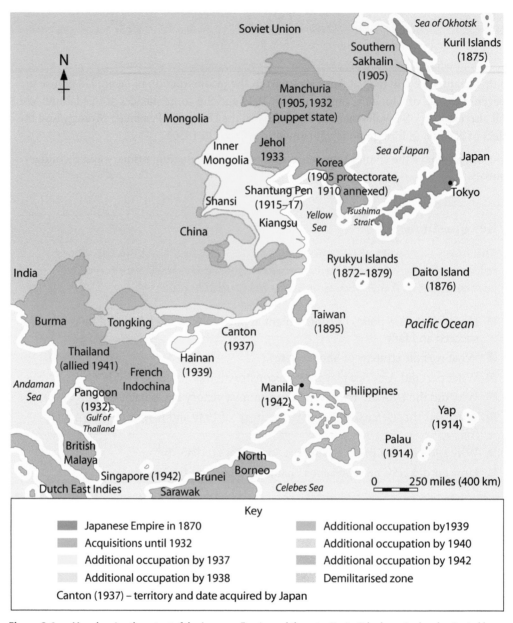

Figure 2.1 Map showing the extent of the Japanese Empire and those territories it had acquired or dominated by 1942.

America soon filled this vacuum by becoming the dominant power in the Pacific, with control over Japan. A wartime song entitled 'To Be Specific, It's Our Pacific' kept up morale amongst a confident American public, as US troops followed a policy of 'island-hopping', driving back Japanese forces with huge loss of life. The devastating impact of the atom bombs dropped on Hiroshima and Nagasaki in early August 1945 forced Japan to surrender unconditionally (see pages 27–28). This gave the USA a sense of invincibility as the only power with nuclear weapons.

Timeline 1945–1951

1945
6 August —————— USA dropped atom bombs on Hiroshima (6 August)
9 August and Nagasaki (9 August).
15 August —————— • Emperor Hirohito announced surrender of Japan.
• MacArthur became Supreme Commander of US occupation forces in Japan.

1946
February —————— Kennan's 'Long Telegram'.
April —————— War crimes trials began in Japan (until 1948).
June —————— Civil war resumed in China.
—————— *Bell Trade Act* gave USA preferential trade in the Philippines.

1947
February —————— The Truman Doctrine.
March —————— Churchill's 'Iron Curtain' speech.

1948
August —————— Syngman Rhee elected President of the Republic of South Korea.
September —————— People's Democratic Republic of North Korea set up under Kim Il Sung.

1949
August —————— USSR successfully tested its own atomic bomb.
October —————— • Communist Mao Zedong established the People's Republic of China.
• Truman administration announced a 'Defensive Perimeter Strategy'.
• Huk rebellion began in the Philippines (ended 1951).

1950
February —————— Mao signed treaty of friendship with Stalin.
April —————— NSC policy document recommending huge increase in military funding.
June —————— Korean War began.
1951
September —————— Independence of Japan agreed by the *San Francisco Treaty*.

How did the Truman administration apply containment policy to Asia and where did this succeed and fail?

A democratic Europe was the main priority of Truman, Marshall and Acheson. In Asia, American 'containment' was on a more limited scale between 1945 and 1950, as the USSR's power base was at a further distance geographically and its armed forces were concentrated on its satellite states in Eastern Europe.

The USA sought to establish close relations with Asia and to reconstruct Japan and the Philippines as model states, exemplifying the success of democracy. It intended to uphold capitalism and develop strong economies based on free trade in South-East Asia. Their prosperous economies would help spread the costs of defence.

There was always the danger of 'overstretch' of military resources, but the US monopoly of nuclear weaponry gave a feeling of superiority in the face of Soviet ambitions in China, Japan and Korea. The Truman Doctrine risked provoking military confrontation with the USSR along the **Pacific Rim** (see also pages 47–48 on the Defensive Perimeter Strategy), because of his confidence in US military superiority, and the need to protect American markets and the vital resources in South-East Asia.

The main US strategies were:

- to make Japan into a satellite of the USA
- to extend economic aid to anti-communist forces in China and Indochina
- to establish and defend a ring of offshore Pacific islands as a barrier to the advance of communism and its encroachment on South-East Asian trade
- to prop up non-communist South Korea, though it was of limited US interest.

Truman was prepared to accept the return of the old European imperial powers to South-East Asia to reinforce democracy; Britain and France could then share the costs of strengthening the regimes to deter others from wavering towards communism. Ironically, though it claimed to be anti-imperialist and supported self-determination for free peoples, the USA had ruled its own South-East Asian colony in the Philippines. After the Second World War the USA used its ex-colony of the Philippines to create a 'model state' – a prosperous, democratic, capitalist nation – to encourage other national movements to copy its example of freedom and prosperity, so containing the spread of communism in South-East Asia. George Kennan, in his 'Long Telegram' (see pages 15–16) had said 'world communism is like a malignant parasite that feeds on diseased tissue'. American aid would end poverty and halt its spread.

In Asia, containment policy followed similar lines to those adopted in Europe. Poor countries devastated by warfare and Japanese domination were given economic aid and a US military presence to help them stem the spread of Soviet-inspired communism. But in Asia, unlike Europe, many countries had been under Japanese domination for many years, and these were traditionally poor Third World countries, with no history of democracy or capitalism. Successive US administrations mistook Asian national movements for Soviet-inspired communism (see case study page 24).

What was the strategy of 'model states'?

One fundamental strategy used by successive US administrations was to attempt to create model states in Asia, to show that democracy and capitalism would bring economic prosperity, freedom and happiness. The USA felt that their political system was the best in the world, and that no country would choose communism when they saw the benefits democracy had brought to these model states. They began with their own ex-colony of the Philippines. This artificial imposition of western culture onto another country is an example of **cultural imperialism**.

Pre-1935 US colonial economic policy in the Philippines

American companies bought up vast areas of land in the Philippines to open up the trade of South-East Asia to America. The country became dependent on US markets to sell its goods, which included rice, tobacco, sugar, coconuts, timber, rubber and pineapples. US capitalist practices were patchy, but the Filipino landed classes prospered from a boom in rice and sugar prices. They realised their wealth depended on US support.

Pacific Rim

The islands around the rim of the Pacific Ocean, such as the Philippines, the Ryukus, the Kuril Islands and the Aleutians off the coast of Alaska.

Cultural imperialism

Refers to promoting or artificially imposing the culture of a large, economically or militarily powerful nation onto a smaller, less important one. In the Philippines and Japan, 'cultural imperialism' was an active, formal policy but the term may also refer to a general attitude. The term is usually used in a pejorative sense, usually alongside a call to reject foreign influence.

BIOGRAPHY

Manuel Roxas (1892–1948)

First president (1946–48) of the Republic of the Philippines. Roxas was a Catholic lawyer who began his political career in 1917. An advocate for Philippine independence from the USA, he was a member of the convention that drew up a constitution under the revised *Philippine Independence and Commonwealth Act* (Tydings-McDuffie Act; 1934). He collaborated with the pro-Japanese administration during the Second World War but was defended in post-war trials by General MacArthur. He became president of the Philippines when independence was achieved in 1946. Roxas managed to get rehabilitation funds from the USA but was forced to allow US military bases and to make other major concessions. His government was marred by corruption and police brutality, setting the stage for the Hukbalahap (Huk) Rebellion.

Manuel Roxas, first President of the Philippines making a speech, in 1946.

The Hukbalahap (or Huks)

A successful anti-Japanese guerrilla group during the Second World War. By the war's end they had seized most of the large estates, established a government, and were collecting taxes. The Huks rebelled after they were prevented from taking government seats to which they had been elected.

However, there was a widening gap between rich and poor, which led to peasant unrest, and an independence movement began to develop.

The Philippines national movement during the Second World War

In 1935, when the Philippines became semi-independent after nearly 40 years of American colonial rule, its President asked General Douglas MacArthur to set up a Philippines army with himself as Field Marshall. However, he badly underestimated the strength of the advancing Japanese, and was defeated in a bitter Philippines campaign in 1941–42. Japan seized the Philippines forcing both the President and MacArthur to leave. MacArthur was famously reported as saying 'I shall return', and was given command of US forces in Asia.

Japan established an authoritarian government in the Philippines, declared martial law and used the Filipino economy to support the needs of its advancing troops. Some Filipinos sided with the Japanese, but the **Huks** harassed Japanese forces, led guerrilla raids and assassinated collaborators. They carved out 'liberated zones' north of Manila, mobilising peasants to maintain the agricultural estates abandoned by landlords. The Huks also worked with the US forces against the Japanese, though on some occasions they clashed with US troops over scarce resources. Approximately one million Filipinos died in the four years of the Second World War.

The USA recognised the importance of the region to the stability of South-East Asia. It gave the Philippines independence on 4 July 1946, seeing the hypocrisy of keeping a colony in light of its anti-imperialist wartime policy against Germany and Japan.

ACTIVITY

Read the case study on the Philippines on page 24.

How well did the USA achieve their aims of:

- creating a model state of freedom and democracy

- a prosperous Filipino economy

- a market for US goods

- a source of raw materials for US military operations in the region

- a strong political ally in the front line of defence of South-East Asia?

Provide evidence for and/ or against each point in turn.

Case study

The Philippines as a model state

President Truman used Filipino independence as a means of ensuring US dominance in the Pacific and so strengthening the Pacific Rim Defensive Perimeter Strategy. However, he resisted any suggestion that the USA was in fact treating it as a colony, in case this provoked a revival of European imperialism. Instead, he emphasised two features of the newly-independent state:

■ its measures to prevent European dominance of its markets and materials

■ its democratic values of freedom and liberty.

It was intended to be a shining example of capitalist prosperity and democracy to encourage other states in the area to resist the spread of communism.

The Philippines economy

The economic aim was to reinstate US 'open door' free trade policy in the region, to make the former colony:

■ a market for US goods

■ a source of raw materials for US military operations in the region

■ a source of materials for a reconstructed Japan (see page 26–27)

■ a strong political ally in the front line of defence of South-East Asia.

$620 million of US investment was injected into the Filipino economy to defend it from the poverty which might allow it to fall to communism. Some of this was used to restore the infrastructure: hospitals, factories, roads, bridges and residential areas. $100 million was given as surplus military property, but most went to individuals to re-distribute land and wealth. In practice, the groups dominant in pre-war Philippines society were restored to their previous status.

The *Bell Trade Act* of 1946 protected American domestic producers with preferential trade concessions, while quotas were imposed on Filipino products competing with US ones. Filipino market places were flooded with cheap US goods. This was widely seen as unfair, but a Republican senator wrote,

'We have [our] interests to look after too. It is not that we do not desire to be helpful to the Philippine people. God knows, I would give them the shirt off my back, if I had another one to replace it. In other words, I would give them half. But we have certain obligations here and we can't let our hearts run away with us altogether.'

(Senator Harold Knutson, Senator of Minnesota, 1946.)

The imposition of democracy and the Huk rebellion

America's political intention was to establish democracy in the Philippines, and here it set a precedent by choosing a man rather than a national liberation movement – a flawed policy later followed in South Korea and South Vietnam. MacArthur's support helped **Manuel Roxas** win the first presidential election, even though he was unpopular as a double agent and collaborator during the War. The literate upper classes of Filipino society dominated the voting. In 1946, Roxas corruptly secured the passing of the US preferential trade agreement, the *Bell Trade Act*, by silencing its critics.

Strategically placed US military bases were justified as a 'stabilising' influence. Their purpose was to maintain the Philippines within the US sphere of influence and to support the reinstated Filipino elites. Yet State Department officials accepted that the Philippines faced no outside threat. Roxas set up a Philippines Military Police under the control of the US Army. It was full of opponents of the Huks, and unleashed brutal repression of their reformers and peasant supporters. The USA saw Huks as a threat to their plans, as they were known to be a popular guerrilla movement with political organisations in the villages. The powerful pre-war landlords were restored. In 1949–51 the Huks led an armed rebellion to gain political rights, improve working conditions and remove unfair US trade restrictions. American troops crushed the rebellion; they disarmed the Huks and imprisoned their leaders. Cold War rhetoric was used to brand them 'communist' or 'communist inspired', to justify US actions.

The policy of the 'model state' applied to the Philippines was a pattern to be followed later in South Korea, with very limited success, and South Vietnam, where the outcome proved a disaster for the USA.

ANALYSIS

Interpretations of US policy in the Philippines

Contradictions in US policy

- The Philippines would have independence, but also a role in launching attacks.

- The USA wished morally to support Asian nationalist movements but needed to use Asian economies to support the rebuilding of Europe.

- Philippine independence was under US economic and political control.

Criticisms of US policy

- The French copied this model in Laos and Cambodia with disastrous results.

- In Indonesia, the Dutch used it to hand power to Sukarno, an unpopular dictator.

- The USA was hypocritical: a neo-colonial power which preached anti-imperialism.

- A similar policy proved disastrous for the USA in South Korea and South Vietnam.

Sources

A **The US High Commissioner to the Philippines states American strategy there.**

A US presence in the islands is not merely for the protection of the Philippines, nor even for the defence of the United States. These bases are expected to be secondary, supporting installations for supply, repair and staging activities for all our armed forces in the Far East. Committed as we are to a long-time occupation of Japan, to a strong policy in Asia, the Philippines are designed to play a major role in US diplomacy in the Far East.

From a speech by Paul Mc Nutt, 1946

B **A group of leaders of the American armed forces advise the Truman administration on the importance of the Philippines to US foreign policy.**

The United States bases in the Philippines should be considered, not merely as outposts, but as springboards from which the United States armed forces may be protected.

From a report by the US Joint Chiefs of Staff

C **A modern US historian gives his view of US policy in the Philippines.**

American leaders were not blind to the fact that their Filipino protégés were usually undemocratic and often corrupt, sometimes embarrassingly so. But while Washington remained convinced that communism posed a grave threat to the security of Asia and the peace of the world, the United States was willing to overlook such defects.

From: H. W. Brands, *Bound to Empire: The United States and the Philippines*, 1992

ACTIVITY

Evaluate Sources A, B and C as evidence for US containment strategy in the Philippines and in Asia.

Stretch and challenge

What lessons might the USA have learned from the experience of creating a 'model state' in the Philippines?

First define what is meant by a 'model state'. Then consider:

■ attitudes towards landed elites and national movements
■ political problems in imposing democracy successfully from above
■ economic problems in creating a free market for trade in South-East Asia
■ military problems in defending the Philippines
■ the role played by MacArthur
■ the Philippines' role in US 'Defensive Perimeter Strategy'.

Judgement: Assess the effectiveness of the US policy of the 'model state'.

■ Organise your ideas into political, economic, social and military aims.
■ Draw up a list of facts relevant to these ideas.
■ Judge whether the policy was 'effective' or 'ineffective'.

What part did America play in the reconstruction of Japan, 1945–51?

Figure 2.2   A cartoon by David Low published on 28 August 1945 in the *Evening Standard*. The banner in the cartoon quoted Emperor Hirohito's speech accepting surrender, two weeks before, in which he stated that war had 'developed not necessarily to Japan's advantage'. It reads, 'Welcome to inhuman Americans who (by glorious efforts of undefeated imperial general staff) have agreed to postpone war which was developing not necessarily to Japan's advantage'.

Japan was the biggest test of the US policy of creating 'model' democratic, prosperous, capitalist states in Asia. At Potsdam, Truman described the Japanese as 'savages, ruthless, merciless and fanatic'. The Japanese feared the USA would adopt a severe line in reconstructing their devastated country. Yet, by 1951, the year in which a peace treaty finally ended the state of war between the USA and Japan, the 'savage' had been successfully turned into a democratic, business-orientated ally.

ACTIVITY

1   Explain the message of the cartoon entitled 'Tokyo Reception' (Figure 2.2).

2   Compare Sources A and B below as evidence for views on the Japanese situation towards the end of the Second World War.

■   How can you use their provenance (authorship; date; purpose; audience; nature and tone) to answer the question in the context of war events and propaganda?

■   How do their similarities and differences in content help you answer the question?

■   Supported by your answers to the questions above, which would you judge to be the more useful or reliable source in answering the question?

Sources

A In 1944, a secret US intelligence report to General MacArthur presented the former brutal Japanese enemy as weak.

In every sense of the word the Japanese are little people. Some observers claim there would have been no Pearl Harbor had the Japanese been three inches taller. Japan is a land of diminutive distances. Japanese houses are artistic but flimsy and cramped. The people, tiny in stature, seem to play at living. To a Westerner, they and their country possess the strange charm of toyland. Centuries of isolation have accentuated their restrictive outlook on life. Being little people, the Japanese dreamed of power and glory, but lacked a realistic concept of the material requirements for a successful world war. Moreover, they were totally unable to envisage the massive scale of operations in which the United States is now able to indulge.

B Emperor Hirohito's Declaration accepting the armistice, nine days after the dropping of the first atom bomb on Hiroshima, August 1945.

If we should continue to fight, it would not only result in an ultimate collapse and obliteration of the Japanese nation, but it would also lead to the extinction of human civilisation. We should atone ourselves before the hallowed spirits of our imperial ancestors. This is why we have ordered the acceptance of the provisions of the joint declaration of the powers. Let the entire nation continue as one family from generation to generation, ever firm in its faith that its divine land will never perish, and mindful of its heavy burden of responsibilities, and the long road before it. Unite your total strength to be devoted to the construction for the future. Cultivate the ways of rectitude, nobility of spirit, and work with resolution so that you may enhance the innate glory of the Imperial State and keep pace with the progress of the world.

To the Japanese, unconditional surrender was so dishonourable and shocking that they would prefer to face death rather than such shame. Yet the Emperor was forced to agree to unconditional surrender on 2 September 1945. US atomic bombings of Hiroshima and Nagasaki had caused the horrific deaths of 210,000 civilians from burns, radiation and related effects and there was therefore no other option.

Figure 2.3   Aerial view of Tokyo flattened by Allied bombing, 1945

How serious was the situation in Japan in 1945?

Japan was perhaps the prime target for the spread of communism in Asia because its post-war situation was very grave. The Emperor remained a symbol of continuity, but there was no political system and social ties had been broken. Japan had suffered widespread devastation and high casualties. Almost three million Japanese had been killed (3% of the 1939 population), including more than half a million civilians. The islands were already short of food before three million scattered troops began to be shipped home.

Economically, Japan had been one of the five powerhouses of global production and possessed a skilled workforce and industrial plant. Now there was low industrial and agricultural output, spiralling inflation, a black market and looting. The economy had been devastated. Just two million of Tokyo's seven million population remained in the city. Japan was potentially an obvious target for Soviet expansion.

There were large numbers of poor, homeless and hungry people, but orphans, widows and single women were particularly badly hit. Some women were recruited as prostitutes by Japanese officials offering them food and shelter. This became known as the Recruitment and Amusement Association (RAA) and was set up to save other Japanese females from rape by occupation forces, and so preserve the purity of the Japanese nation (see Source below).

ACTIVITY

Analyse the reasons why Japanese women swore the oath to the RAA.

Source

Some women swore this oath to serve their country by building good relations with the occupations forces, and keeping them contented to lower their potential aggression.

We have been pierced with grief and endless sorrow and are about to sink to the depths of perilous, boundless desperation. We have been assigned the dangerous task of comforting the occupation army as part of the urgent national measures for post-war management. The order is heavy and immense, and success will be extremely difficult. We unite to sacrifice ourselves, to defend the purity of our race. We are not compromising our integrity or selling our souls. We are paying an inescapable courtesy, to contribute to the security of our society. We are offering ourselves to defend our nation.

Most of these women were extremely naïve and thought their role honourable. One of many who committed suicide was a typist who had been expected to entertain as many as 60 American GIs in one day.

The US occupation of Japan under General MacArthur

The threat of confrontation made Stalin back down on his request to accept the surrender of Japanese forces in northern Japan. Truman firmly refused to divide Japan into multinational zones like those in Germany. Though a four-power allied Joint Council was set up, Stalin agreed that all decisions concerning Japan should be made by **General Douglas MacArthur**, Supreme Commander of the Allied Powers of occupation. Perhaps Stalin felt the USA might in turn accept Soviet control of Eastern Europe.

BIOGRAPHY

General Douglas MacArthur (1880–1964)

Douglas MacArthur became the US army's youngest general and Chief of Staff in 1930. In 1935 Roosevelt granted him $10 million to mobilise the Philippine Army to defend the Philippines. The day after Pearl Harbor, Japanese air strikes on the Philippines destroyed half MacArthur's air force. He was appointed Supreme Commander of the US forces in the Southwest Pacific Area, and developed his 'island hopping' tactics to defeat the Japanese, who surrendered to him in 1945. On the outbreak of the Korean War in 1950, MacArthur was appointed commander of the United Nations forces. Truman and Dean Acheson told MacArthur to limit the war to Korea. MacArthur disagreed and was removed from his command.

Truman kept the promise made to Stalin at Yalta and allowed Soviet occupation of the Kuril Islands. This caused bitter protests by Republicans in Congress. The American press believed the decision threatened the security of the USA and its future role in Japan. The US Ambassador to China, Patrick Hurley, resigned his post and accused the US State Department of being subverted by 'communists' and 'imperialists'.

ACTIVITY

Draw a mind map of MacArthur's objectives for Japan using the Source below.

Source

As the US forces move into Japan, MacArthur is issued with this directive from the Truman administration.

Your ultimate objectives are to:

- *ensure that Japan will never again be a threat to global peace and security*

- *bring about a peaceful and responsible government, which will respect the rights of other states and the principles of the United Nations Charter.*

Your means of achieving these objectives:

- *limit Japan's sovereignty to the islands of Honshu, Hokkaido, Kyushu, Shikoku*

- *completely disarm and demilitarise Japan*

- *encourage the Japanese people to desire individual liberties and respect for fundamental human rights, particularly freedom of religion, assembly, speech and the press.*

- *encourage the Japanese people to form democratic and representative organisations*

- *afford the Japanese the right to develop for themselves an economy which will meet their peacetime requirements.*

From: *US Post-surrender Directive on Japan*, August 1945

Which strategies guided US reconstruction of Japan?

US policy went through four stages.

Stage 1: 1945 punish and reform – remove Japan's military forces, introduce democracy.

Stage 2: 1947 'soft' Cold War policy – making Japan prosperous to keep it out of the Soviet sphere of influence

Stage 3: 1949 'hard' Cold War policy – an active role for Japan in the US containment policy.

Stage 4: 1951 'integrated' Cold War policy – when treaties recognised the official status of Japan at the centre of a US defensive strategy.

These treaties put a remilitarised and economically-strong Japan at the heart of a triangle of US South-East Asian bases and trading links. This stage was a response to the Korean War (see Chapter 3, page 51).

Stage 1: 1945 punish and reform – remove Japan's military forces, introduce democracy

During this period, US feelings of fear and hatred of the Japanese lingered, after horrific stories of torture and mistreatment of US prisoners of war. However, in the light of the UN emphasis on human rights, MacArthur adopted a cautious policy in punishing the previous regime. War crimes trials took place over a period of two years, from May 1946 to November 1948, being gradually phased out after 1947. The Japanese were surprisingly supportive of the trials. They agreed to co-operate as long as MacArthur kept his promise to exempt Emperor Hirohito from trial. He symbolised the independent survival of the Japanese nation; their main priority. Many defendants were found not guilty and some were granted immunity, including those who had taken part in bacteriological experiments. This was a far cry from the Nuremberg trials (see Source below).

Source

A 1997 Japanese lawsuit seeks compensation for Chinese victims of Japan's germ warfare.

Former members of Unit 731, which specialised in germ warfare, have been confessing crimes. Chinese researchers say they keep uncovering new sites where anthrax, typhoid, plague and other diseases were spread, wiping out perhaps hundreds of thousands of Chinese. Another 10,000 or more Chinese,

Russians and perhaps some American prisoners of war as well, researchers say, were killed in ghoulish experiments. Japanese officials insist they lack proof, although by other accounts they have sealed wartime archives returned to them by the American authorities in the 1950s.

From: Ralph Blumenthal, 'The World: Revisiting the Second World War Atrocities; Comparing the Unspeakable to the Unthinkable', *New York Times*, 7 March 1999

ACTIVITY

How useful is this Source as evidence for US weakness in imposing their policy of retribution?

How was Japan demilitarised and disarmed?

MacArthur ordered the dismantling of the Japanese army, destruction of its weapons and the exclusion of former military officers from leading political roles in the new government. Two hundred thousand alleged 'militarists' were purged from public life. Many rich landlords, who had supported war and aggressive expansion, now lost their power to tenant farmers.

In November 1945, MacArthur ordered a tax on Japanese wartime profits and ended the payment of compensation. His aim was to keep inflation in check and allow more control over the economy. These policies were openly opposed by the Finance Minister, Ishibashi Tanzan, former editor of a pacifist journal, *The Oriental Economist*. MacArthur extended the purges to those previously involved in media and local government and Ishibashi was forced to resign.

The repatriation of prisoners of war was in itself a success, though defeated veterans were unpopular and treated as outcasts (see Source below). Some had been indoctrinated by communist propaganda and felt bitter towards their officers and commanders. However, of the 400,000 Japanese prisoners thought to be still held by the USSR, by the end of 1949 only 94,000 had been located, while another 300,000 or so remained unaccounted for. Not until 40 years later did the USSR publish the names of 46,000 prisoners buried in Siberia. On the other hand, there was also bitterness among US prisoners of war, who claimed to have suffered torture and starvation at Japanese hands. This gave the occupation forces a very negative view of the Japanese.

Source

An anonymous letter from a Japanese ex-soldier, published in the *Asahi Shimbun*, a Japanese newspaper on 9 June 1946. It stated:

I returned to Japan from the southern regions on 20 May. My house was burned, my wife and children missing. What little money I had was quickly consumed by the high prices, and I *was a pitiful figure. Not a single person gave me a kind word. Instead, they cast hostile glances my way. Tormented and without work, I became possessed by a devil*.*

From an anonymous letter published in the *Asahi Shimbun* newspaper on 9 June 1946

* The 'devil' he referred to was the compulsion to turn to crime, and this man was typical of the many who became involved in robbery and murder.

SON OF HEAVEN LEADS WORLD TO DEMOCRACY! FACE! BANZAI!

Figure 2.4 A cartoon by David Low, published in the *Evening Standard*, 19 October 1945.

ACTIVITY

Analyse and discuss the message of the cartoon (Figure 2.4) as evidence for US democratisation of Japan.

How was Japan given democracy?

In 1946, MacArthur's officials drafted a new constitution, renouncing war. The Japanese were able to agree to it only because they had the protection of the US nuclear shield. This is what it stated:

'Aspiring sincerely to an international peace based on justice and order, the Japanese people forever renounce war as a sovereign right of the nation and the threat or use of force as a means of settling international disputes. To achieve this aim, there will never be any land, sea or air forces maintained. The right of the state to declare war will not be recognised.

(Japanese constitution. Article 93 November 1946.)

31

The new democratic Japanese constitution, which came into effect in 1947, imposed major changes from the previous rigid authoritarian system. It guaranteed basic freedoms and civil liberties:

- Political parties, including the Communists, were allowed to exist and political prisoners were released.
- Women were to gain equal rights, more equality than US women had.
- Noble status was abolished and Christianity was tolerated alongside Shinto, giving religious freedom.
- Emperor Hirohito was removed from politics to become a patriotic symbol of Japan.

However, MacArthur himself became the new 'god-like' figure for the Japanese. US analysts recognised that the Japanese culture had a tendency to worship those who had power and strength. This attitude was hardly a basis for democracy.

Sources

(A) An anonymous Japanese citizen gives his views on the plan for Japanese democracy

Your Excellency General MacArthur;

Having received Your Excellency's overall support, this progressive constitution clarifies Japan's future. The American form of democracy under the emperor system seems to me a Japanese-style democracy. I express my full support and the support of the Japanese people. This will mean an end to debates on the emperor system, the rejection of communism, and the importing of American-style democracy. This is natural, since the United States sacrificed the most during the war against Japan. The question of whether Japan should follow American or Soviet lines has been resolved. Japan will benefit from American culture in general and movies will likely be imported in large numbers.

From a letter to General MacArthur on 11 March 1946

(B) The organisers of the May Day left-wing rally express their gratitude to the Supreme Commander of the Allied Powers and the Allied Powers for their Japanese reconstruction policy.

We express our sincerest appreciation for the measures taken by the Allied Powers to liberate the people, grant freedom, and extend the rights to labour and agricultural groups. Inspired by this, we hope to:

- *uproot feudalistic and despotic oppression*
- *establish a popular government, based on the true will of the people never to break the peace of the world again*
- *achieve political, economic and social conditions which will not jeopardise the livelihood of the people*
- *and be recognised internationally as a peaceful and democratic nation.*

May Day Committee, letter, May 1946

ACTIVITY

Compare Sources A and B as evidence for the reasons why the Japanese people accepted US-imposed democracy.

Stage 2: 'soft' Cold war policy – making Japan prosperous to keep it out of the Soviet sphere of influence

The American guiding principle of Japanese economic reconstruction was to integrate Japan and South-East Asia into a 'great crescent' of anti-communist capitalist states to contain communism in the Far East. Japan was to be a shining example of the power of democracy and a free market. However, it seemed to some observers that the USA was dusting off Japan's plans for a **'co-prosperity sphere'**, which had brought defeat in the Second World War, and applying it themselves.

As in Europe, Americans worried about the attraction of communism to a defeated and demoralised people. Japan, with its large population, had depended on overseas imports of food and raw materials. In 1945, these had dried up and Japanese trade had collapsed. Until

1947 there was little improvement. Industrial production was low, exports weak and food costly due to shortages.

Prime Minister Shigeru Yoshida (see also page 35) saw the vital importance of economic development and was determined to retain Japan's national identity. At first the **Zaibatsu** remained in control of business. Japanese civil servants continued to plan the reconstruction of the economy. They advised producing high-grade machine tools and ultra short-wave communications as a priority.

What economic changes made Japan a fortress of capitalism during this stage?

In 1947, the Chairman of Chrysler and a group of American businessmen ended Zaibatsu privileges and helped set up a Japanese car industry. In 1949, Congress authorised $500 million per annum in aid to Japan, to allow the purchase of the foodstuffs and raw materials essential to Japanese economic growth.

Approximately 5.8 million acres, about 38 per cent of Japan's cultivated land, were purchased from the landlords under the government's reform program, and resold at extremely low prices to the farmers who worked them. By 1950, three million peasants had their own land, breaking the domination of landlords over centuries.

George Kennan suggested restoring the influence of former Japanese politicians and businessmen. The USA and Japan co-operated to build up foreign trade, excluding the communists from involvement in this. The Ministry of Trade and Industry built on previous successes, and the Americans fixed the exchange rate to boost exports. The Japanese economy began to prosper (see Table 2.1).

What was the social impact of US occupation?

The Japanese embraced defeat and welcomed change. They quickly recognised the superior strength of the USA and respected it. Most Japanese did not understand 'democracy' after centuries of repressive all-powerful regimes. They thought it meant 'freedom', and that was enthusiastically welcomed, far preferred to Soviet communism. Many young people became quite extreme in their political, social and sexual behaviour. They blatantly chewed gum as a sign of their freedom. Women happily gave up drab baggy trousers for US-style skirts, stockings and perms. Men wore brash American casuals. The Japanese became Westernised, but only superficially. At a fundamental level, the flood of letters to MacArthur (see Source A opposite) showed that they had exchanged one 'god', the Emperor, for their American 'god', MacArthur. Japan had not discovered the independent thought necessary to create its own democracy, though democracy did seem to have been successfully imposed on it. Some might argue, of course, that it is a contradiction of terms to suggest that democracy can be imposed from above.

Stage 3: 'hard' Cold War policy – an active role for Japan in the US containment policy

The CIA saw Japan's role as crucial for the Cold War balance of power in the Far East. If the communists controlled a rearmed Japan they could use its location and industry to:

- protect communist-controlled lands in Asia
- break through US defences in the western Pacific
- strengthen Soviet control of Pacific shipping and sea-power
- launch an aggressive policy in South and South-East Asia
- free up communist forces for use elsewhere.

Co-prosperity sphere

In theory, the Greater East Asia co-prosperity sphere reflected the desire for a self-sufficient bloc of Asian nations, led by the Japanese and free of Western powers. In practice, it was propaganda to justify the manipulation of local populations and economies by aggressive puppet governments for the benefit of Imperial Japan.

Zaibatsu

Large, powerful companies in industry and banking which had dominated the economy before and during the war; for example, Sony, Toyota and Honda.

1947	$174 million
1948	$258 million
1949	$510 million
1950	$827 million

Table 2.1 Japanese export values, 1947–1950

If the Western democracies allied with a rearmed Japan, they would gain:

■ industrial and military resources

■ a potential military base in north-east Asia

■ protection for US defensive outposts in the western Pacific

■ a shining example to encourage other non-communist countries to fight against communism.

In March 1948, George Kennan visited Japan to discuss with MacArthur the means of reaching a peace treaty with Japan to give it independence. MacArthur's hold on policy began to loosen. Truman had been unexpectedly re-elected in 1948, despite Republican pressure and McCarthyist attacks on his foreign policy. He feared tight occupation controls might damage Japanese goodwill and drive them into the arms of the USSR. The Japanese Communist Party was gaining support, encouraged by the Soviet mission in Tokyo.

By 1949, there was a 'Red Scare' in the USA. In Japan, the year opened with a series of industrial strikes. The Japanese Communists polled three million votes in the elections. The US State Department increased its control of Japan. Government workers were forbidden to strike and US occupation authorities started arresting communist sympathisers in the Japanese trade union movement. A 'Red Purge' began, eroding the democracy that MacArthur had imposed. Containment of communism was necessary before the Americans could start giving the Japanese more responsibility for day-to-day government. Only then would there be a basis for a Japanese peace treaty.

Removing Japan's armed forces caused problems for the USA in preparing Japan for independence. To defend Japan, Kennan recommended long-term control of Okinawa, expansion of the naval base at Yokosuka and the creation of a 'National Police Reserve' of 75,000 men – in fact they were a lightly-equipped army. The USA were also back-tracking on their disarmament policy for Japan.

The final stage of Japanese reconstruction happened after 1950 and was a response to the Korean War.

Stage 4: integrated Cold War policy – when treaties recognised the official status of Japan at the centre of a US defensive strategy

When the Korean War broke out, in June 1950, Japanese rearmament became essential, making the USA look hypocritical for having disarmed it in the first place. Yoshida called the Korean War 'a gift from the gods', as it gave a huge boost to the Japanese economy. The US government bought war supplies worth $500,000,000 from Japan. By 1952 the Japanese forces had tanks and artillery, and by 1954, a 130,000-strong army. China's involvement in the Korean War led to the full enforcement of a Japanese trade embargo with China, preventing Japan from trading with China. The war also brought forward the signing of the *San Francisco Peace Treaty* marking the end of the Allied occupation and the start of Japanese independence.

How much independence did Japan gain?

The terms of the *San Francisco Peace Treaty*, 8 September 1951, were as follows:

■ full sovereignty

■ reparations by negotiation

- loss of all land surrendered at the armistice to the USA, including Korea, Taiwan, the Kuril Islands and South Sakhalin (perhaps if Korea had been retained by a US-dominated Japan, there might have been no Korean War)
- Taiwan not to return to communist China nor South Sakhalin to the USSR
- US occupation forces to withdraw no later than 90 days after the treaty.

In fact, on the same day, another treaty allowed US land, air and sea forces to be stationed in and about Japan 'to defend against outside attack and internal riots started by a foreign power'. Japan promised not to allow any other country to station troops on its territory without the permission of the USA. Japan also signed a trade treaty with Taiwan, not communist China.

What was the importance of Shigeru Yoshida?

Right-wing Prime Minister Shigeru Yoshida showed patience and caution in dealing with MacArthur and the Americans. He astutely pointed out that the US had once been a colony of Great Britain and was now the more powerful of the two. The same could happen to if Japan became a colony of the US.

Yoshida wore a kimono and white oriental 'toed socks', smoked expensive cigars, travelled in a Rolls Royce and sent flowers and fruits to MacArthur's wife. He had firm control of the Japanese government despite his easygoing outward appearance. As a trained diplomat, he realised Japan had no choice but to co-operate with the US occupiers, but he spoke his mind and played their factions off against each other.

BIOGRAPHY

Shigeru Yoshida (1878–1967)

Shigeru Yoshida became the 45th prime minister of Japan on 22 May 1946. His pro-American and pro-British ideals and his knowledge of Western societies, gained through education and political work abroad, made him the perfect candidate in the eyes of the post-war Allied occupiers. After being defeated in the election one year later, he returned to the post as the 48th prime minister on 15 October 1948. Under Yoshida's rule, Japan began to rebuild its lost industrial infrastructure and emphasised unrestrained economic growth. Many of these concepts of Japan's political and economic policies still continue today. His administration openly encouraged a '3-S' policy: 'sports, screen and sex'. This was a change from strict pre-war censorship. He was retained in three succeeding elections and was finally ousted on 10 December 1954. He retired from politics in 1955 and died in 1967, aged 89. Yoshida's grandson is a Japanese politician and the current Prime Minister of Japan.

Yoshida's reputation and career had its ups and downs, but he is now seen as a national symbol of Japan's transformation into a successful modern state.

Positive interpretations of Yoshida

- He represented the recovery of the 'civilian old guard'.
- He made patriotic democracy the basis for the new Japan.
- He restored Japan's reputation, respect and security among non-communists.
- He resisted US pressures for rapid Japanese rearmament and rearmed slowly.
- He maintained neutrality in the Cold War as far as was possible.

Negative interpretations of Yoshida

■ General MacArthur said he was 'monumentally lazy and politically inept'. Many westerners found him puzzling and exasperating.

■ International respect for Japan was limited; it was seen as a lackey of the USA.

■ He failed to exploit Anglo-American disagreements on recognition of Communist China to benefit Japan.

■ He tried to avoid a Japanese revolution by stifling 'dangerous thoughts' like McCarthyism in the USA.

To what extent did the US policy of Japanese reconstruction live up to its objectives?

Japan seemed to be the only area in South-East Asia where the USA could rightly claim success. In April 1952, the US occupation of Japan formally ended and it regained its independence as the key ally of the US in Asia. Japan lay at the heart of a linked economic network of friendly states with front-line military posts in the Pacific.

Source

General MacArthur's address to the United States Congress, five months before the signing of the *San Francisco Peace Treaty* giving independence to Japan.

Since the war, the Japanese people have undergone the greatest reformation recorded in modern history. From the ashes left in the aftermath of war, they have erected in Japan a system *dedicated to the supremacy of individual liberty and personal dignity. They have done this with a commendable will, eagerness to learn, and marked capacity to understand. In the process a truly representative government has been created, committed to the advance of political morality, freedom of economic enterprise, and social justice.*

From a speech by General Douglas MacArthur, 19 April 1951

ACTIVITY

How reliable and useful is the Source above as evidence for the success of America's reconstruction of Japan between 1945 and 1951?

The 'free world' view

Even before the Truman administration was over, it was commonly accepted that Japan was the one area in Asia where US post-war foreign policy was a success. The USA had made Japan a model democratic state (see also pages 22–26), given it stability and then reversed its removal of armed forces to make it a valuable Cold War ally. The USA had established a conservative, strongly anti-communist government by mutual co-operation, and made public opinion friendly towards the USA. In contrast to China, Korea and South-East Asia, it was a beacon of enlightened 'free world' policies. The US government claimed to have reversed its disarmament policy in Japan only as a response to a communist threat to Japan, Korea and the rest of Asia.

The Japan-centred view

Recent historians emphasise the part played by Japan itself in its reconstruction, both positive and negative. Their views are that previous Japanese policies continued, Japanese businessmen played a major part, and that US bases and forces were there before the Korean War began, allowing the USA to draw troops from them for use in that war. Japan itself is now seen to have played a major part in US strategies for the Pacific region.

The US imperialist view

Some recent research emphasises American repression in Japan, recorded by Japanese sources at the time. US bases are now sometimes seen as the cause of rising Cold War tensions in 1949, rather than a response to them. Many countries that had suffered under Japanese imperialist rule feared that the USA was building up their oppressor to impose a new US-backed imperialism on them. Preventing Japan from trading with China and using it as a 'workshop' for the economy of the whole of South-East Asia made Japan the greatest 'domino' in the US Defensive Perimeter Strategy. If it fell to communism, it would cause the collapse of the whole strategy.

ACTIVITY

1 Which of the following interpretations is most convincing?

- The 'free world' view
- The Japan-centred view
- The US imperialist view

Form your own judgement and support it in debate.

2 In groups, argue which of the following views best describes US policy towards Japan between 1945 and 1950.

Group 1	Group 2
Severity	Human rights
Continuity	Change
Democracy	Military dictatorship
Freedom	Imposed control
An 'open door'	A closed economy

Why did the USA fail to prevent a communist victory in China in 1949?

The Chinese Civil War

Estimates suggest China's population in 1945 to have been more than 500 million. Authoritarian emperors had ruled it from the **Forbidden City** in Beijing (Peking) for centuries, holding back its progress. However, a history of Western influence in China provided the backdrop for rapid political change in the early 1900s. Western traders had established settlements in Shanghai and other major ports. They lived apart from the Chinese and enjoyed a privileged lifestyle. In 1911, **Sun Yat-sen** (Yixian) led a nationalist revolution and made the country into a Republic. But despite his efforts, war lords ravaged and divided the country.

In 1925, on Sun's death, a young army officer named **Jiang Jieshi** (Chiang Kai-shek) assumed the leadership of the **National People's Party (the Kuomintang)**. The Russians offered money and weapons to an emerging Chinese Communist party, the **CCP**, in return for their acceptance into the Nationalist party (Kuomintang). Jiang allied with the CCP to crush the war lords and drive out the Westerners who were draining the Chinese economy. As he approached Shanghai the Westerners rushed in reinforcements, so he decided to make an alliance with them to strengthen the Chinese economy. The CCP refused to accept

Forbidden City

Lying at the centre of Beijing, the Forbidden City, called Gu Gong in Chinese, was the imperial palace during the Ming and Qing dynasties. Now known as the Palace Museum, it is located to the north of Tiananmen Square.

The Kuomintang, or National People's Party

A highly centralised, hierarchical, and authoritarian party/government, the Kuomintang, led by Generalissimo Chiang Kai-shek, ruled China from the 1930s through the Second World War. Defeated by the Chinese Communists led by Mao Zedong in the civil war which ended in 1949, the vestiges of the Kuomintang withdrew to the island of Taiwan and there re-established the government of the Republic of China.

CCP

The Chinese Communist Party.

this, and so began the prolonged Chinese Civil War between 1927 and 1949. Jiang's Nationalists (the Kuomintang) set out to destroy the CCP.

The CCP

A political party founded in China in 1921 by Chen Duxiu, Li Dazhao, Mao Zedong, and others. It grew directly from the reform-oriented May Fourth Movement and was aided from the start by Russian organisers. Under Russian guidance, the CCP held its First Congress in 1921; the Russians also invited many members to the Soviet Union for study and encouraged co-operation with the Chinese National Party. This co-operation lasted until 1927, when the communists were expelled. War with the Japanese broke out in 1937 and led to a temporary alliance between the CCP and the Nationalists. After the Second World War, the CCP participated in US-mediated talks with the Nationalists, but in 1947 the talks were abandoned and civil war resumed. The CCP increased its already strong rural base through land redistribution, and in 1949, under Mao, it took control of mainland China. After Mao's death in 1976, the party moved steadily toward a free market economy.

In 1931, Japan annexed Manchuria, an industrial province in northern China, and set up the state of Manchukuo under a puppet head of state. He was the last Chinese emperor of the Quin dynasty, an insult to the new Chinese nationalist government.

In 1936, **Mao Zedong** (Mao Tse Tung) rallied the Chinese to form a united front against Japan, giving the CCP a reputation as freedom fighters. However, Jiang Jieshi (Chiang Kai-shek) did nothing and lost support, enabling the Communists to capture him. He was forced to promise to end the civil war and form a united front, but he saw this only as a breathing space before the civil war began again.

In 1937, a full-scale Japanese invasion of China was launched from Manchukuo and various points along the coast. This caused the Nationalists and the CCP to become allies. Japan bombarded and captured Shanghai, Nanking and other cities. Japanese occupation inflicted great suffering on the Chinese people, and Jiang, his wife and government were forced to retreat to Chungking, further inland. The **League of Nations** was powerless, as Japan had left it in 1933 after complaints over its annexation of Manchuria. The West was sympathetic, but did nothing to help as they did not wish to risk war with Japan over China.

League of Nations

The League of Nations was an inter-governmental peace-keeping organisation founded as a result of the *Treaty of Versailles* (1919). From 28 September 1934 to 23 February 1935, it had 58 members, but the USA never joined. The League's goals included upholding the new found Rights of Man, disarmament, preventing war through collective security, settling disputes between countries through negotiation, diplomacy and improving global quality of life.

Jiang's American-educated wife visited the USA and gained public support by her eloquence on China's behalf. She drew attention to the brutality of the Japanese. Roosevelt gave loans to the Nationalist Chinese to buy modern weapons, delivered by sea to Burma and then via the Burma Road to Chungking. The ***Lend-Lease Act*** meant US munitions could be sent direct to China. Jiang pressurised the Communists to such an extent that they were forced to retreat to north-west China. This retreat was led by Mao and known as the Long March.

The USA enters the Second World War

Japan's attack on Pearl Harbor in 1941 allowed both Britain and the USA to give open aid to the Chinese. However, the rapid advance of the Japanese through the Pacific drew Western forces away from mainland China. General Joseph Stilwell (head of the US army forces in China, Burma and India) was sent to advise Jiang's government. He had long experience of the country and his task was to defend the Burma Road. Chinese Communists received no US aid and had to fend for themselves. Then, in 1944, for the first time, the Americans made contact with Mao's forces and were impressed. However, in the

BIOGRAPHY
Sun Yat-sen (1866–1925)

Sun Yat-sen studied medicine in Hong Kong but became interested in politics and established the Revive China Society. In 1895 Sun was forced into exile. He lived in Japan, the USA and Britain. While in London he was imprisoned in the Chinese embassy. The British Foreign Office obtained his release, or he might have been executed. The Qing dynasty was finally overthrown in the Chinese Revolution of 1911. Sun briefly became President and established the National People's Party. When the party was suppressed by a war lord in 1913, Sun escaped to Japan. He returned to lead the Nationalist Party (Kuomintang), which gradually increased its power in China. In 1924 it adopted the 'Three Principles of the People' (nationalism, democracy and social reform). Sun died of cancer in Beijing in 1925.

BIOGRAPHY
Jiang Jieshi (1887–1975)

Jiang Jieshi (also known as Chiang Kai-shek) joined the army and became a supporter of Sun Yat-sen, the leader of the Nationalist Party. When Sun Yat-sen died in 1925, Jiang became the Nationalist leader. He defeated the communist army and forced the survivors to make the famous Long March to Shensi in north-west China. Jiang lost control of the coastal regions and most of the major cities to Japan. To beat the Japanese he collaborated with Mao Zedong and his communist army. After the bombing of Pearl Harbor, Jiang and his government received considerable financial support from the United States. As soon as the Japanese surrendered, the Chinese civil war began again. Jiang fled to Taiwan in 1949 when China became the People's Republic of China. He died on 5 April 1975.

BIOGRAPHY
Mao Zedong (1893–1976)

Mao led the Chinese Communist Party to victory in the Chinese Civil War, and was the leader of the People's Republic of China (PRC) from its establishment in 1949 until his death in 1976. He won the leadership of his party and wide peasant support during the Long March of 1934–35, a military retreat from the Chinese Nationalist army, in which the Communists covered 12,500 kilometres in 370 days and only one-tenth survived. The route passed through some of the most difficult terrain of western China. 'Chairman Mao' is officially held in high regard in China where he is known as a great revolutionary, political strategist, and military mastermind who, through his policies, transformed the country into a major world power. Additionally, Mao is viewed by many as a poet, philosopher, and visionary. However, Mao's 'Great Leap Forward' and the 'Cultural Revolution', are seen to have caused severe damage to the culture, society, economy and foreign relations of China, as well as a probable death toll in the tens of millions.

The *Lend-Lease Act*

On 11 March 1941, Congress passed the *Lend-Lease Act*. This gave President Roosevelt the powers to sell, transfer, exchange and lend equipment to any country to help it defend itself against the Axis powers. A sum of $50 billion was granted by Congress for Lend-Lease. The money went to 38 different countries.

ACTIVITY

Consider the Republican view that treachery by Truman's Democrat administration was the main reason for the 'fall' of China to Communism in 1949.

(Look back at page 15 for information on the Republican and Democrat parties.)

McCarthyism

A wave of anti-communist paranoia, which swept through America in the early 1950s. It was named after its loudest disciple, Senator Joseph McCarthy, who claimed to know the names of Soviet-inspired infiltrators: 'the enemy within'. Resultant charges led to interrogations of many people, including Hollywood stars, by Congressional committees. By the 1950s, this paranoia had shifted to fears of nuclear proliferation and global destruction.

USA there was reluctance to equip communist Mao's forces, especially because Jiang mistrusted him.

The effect of the Yalta conference on China

At the Yalta conference in February 1945, Stalin made a deal with Roosevelt to get revenge for Russia's humiliating defeat by Japan in 1905 (the Russo–Japanese war). In return for Soviet help to share the costs of ending the war against Japan, Roosevelt gave the USSR:

- the islands of South Sakhalin and the Kurils
- control of Outer Mongolia
- two ice-free Pacific ports
- control of two railways in Chinese-owned Manchuria.

Roosevelt appeared to be encouraging Soviet expansion in Asia. Truman confirmed the deal at the Potsdam conference, but it turned out that buying Stalin's support was unnecessary. The US bombings of Hiroshima and Nagasaki ended the war just days before the USSR 'liberated' Manchuria and took control of the industrial powerhouse of China. Mao's CCP forces joined in Stalin's invasion of Manchuria and began to receive Japanese weapons and ammunition from the USSR, as they stripped the industrial province of its resources.

Republicans blamed the Democrat administration for a 'shameful betrayal' at Yalta and Potsdam. Right-wing US politicians looked for communists inside Truman's Democrat administration. The seeds of **McCarthyism** were sown, and anti-communism was soon to become the dominant theme of American politics.

China's civil war resumes

After the surrender of Japan on 10 August 1945, Jiang's Nationalist China was admitted to the UN as a permanent member of the Security Council. Patrick Hurley, US ambassador to China, managed to get Mao and Jiang to meet in August 1945, but there was no chance of the two sides reaching a compromise and the fighting resumed in 11 of China's 28 provinces.

The USA still hoped to maintain Nationalist China as an ally to stop the advance of communism. Truman wished to avoid a renewal of the Chinese civil war. US forces were over-stretched in Europe and Asia. Furthermore, in 1945, although the USSR was prepared to recognise the Nationalist government of China, it was likely to support the CCP if fighting resumed. The USSR might also take advantage of a renewed civil war to take more territory.

General George Marshall was sent to persuade Mao and Jiang to form a government of national unity. The USA offered massive financial aid to repair the devastation of the previous eight years and more. Marshall described this as 'pouring sand down a rat-hole'. The terms Mao requested would take away Jiang's 'trump card', the strong Nationalist army which alone had kept him in power, whereas Jiang wanted nothing less than total submission to him by the Communists. Neither side would give in, so in 1946 the Chinese civil war broke out again. US relations with the USSR declined and Mao expressed his hostility towards what he considered to be a weak and reactionary USA (see Source opposite).

Source

Mao Zedong comments on the atom bomb in a newspaper interview with Anna Louise Strong, an American journalist working in China.

The Soviet Union defends world peace and is a powerful factor in preventing the domination of the world by US reactionaries. The existence of the Soviet Union makes it absolutely impossible for the reactionaries in the United States and the world to realise their ambitions. That is why the US reactionaries rabidly hate the Soviet Union and actually dream of destroying this socialist state. The atom bomb is a paper tiger which the US reactionaries use to scare people. It looks terrible, but in fact it isn't. Of course, the atom bomb is a weapon of mass slaughter, but the outcome of a war is decided by the people, not by one or two new types of weapon.

All reactionaries are paper tigers. In appearance, reactionaries are terrifying, but in reality they are not so powerful. From the long-term point of view, it is not the reactionaries but the people who are really powerful.

From a newspaper report, August 1946

The USA soon realised that Mao was right to think that the 'bomb' was a 'paper tiger'. The impact of nuclear weapons was too devastating to make them usable, while military cutbacks and concessions to Stalin had made the USA appear as weak as the appeasers of Hitler.

Should the Truman administration have continued supporting the corrupt Nationalist government?

Truman always considered Japan to be his priority, and did not wish to become embroiled in wars on mainland Asia. However, there was now a serious threat of Soviet expansion into China. Though the two warring sides signed a military truce, the main problem lay in communist control of Manchuria. Stalin dismantled Manchuria's industry and transported its machinery back to the USSR. This undermined the Chinese economy.

Galloping inflation hit the rest of China. Between 1946 and 1948, prices doubled 67 times, encouraging a black market and widespread corruption amongst officials. Jiang had already alienated the businessmen who had supported him. Though the USA were well aware of the corruption of Jiang's administration, they wished to contain communism (see page 21). They therefore increased their aid to the Nationalists, supplying aircraft and sending teams to Taiwan to train their troops. However, Jiang's armies lost 45 per cent of their men in four and a half months. Of the American equipment on loan to Nationalist forces, 80 per cent was lost, with 75 per cent of this falling into communist hands. Jiang's troops often turned and fled rather than facing the enemy.

His army also had a reputation for arrogance and cowardice, and were accused of looting and stealing. He was so unpopular that he had to use force to retain areas he had previously controlled, imprisoning suspects without trial. He chose his generals for their personal loyalty rather than their ability. Jiang failed to defend the Yangtze River in his attempt to open a route to Manchuria from the south. He tended to interfere in the chain of military command, breaking up his forces to target towns rather than meeting his communist enemies in battle in their rural base.

On the other hand, Mao gained control of Manchuria by maintaining his forces at 2.7 million. The CCP showed few openly Marxist principles. They were a powerful force among the peasants and seemed to stand for democracy, freedom and individual liberty. As a party based in the countryside, they used moderate reform policies in areas under their control,

ACTIVITY

Look at the Source above. What is the evidence for Chinese attitudes to US military strength in August 1946?

lowering interest rates and reducing rents rather than seizing land for the peasants. They also allowed all groups to take part in local government in the areas they controlled, though they did approve CCP candidates.

In areas which Jiang had alienated, the CCP gained at least the neutrality or indifference of local people, even if they did not offer them active support.

Figure 2.5   Chinese propaganda poster entitled 'Mao Zedong leading the peasants in the Chinese Revolution of 1949'.

ACTIVITY

Discuss the use of this poster (Figure 2.5) as propaganda for the Chinese Communist Party.

Jiang's reputation was much higher in the USA than among Americans in China, who had first-hand knowledge of his limitations as a leader. Even the anti-communist US General Stilwell described the Nationalist government as 'corruption, chaos, neglect, taxes, words and no deeds', and acknowledged that, in comparison, the Communists 'raise production and standards of living. They practise what they preach'. Regretfully, but realistically, by mid-1949, the American government realised that in supporting Jiang they had backed a lame duck, and that the imminent communist victory was beyond American control.

Mao's tactics changed from guerrilla warfare to open confrontation with Nationalist forces. In decisive campaigns, Mao gained control of Beijing, Nanking and Shanghai, capturing more than 320,000 Nationalist troops. On 1 October 1949, Mao declared the People's Republic of China (PRC). In December, Jiang retreated with his remaining forces to the island of Taiwan, 100 miles off the Chinese coast, taking China's art treasures and all the funds of the Chinese Central Bank with him. He declared the Republic of Taiwan, set up forward bases on islands just off the coast and vowed to win back China by overthrowing the Communists. On the other hand, Mao's victory inspired other communist national movements in Malay and Indochina.

Sources

(A) The Premier and Foreign Secretary of Communist China comments to the Chinese News Agency in Beijing on US policy in the Far East.

The whole world knows that the US government, in an attempt to annex China, has supported Jiang Jieshi in waging large scale civil war, denying the Chinese people any opportunity to live in independence and peace. The US government is supplying the Jiang Jieshi bandits with aircraft to bomb the mainland of China. Acheson says to the Chinese people 'Why don't you ask for American aid?' But from their personal experience the Chinese people have realised what American so-called 'aid' means. It means death for millions; it means the loss of national freedom and rights. Since the Chinese rid themselves of American 'aid' things have gone well for China, and she has become really independent. The affairs of the Asian peoples will be settled by the Asian peoples themselves, and must never be interfered with by such American imperialists as Acheson and company on the other side of the Pacific.

Zhou Enlai (Chou En-lai), 18 March 1950

(B) Secretary of State Dean Acheson's statement on the Communist victory in China, 1949.

The reasons for the failures of the Chinese National Government do not stem from any inadequacy of American aid. Our military observers on the spot have reported that the Nationalist armies did not lose a single battle during the crucial year of 1948 through lack of arms or ammunition. The fact was that the decay, which our observers had detected in Chongqing early in the war, fatally weakened the resistance of the Nationalists. Its leaders proved incapable of confronting the Communists, its troops lost the will to fight, and its Government lost popular support. The Communists, on the other hand, through ruthless discipline and fanatical zeal, portrayed themselves as liberators of the people. The Nationalist armies did not have to be defeated; they disintegrated. History has proved again and again that a regime without faith in itself and an army without morale cannot survive the test of battle.

Dean Acheson, in Dept of State records, US relations with China, August 1950

SUMMARY ACTIVITY

1 Why did the USA fail to prevent the fall of China to communism? Which of these ideas can you find in Sources A and B?

- Insufficient military aid from the USA.

- Support for an unpopular and corrupt Chinese Nationalist government.

- Poor morale in Jiang's armies; communist propaganda.

- US priorities placing Europe above Asia.

- A strong Chinese independence movement which opposed US imperialism.

- Soviet military support for the CCP.

- Communists within the US administration undermining containment policy.

2 Which of these ideas have been left out of the Sources? Can you find evidence for them in the text of this chapter?

3 Can you think of any reasons not on this list, and can you find evidence for them?

4 Now place all the reasons in order of importance in answering the question.

Examiner's advice

When comparing sources, analyse points of both agreement and disagreement linked to answering the question.

Stretch and challenge

Compare Sources A and B as evidence for the reasons why the USA failed to prevent the fall of China to communism.

First use the historical context to help you analyse the Sources.

- Truman's administration, especially Acheson, came under attack by McCarthy.
- The USSR successfully tested its own atom bomb in August 1949.
- Mao declared the People's Republic of China in October 1949.
- Mao gained $300 million worth of aid from Stalin in December 1949.
- NSC 68 secretly proposed tripling the US armed forces budget in April 1950.
- Communist North Korea invaded democratic South Korea in June 1950.
- Truman approved NSC 68; tripling spending on US armed forces in April 1950.
- North Korean Communist forces quickly overran South Korea by August 1950.

Then use the provenance to help you analyse the similarities and differences of the points made in the Sources.

How realistic were other policies that the Truman administration might have followed to prevent the 'fall' of Communist China in 1949?

There were some factors which might have had an effect, for example:

- placing more US commanders in control of Nationalist forces
- committing US land, sea and air forces to fight in China
- making an even larger financial commitment than the $2 billion given to the Nationalists in grants and credits.

None of these options were realistic. The US armed forces had been scaled down and American public opinion was firmly against fighting a war in China. Giving more US funds to the corrupt Nationalists would have been a huge waste of money. However, Senator Joseph McCarthy suggested another reason for the failure of the Truman administration to prevent the fall of China to communism:

> 'In my opinion, the State Department is thoroughly infested with communists. I have here in my hand a list of 57 cases of individuals who would appear to be either card-carrying members or certainly loyal to the Communist Party. Nevertheless, they are still helping to shape our foreign policy. This fact is known to the Secretary of State, a pompous diplomat in striped pants, with a phony British accent.'

(Joseph McCarthy, speaking to the Women's Republican Club, expresses his fears concerning communist infiltrators within the US government in February 1950.)

ACTIVITY

Discuss the reliability of this statement by Joseph McCarthy.

What was the significance of the 'fall' of China for US foreign policy?

The USA continued to recognise the Chinese Nationalists as the government. Acheson feared that Taiwan would fall to the Communist forces before the end of 1950. If the CCP were to take Taiwan, communists could dominate the sea lanes linking Japan to Malaya which supplied it with tin and rubber. They could also dominate the Philippines, Okinawa and eventually Japan itself. Taiwan's strategic position made it essential to the whole US defensive position in Asia, but Mao considered it to be part of China's territory. However, there was a US consensus not to send in troops to defend Taiwan, due to overstretch. US military strength was too low to deal with emergencies in other spheres of influence. Then, in August 1949, the USSR successfully tested the atomic bomb and the US nuclear monopoly was over. They had lost their nuclear supremacy and now faced potential confrontation with the combined forces of the Soviet Union and Communist China.

Figure 2.6   David Low cartoon published in the *Evening Standard*, 3 January 1950, showing Truman and MacArthur with another US general stationed on the island of Taiwan (Formosa) trying not to recognise the existence of Communist China, which wishes to take its seat on the UN Security Council. They are having a sneak look at the fact that Mao is phoning for support from Stalin. The caption on the cartoon suggests that their attitude in support of Nationalist Jiang Jieshi has alienated Mao and the people of China, so that Mao will not wish to recognise Nationalist control of Taiwan. Taiwan becomes part of the US defensive perimeter of offshore islands, though it is really part of Chinese territory, and Mao is likely to ask for Soviet help to recover it.

Acheson suggested the withdrawal of US support from Nationalist China and recognition of Communist China as a gesture of friendship. He felt it was only a matter of time before Mao and Stalin clashed, as the USSR soon began to absorb the northern provinces of China. Mao was unlikely to want to link his new regime with unpopular foreign control, and would almost certainly be independent of the USSR. Acheson argued that the USA must break its ties with Taiwan to allow the PRC to build better relations with America.

However, Truman refused to accept this advice, in case it confirmed Republican views that his policies were pro-communist. Congress therefore sent further funding to Jiang. When Mao met with Stalin in Moscow (see Sources A and B on page 46) in December 1949, they felt they had been in the right.

The Soviet–Chinese Treaty, 1950

By February 1950, less than five months after the successful Soviet atomic bomb test, Mao signed a *Soviet-Chinese Treaty* giving him $300 million of Soviet aid. The treaty contained a veiled threat to the USA: the promise of mutual military assistance against any aggression by (US occupied) Japan. Mao realised that China could not stand alone, and that the USSR was its only real choice of ally. He said that China would 'lean towards' the USSR and against capitalist imperialism.

What was the significance of Truman ignoring Korea?

One country that the USA had not seriously considered in all its defensive strategies was Korea:

- they had failed to keep it for their Japanese satellite
- they had allowed Stalin to liberate its northern industrial area
- they had not included it in their 'Defensive Perimeter Strategy' (see page 47).

From the start, Truman's administration had wished to use financial aid rather than military force to defend mainland Asia and the Pacific from Soviet expansion. Korea bordered the vast new state of Communist China as well as the tip of the USSR. It was in a prime geographical situation to threaten Taiwan and there was only a token US presence in South Korea. In June 1950 the Cold War became a 'hot war' when the Korean War broke out. This was partly because the Truman administration had omitted Korea from its 'Defensive Perimeter Strategy'.

Sources

(A) **Stalin met Mao Zedong in December 1949 and arranged a $300 million Soviet aid package for Communist China.**

COMRADE STALIN: Soviet troops currently stationed in China will withdraw upon your request.

COMRADE MAO: Soviet presence corresponds well with Chinese interests, as Chinese forces are inadequate to fight effectively against imperialist aggression and you provide a training school for Chinese activists in railroad and industry.

COMRADE STALIN: The withdrawal of troops does not mean that the Soviet Union refuses to assist China, if such assistance is needed. We can stay for as long as 20 years.

COMRADE MAO: You should not rush to withdraw troops. We would like to draw up a credit agreement for $300,000,000 between the governments of the USSR and China. We believe we must first bring order, strengthen our country and then we can talk to foreign imperialists.

COMRADE STALIN: That is a good policy. There is no need for you to create conflicts with the British and the Americans.

(B) **Mao Zedong and Joseph Stalin are shown here at the Soviet leader's birthday celebrations in 1950. Together with Kim Il Sung they may have plotted to invade Japan that year.**

ACTIVITY

Assess Sources A and B as evidence for the effect of US foreign policy on the Sino–Soviet relationship from December 1949.

What was the 'Defensive Perimeter Strategy' of 1949 and why did the Truman administration adopt it?

In March 1948, Kennan (see page 15, Chapter 1) warned that 'we are operating without any overall strategic concept for the entire western Pacific area'. The area had geographical importance as the economic crossroads of the Indian and Pacific Oceans. Asian markets provided the world with 90 per cent of its rubber, 60 per cent of its tin, and essential raw materials such as petrol and timber. The USA saw Asian national movements as 'communist inspired' and feared an expansion of Soviet influence in the area.

The US 'Defensive Perimeter'

Kennan's supporters persuaded MacArthur, in Tokyo, to accept a plan to construct a defensive line of military bases including the Aleutians, Midway, the former Japanese mandated islands, Okinawa in the Ryukyus, the Philippines, Australia, New Zealand, and the British and Dutch islands in the south-west Pacific (Figure 2.7).

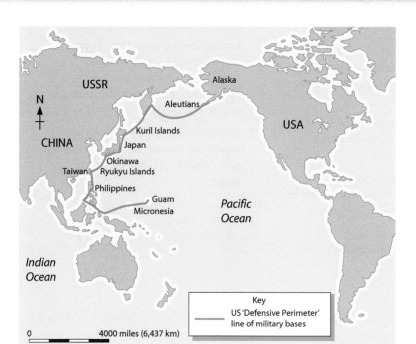

Figure 2.7　The line of the US 'Defensive Perimeter' military bases.

Kennan saw Okinawa as the strong point for control of the ports of north-east Asia from which an amphibious attack could be launched. Military, air and naval bases would be set up on the offshore island chain. The policy took the pessimistic view that the USA would not be able to influence events on the Asian mainland, based partly on the success of Mao Zedong's communist guerrillas in the Chinese Civil War.

This 'Defensive Perimeter Strategy' became a widely-accepted policy by the summer of 1949. The CIA stressed the importance of keeping the offshore islands out of hostile hands, to allow access to the strategic raw materials of India and South-East Asia, especially if the Suez Canal route were to be closed. The Pentagon concluded that 'our position is not directly jeopardised by the loss of China as long as we retain the security of the islands.' This included Japan, Taiwan and the Philippines.

ACTIVITY

Analyse the content and provenance of the Source below as evidence for US attitudes to global defence.

Source

A Democrat senator representing a Republican state, well known for his isolationism and consistently voting against America's military involvement in foreign wars, gives his views on the USA in the role of 'world policeman'.

With the strategic location of airfields from the Philippines to Alaska, on the coast of Asia, from Alaska to the Azores in the South Atlantic, we can drop, at a moment's notice, atomic bombs on any spot on the world's surface and return to our base. With vision and guts and plenty of bombs, ultra-modern planes and strategically located airbases, the United States can outlaw wars of aggression. The world organisation which I am thinking of, is one designed to stop war with the atomic bomb in the hands of the United States as the club behind the door, to be used only when the bandit goes berserk.

From a speech to the US Senate by Senator Edwin Johnson, 28 November 1945

How did differing expectations of the US Defensive Perimeter Strategy contribute to conflict in Asia?

The State Department, the Joint Chiefs of Staff and MacArthur supported the strategy for different reasons:

- The State Department saw the offshore island chain as a detached position from which to encourage Asian national movements.

- The Chiefs of Staff saw it as a low-cost defensive line in the event of war, by relying on it instead of requesting higher funding for adequate forces.

- MacArthur saw it as a series of bases for offensive attacks to regain mainland China.

These differences in expectations were painfully exposed when the Truman administration tried to fit the strategy to Taiwan, Indochina and Korea. The Defensive Perimeter Strategy was similar to the Soviet construction of a defensive buffer against the capitalist West in Eastern Europe. The USA aimed to avoid having to deploy troops on mainland Asia by constructing a 'defensive wall' against Soviet aggression in the Pacific. However, at the heart of the strategy stood a US satellite, the newly-reconstructed Japan, causing outrage among countries which had been brutalised by Japanese annexation and occupation during the Second World War.

Why and how did the Truman administration support South Korea, 1945-50?

In August 1945, Korea was liberated from Japanese control by Soviet troops from the north and American troops from the south. The country was temporarily divided at the 38th parallel of latitude. However, each occupying force developed its sector in accordance with its own political principles and each wished to rule a united and independent Korea.

In 1948, a Soviet-sponsored communist regime under Kim Il Sung was set up in North Korea. It won support through carrying out land reform. A US-backed right-wing government led by Syngman Rhee was elected under UN supervision in the South, but was corrupt and brutally suppressed left-wing opponents. A Joint Commission, set up by the United Nations, failed to establish a 'trusteeship' government to unite the country.

In 1949 both the Soviet and US occupying forces withdrew from Korea, but while Stalin left Soviet military advisers and armed forces in the North, the US refused to equip the South with troops for fear of a civil war breaking out. Clashes occurred along the 38th parallel, in which many Koreans were killed. Rhee's government lost the propaganda war against the Communists, and its brutal police methods led to a heavy defeat in elections of May 1950. The USA knew that, in order to contain communist expansion and prevent Soviet influence encroaching on Japan, they would have to help prop up Rhee's government.

The Defensive Perimeter Strategy was deliberately constructed to defend Japan, the Philippines and South-East Asian resources and trade, so that the USA would not have to make costly interventions in mainland Asia. It was a half-measure designed to protect US interests and 'free world' democracy in a time of military overstretch, when the main priority was Europe. Unfortunately, once China fell to the Communists and the USSR developed its own atomic bomb, the USA was forced to change its policy and triple its military spending (**NSC 68**) to hold back communist expansion in Asia.

How far did NSC 68 represent a change or a continuity of policy?

On 14 April 1950, a joint State-Defence Department Group issued NSC 68 (see pages 66–67, Chapter 3). It suggested the tripling of America's defence budget to build up a massive US military presence to combat the advance of the USSR. The annual cost was estimated in the region of $50 billion. Though its suggestions were remarkably similar to Kennan's 'Long Telegram', NSC 68 became one of the most critical planning documents of US Cold War strategy. In his memoirs, published in 1969, **Dean Acheson** called NSC 68 'a blunt but effective propaganda tool' to manipulate public opinion into agreeing to military funding, as there was no tradition in the USA of raising tax for military spending in peacetime. Unfortunately, its propaganda impact on the USSR was limited by its secrecy and by Truman's delay in seeking its approval in Congress. If Kim Il Sung and Stalin had known of its existence, South Korea might not have been invaded by the Communist North in June 1950.

Conclusion

1945 began with the USA and USSR allied against common enemies, but Cold War ideological tensions soon emerged and American foreign policy changed. Between 1945 and 1950, the USA prioritised the containment of Soviet Communism in Europe, the heart of established democracy. However, they perceived a global communist threat, and hoped that blocking opportunities for Soviet expansion might lead the USSR to collapse. Conciliatory policies at the conferences of Yalta and Potsdam had allowed Stalin a presence in Asia. From 1947, US policy shifted to Cold War containment of communism in Asia by giving economic aid to Japan, the Philippines and Jiang Jieshi's Chinese Nationalists. Korea was the exception, as it contained no resources valuable to the West. But Truman was slow to realise which Asian national movements had only remote links to Soviet influence. In China, US economic aid failed, powerless to prevent Mao's victory in the Civil War.

Right-wing opponents accused Truman's administration of being 'soft' on communism, leading him to harden policy by accepting NSC 68. The USA refused to recognise Communist China and continued their economic aid to the Nationalists in Taiwan. It joined the Philippines, Okinawa and the Aleutians in a chain of offshore Pacific islands with US front-line military and naval bases. At the heart of this 'defensive perimeter' lay the US

NSC 68

A US National Security Council review document that proposed the tripling of America's defence budget to build up a massive US military presence to combat the advance of the USSR.

BIOGRAPHY

Dean Acheson (1893–1971)

From an East Coast élite background, Acheson trained as a lawyer before entering politics. He helped consolidate the Truman Doctrine, Marshall Aid and NATO. He was blamed by some for the Truman administration's weakness over China and Korea. He retired in 1953 but continued to advise Kennedy, Johnson and Nixon as one of the Wise Men. (See also page 14.)

satellite of Japan, which was by 1950 newly reconstructed as a shining model of capitalist economic prosperity and democracy. The USA hoped this would deter other states from falling to communism, but it only managed to alienate Asian countries devastated by Japanese imperialism. The USA was oblivious to this fact, but it did begin to realise that, in Asia, the popularity of communism within national movements was due to circumstances beyond the control of either itself or the USSR. No amount of American resources and willpower would be able to contain it.

The USA made the mistake of not including Korea in its strategies, due to the pessimistic view that the USA would be unable to influence events on mainland Asia. US military cutbacks after the Second World War meant that a presence in Korea would have caused overstretch, because the bulk of their remaining troops were concentrated in Europe. This message was not lost on Stalin, Mao and the leader of North Korea, Kim Il Sung, who all realised that America was not in a position to contain communism in Asia. Now there was a Soviet nuclear capability, concentrating on Japan proved to be a rather short-sighted policy. When the Korean War began in June 1950, US troops found themselves suddenly propelled from their comfortable roles in Tokyo into the harsh realities of warfare less than five years after the end of the Second World War. From 1950, the USA embarked on a policy of full-scale military intervention in Asia.

Skills practised

In this chapter you have:

- learned and practised the skills of source analysis, comparison and evaluation
- had to link sources to a question in order to answer it
- studied the contextual information to understand these sources and their provenances
- gained knowledge of continuity and change in US Cold War strategies in Asia.

 Exam café (pages 174–190) will help you further in revising the content and practising the skills of source interpretation against exam-style questions.

Bibliography

Dower, J. (1996). *Japan in War and Peace: Essays on History, Culture and Race.* London: Fontana.

Dower J. (2000). *Embracing Defeat: Japan in the Aftermath of World War II.* London: Penguin.

Hanhimäki, J. M. and Westad A. (2003). *The Cold War: A History in Documents and Eyewitness Accounts.* Oxford: Oxford University Press.

Rinjiro, S. (2001). *Dear General MacArthur: Letters from the Japanese during the American Occupation.* Lanham, Maryland: Rowman & Littlefield.

Tyner, J. A. (2007). *America's Strategy in South East Asia: From Cold War to Terror War.* Lanham, Maryland: Rowman & Littlefield.

How far did the Korean War and its origins (1950–53) change the US conduct of the Cold War in Asia?

3

In this chapter, we will look at the origins of the Korean War and the role played by the United Nations, the USA, the USSR and China. The Korean War had considerable impact in shaping future American foreign policy in Asia, and provided a 'dress rehearsal' for the Vietnam War. We will consider why the Korean War caused a serious disagreement between Truman and MacArthur, which set a precedent for US Presidents having more say in the conduct of future wars. We will look at the military, strategic and financial consequences of the Korean War, its impact on Cold War politics and shifts in the balance of power.

During the course of the chapter you will build up more experience in the skills of source analysis, interpretation and evaluation.

Key questions

In this chapter, we will discuss and analyse the impact of the Korean War (1950–53) on US conduct of the Cold War in Asia. The key questions for evaluation are:

- What were the origins of the Korean War?
- Who was responsible for the division of Korea?
- How did the USA attempt an international solution to the Korean problem by 'collective security' in 1947?
- How did the Korean War cause disagreements between Truman and MacArthur?
- What were the military, strategic and financial consequences of the Korean War?

What were the origins of the Korean War?

Like China, Korea had a long history of authoritarian government (see Timeline overleaf) and, during the early twentieth century, developed local nationalist and communist movements. However, one key difference between the two countries was that the Chinese had an established national, if corrupt, government when the Japanese invaded in 1937, whereas Korea had fallen under Japanese imperial control as early as 1910 and their independence movements had been suppressed or forced into exile. Therefore, Korea had not experienced national independence and the inevitable civil war between its democratic and communist forces had been postponed.

The USA had more pressing concerns than the local disputes inside one of many 'Third World' countries on mainland Asia, so did not include Korea in its defensive strategies. Nationalist China was a US ally and its province of Manchuria bordered Korea. Even when wartime agreements during the Second World War allowed the USSR to liberate Manchuria, US strategies were so preoccupied with defeating Japan that they failed to consider Korea as a temptation for Stalin. Its geographical location placed it, after all, within striking distance of a reconstructed Japan and possible control of trade in South-East Asia. The Truman administration was preoccupied with the Cold War in Europe and failed to see any useful resources in Korea.

Timeline 1905–1953

1905	Korea became a protectorate of the Japanese Empire.
1910	Korea became a formal Japanese colony.
1919	Widespread protests in Korea against Japanese colonial rule.
1943	Cairo Declaration for Korean independence 'in due course'.
1945	
February	USSR and USA agree to a four-power trusteeship for Korea.
August	USA propose 38th parallel as temporary dividing line between forces of USA and USSR in Korea.
September	Korean People's Republic announced, independent of Japan.
October, November	Syngman Rhee and Kim Ku return to Seoul from USA and China.
December	Moscow conference: joint Soviet-American Commission to oversee process for Korean independence.
1946	
February	Syngman Rhee became chair of the Representative Democratic Council in Seoul, South Korea; Kim Il Sung became leader of People's Committee in North Korea.
July	North Korean Workers' Party established.
October	Elections for South Korean Interim Assembly.
1947	
November	United Nations Temporary Commission on Korea set up to oversee elections in all Korea.
1948	
February	• North Korean People's Army set up. • US occupation commander, John Hodge, announced South Korean elections for early May.
15 August	Republic of Korea established, with Syngman Rhee President; Democratic People's Republic of Korea established under Kim Il Sung.
1949	
March	Kim Il Sung visited Moscow and met Stalin.
1 October	People's Republic of China established under Mao Zedong.
1950	
March	Kim Il Sung gained Stalin's backing for an offensive against South Korea.
April	Truman approved NSC 68.
August–September	Battle of Pusan Perimeter.
September	US/UN Inchon landing and Seoul re-taken.
October	US advance to the Yalu River; Chinese intervention and escalation.
1951	
April	MacArthur dismissed; stalemate began.
1952	
November	Eisenhower elected President.
1953	
27 July	Final peace treaty signed at Panmunjom, but not by South Korea.

What part did Korean nationalism play in the origins of the Korean War?

Korea was known as 'the Land of the Morning Calm'. It is a mountainous 680-mile long peninsula, with shores on the Yellow Sea and the Sea of Japan, and a land border with Manchuria. The proximity of Korea to Manchuria, China, Japan, the USSR and the Soviet-held Kuril Islands and Sakhalin played a significant role in the Korean conflict. The borders between these states and northern Korea all followed the lines of rivers.

Only the north of Korea has resources of iron, lead and coal, and this is a barren mountainous area, freezing in winter and sweltering in summer. After centuries of rule by the authoritarian **Choson** dynasty, it became a Japanese colony in 1910. Like China, it was aware of Western ideas of national sovereignty, thanks to missionaries, foreign officials and journeys to the United States. Korean nationalism, organised in the '**Independence Club**', developed into an anti-colonial, anti-Japanese movement with a slogan of 'Korea for Koreans'. Woodrow Wilson's ideas of 'national self-determination' inspired a million-strong rally in 1919.

Two key figures were later to play the main parts in the outbreak of the Korean War. The first was **Syngman Rhee**, a Christian who became a founder member of the Independence Club. He served a five-year jail sentence and after his release in 1904, he became 'westernised' by living in Hawaii and the USA for most of his life. He was awarded an M.A. from Harvard and a PhD from Princeton, the first Korean to gain an American doctorate. He was therefore well-suited as delegate to attend the Paris Peace Conference after the First World War to request Korean independence. However, the US government refused to grant passports to the delegation. Instead, Rhee became President of the Provisional Government set up by the exiled independence movement in Shanghai, China in 1919. In the 1920s, he went to Washington to lead the attempt of the Provisional Government of Korea to get American or European help for Korean independence. He made no progress thanks to strong right-wing attitudes in Korea, American isolationism and the weakness of the League of Nations. Rhee attended its debate on the Japanese invasion of Manchuria in 1931. The League condemned Japanese imperialism but took no action.

Choson dynasty

'Choson' was the family name of the last emperors to rule Korea.

'Independence Club'

This was the name for the Korean nationalist movement.

BIOGRAPHY

Syngman Rhee (1875–1965)

Rhee was the first president of South Korea, though he only ever had minority support. His presidency, which started when he was 73 years old, lasted from August 1948 to April 1960. His role remains controversial, affected by Cold War tensions on the Korean peninsula and elsewhere. Rhee was a right-wing anti-communist, regarded in the USA as a strong man who led South Korea through the Korean War. His presidency ended in resignation following popular protests against a disputed election. He died in exile in Hawaii in 1965 aged 90.

By the outbreak of the Pacific war in 1941, Rhee was known to be a leader of the Korean national independence movement, though Kim Ku had replaced him as President of the Provisional Government of Korea in 1926. Kim Ku believed it was acceptable to use violent paramilitary groups to force Japan to end Korea's colonial status. By the time Rhee returned to South Korea in 1945, he was a right-wing conservative, aged 70.

3 How far did the Korean War and its origins (1950–53) change the US conduct of the Cold War in Asia?

The second key figure in the Korean national movement was Kim Il Sung, a communist aged 29 at the outbreak of the Pacific War in 1941. The Bolshevik revolution of 1917 had acted as an inspiration to some Korean nationalists. Some turned to Marxism because they mistrusted the promises of Western democracies to support Asian national movements. Under Japanese imperial control, colonial police infiltrated, imprisoned and killed members of their groups. The communists went into hiding or set up groups in exile in China or Soviet Siberia. Most of them entered North Korea in 1945 with the Soviet liberating forces. Kim Il Sung was one of them.

Many other Korean communists had close links with the USSR or China. One such influential communist was Nam Il. Born in Russia to Korean immigrant parents before the Revolution, he served in the Soviet army during the war, returned to Korea as part of the occupying force and became Deputy Minister of Education in the North Korean Government up to 1950. Some influential Korean exiles such as Kim Tu-bong joined the CCP (Chinese Communist Party) and commanded the Korean Volunteer Army during the Chinese Civil War. Kim Tu-bong was leader of the North Korean Workers' Party after 1945. Mu Chong was also influential as the commander of the Korean Volunteer Army in China. He briefly commanded the Second Corps of the North Korean army during the Korean War, but was later purged by Kim Il Sung. **Pak Hon Yong** played a major part in the communist underground movement inside Korea. He served two jail terms and was forced to pose as a bricklayer to avoid arrest during 1939.

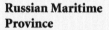

BIOGRAPHY

Pak Hon Yong (1900–1955)

Pak Hon Yong participated in the founding of the Korean Communist Party (KCP) in 1925. From this time until the end of the Second World War, his activities were underground. Late in August 1945, the KCP was re-established; it had been officially disbanded in 1928. Pak Hon Yong became its secretary. On 5 January 1946, as a representative of the KCP, he announced support for the decision of the Moscow Conference of Great Powers (UK, US, Soviet Union), and said that Korea was now in the process of a 'democratic revolution'. In December 1946, he organised the South Korean Workers' Party, and became its first secretary. In September 1948, while keeping his role as secretary of the South Korean Workers' Party, he became Deputy Prime Minister and Foreign Minister of North Korea. Pak was arrested on 3 August 1953 in a purge of the South Korean Workers' Party faction by Kim Il Sung. On 15 December 1955 he was sentenced to death and immediately placed before a firing squad.

Russian Maritime Province

Russian territory in East Siberia, a coastal strip along the Pacific from Korea to the Arctic Ocean, including part of the island of Sakhalin and several small offshore islands.

Kim Il Sung's reputation rested on an attack on Pochonbo, near the Manchurian border, when his guerrilla group killed some Japanese policemen in 1937. The Japanese gave the incident considerable publicity. Kim's 300 guerrillas fought alongside the 20,000 Chinese guerrilla fighters who targeted Korean collaborators as well as Japanese officials. They endured harsh conditions and often went cold and hungry. When the Japanese stepped up their attack on partisan guerrillas in 1941, Kim fled to the **Russian Maritime Province**. Though still only 33, he became a Major in the Soviet army and was with the Russian forces that entered Korea to liberate it. Though in 1945 he had only been a junior member of the Korean Communist Party (KCP) compared to many others, Soviet support made Kim the most prominent member of the KCP after 1948.

Figure 3.1 A propaganda poster showing Kim Il Sung 'guiding the construction of communism'.

What was US policy towards Korean nationalism up to 1945?

As early as the 1922 Washington Conference, a new security policy for the Pacific had been discussed to replace the expired Anglo-Japanese military alliance. The situation became more pressing after 1931, when Japan invaded Manchuria and the League of Nations proved powerless to halt Japanese imperialism. However, Korea had limited interest for Americans after the attack on Pearl Harbor in December 1941. Not until 1943 did the USA realise the potential danger to US interests in the Pacific if the USSR were to occupy Korea exclusively, menacing Japan and China.

'Trusteeship' became the guiding principle of US foreign policy in Asia in August 1941, when the Atlantic Charter was signed, setting up the United Nations. The idea was a variation of Woodrow Wilson's mandate system that aimed to prepare ex-colonies for independence. Trusteeship would involve the Grand Alliance and other colonial powers working together. Their task would be to protect newly-liberated ex-colonial countries and prepare them politically, economically and socially to rule themselves. In 1943, Roosevelt suggested Nationalist China as one of four 'global policemen', alongside the USA, Britain and the USSR. The objective was to contain Soviet influence in four spheres of the world, using a trustee policy that would extend to Korea and Vietnam.

At the Cairo Conference in November 1943, Roosevelt and Jiang Jieshi rejected the idea of recognising Kim Ku's Provisional Government of Korea. Instead, the principle of Korean independence 'in due course' was accepted. This would mean perhaps 40 years of trusteeship, supervised by the Great Powers but with no foreign troops stationed in Korea. Stalin approved this decision at Cairo and again at Yalta in 1945. However, neither meeting discussed any arrangements for the period before trusteeship was set in motion.

Was Truman to blame for the failure to discuss Korean independence at Potsdam in 1945?

When Stalin met Truman at Potsdam, he perceived a change in US policy from the conciliation of Roosevelt, which made him mistrust the Americans. Stalin reported to his Chinese communist allies that the USA was co-operating closely with Britain, and together they saw '**trusteeship**' as a means of extending their imperial power. The CCP consequently viewed the USA as a reactionary power whose anti-imperial statements were hypocritical.

Trusteeship

The United Nations Trusteeship Council, one of the principal organs of the United Nations, was established to help ensure that non-self-governing territories were administered in the best interests of the inhabitants and of international peace and security.

3 How far did the Korean War and its origins (1950–53) change the US conduct of the Cold War in Asia?

Stalin also reported to the Chinese communists that the USSR and the USA had made no binding commitments about the future of Korea. He was correct in that no arrangements were in place for dealing with the area once Japan had surrendered. The entry of the USSR into the Far Eastern arena of the Second World War and the dropping of the atomic bomb altered the speed of events. The two superpowers found themselves dealing with Korea on a day-to-day basis, with the USA the dominant power in the region. Stalin decided to take advantage of any opportunities which came his way in Asia.

Who was responsible for the division of Korea?

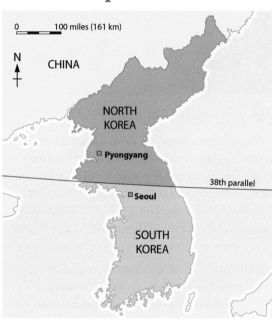

Figure 3.2 Map of Korea in 1945, divided along the 38th parallel.

ACTIVITY

Discuss the potential problems in setting up a trustee government for an independent Korea. What interim arrangement would you make before the new government was in place?

Military factors

At the Potsdam conference of July and August 1945, it was agreed that the USA and the USSR should liberate Korea as quickly as possible to minimise casualties. The speed of Japanese collapse meant that US troops were several hundred kilometres away when Soviet forces entered Korea on 12 August 1945. US forces were unable to arrive until 8 September so, if Stalin had wished to seize the whole of Korea, it is unlikely they could have stopped him. He might have made Korea into an Asian version of his Polish satellite state in Europe.

Truman's advisers hastily improvised, by suggesting a line where Soviet forces should halt their advance, at the 38th parallel of latitude. Stalin readily accepted. He may have hoped to gain a better bargaining position in Eastern Europe if he co-operated in the Far East. He may have suspected Truman of a secret deal with Japanese troops to hold back the Soviet advance, but he also wished to avoid confrontation with the superior US forces in the Pacific after the bombings of Hiroshima and Nagasaki.

Jiang Jieshi's regime in Nationalist China was at that time a US ally, and Korea bordered Chinese-owned Manchuria, which the USSR liberated in 1945. Stalin saw North Korea as a useful buffer against US expansion, especially if the Chinese Civil War resumed. The USA might use Korea to help Jiang win victory. If the USA dominated the Pacific, it would be very difficult for the USSR to have influence in the Korean peninsula.

The USA was more interested in Japan and did not have the forces to police mainland Asia. The situation was unlike that of Europe, as there was no physical barrier, only an imaginary line between North and South. Koreans could move freely across the notional boundary. In 1945, however, both superpowers hoped that Korea would be united 'in due course'. Stalin seized the opportunity to dominate the more industrial North of Korea, which contained valuable supplies of lead, coal and iron, hoping to develop a Soviet trading partner in the future.

Kim Il Sung entered North Korea with the Soviet forces and was supported by their commanders, **Colonel Alexandre Ignatiev** and **General Terentii Shtykov**. These were the real rulers of North Korea. In 1946, a military academy was set up in Pyongyang, and a revolutionary army began to emerge under the leadership of Choe Yong-gon. He became North Korea's first Minister of National Defence until the outbreak of war in 1950. The North Korean Communist Party (**NKCP**) was also deliberately co-ordinated with that of China, by Koreans who returned after fighting in Manchuria against the Chinese Nationalists. Korean armed forces could train in China, then move men and armaments across the border in preparation for crossing the 38th parallel to unite Korea.

How did the US military government alienate the South Koreans?

In the southern occupied area, the USA controlled a majority of the Korean population and the capital, Seoul. In September 1945, Lieutenant-General John Hodge set up a US military government there to rule South Korea. Unlike Japan, South Korea was not disarmed. The USA fully intended to withdraw its forces from Korea at the earliest opportunity.

MacArthur had ordered Hodge to be 'semi-friendly', to treat the Koreans as 'liberated people' and 'create a government in harmony with US policies'. But what were US policies towards Korea? MacArthur had publicly stated that the American Defensive Perimeter ran along a string of islands from the Aleutians to the Philippines with Japan at its heart, excluding Korea. In practical terms, the USA had intervened in the Korean peninsula against their stated strategy and Hodge had to improvise with limited numbers of troops.

The 14 US soldiers who reached Seoul in Hodge's advance party were surprised to find a city of horse-drawn carts. They were alarmed at the disorder in the provinces and the bewildering range of political groups competing for their attention. Hodge had no experience of civilian government and mistrusted the exiled Provisional Government that soon arrived from Shanghai. To Hodge, the Japanese seemed the only stabilising influence he could rely on. 'Koreans are breeds of the same cats as the Japanese' he said, referring to the large numbers of Korean collaborators who had fought in the Japanese army. This outraged Korean Nationalists who had suffered decades of Japanese oppression.

The US military government saw Koreans as unruly and uncooperative, in contrast to the docile Japanese. The only officials the Americans could communicate with were Japanese.

The US attitude to Korean Nationalists

Hodge mistakenly saw many nationalists as communists. Therefore, he kept the previous Japanese government framework and even its unpopular personnel. This alienated the local people, who wished to see collaborators brought to justice. Few Koreans grasped the terms 'communist' or 'democrat', and none of them had had administrative experience for 40 years. They thought Hodge was favouring the Japanese and that their oppression of Korea would continue. Tempers began to flare against the American occupiers. The US occupiers mistrusted and suppressed Korean nationalist groups.

Colonel Alexandre Ignatiev

A highly-influential figure in the Soviet civil administration.

General Terentii Shtykov

Head of the Soviet civil delegation to the Joint Commission and later Soviet ambassador to the Democratic People's Republic of Korea (DPRK).

3 How far did the Korean War and its origins (1950–53) change the US conduct of the Cold War in Asia?

As early as 11 September, MacArthur instructed Hodge to remove all Japanese officials immediately. Over a four-month period, 70,000 Japanese colonial civil servants and 600,000 Japanese soldiers and civilians were transported home, leaving behind their houses, factories and possessions. But by then the South Korean population had already been alienated.

How did the US military help Rhee to power in the south?

Syngman Rhee's backing by the US military government was a decisive force in his rise to power. Yet the State Department, after long acquaintance with him, had denied him a passport as they saw him as a dangerous troublemaker. Hodge secretly planned and carefully orchestrated Rhee's return to Seoul in October. He travelled in one of MacArthur's aircraft, stopped off at Tokyo en-route and was presented as the chosen leader of a new civilian government. His advantages to Hodge were that he was westernised and had been outside the factional tensions within Korea.

It was Kim Ku, newly returned from Shanghai as President of the **Korean Provisional Government**, who represented the Korean national movement. But his nationalist groups criticised Hodge's policies, so Hodge saw them as a Soviet-inspired threat to the USA. During the winter of 1945–46, the US military government suppressed this movement, but soon realised that the country was seething with political unrest.

Hodge became more wary of what he suspected to be Soviet-inspired communist infiltration into the South, of which the Japanese had already made him aware. He wished to withdraw US troops as soon as possible, so urgently needed a solution. All Koreans had one common aim: to establish national unity and independence. As time went by, this desire was likely to foster respect for Soviet strength. Free elections might result in a communist-led Korea.

> ### ACTIVITY
>
> Find factual examples of the view of Roger Makin, a British Foreign Office senior official, that:
>
> *'The Americans go for a man rather than a movement. They have always liked the idea of dealing with a foreign leader who can be identified and perceived as 'their man'. They are much less comfortable with movements.'*

How did the Soviet forces help Kim to power in the North?

The Soviet occupation force greatly helped Kim Il Sung's rise to power. The police enforced obedience to state policy by establishing communist groups who indoctrinated the local population. Stalin realised that Korean public opinion was leaning towards supporting the stronger Soviet political force, and that was likely to be communism if the democratic process took its course in the South. He decided on a 'united front policy', co-operating with non-communists, such as the Christian Cho Mansik, and keeping ties with South Korean communists such as Pak Hon Yong. Kim Il Sung took control of the government in Pyongyang with Soviet support, ignoring more experienced members of the Korean communist movement.

Kim consolidated his power in the north by becoming Premier of the Democratic People's Republicof Korea (**DPRK**) in 1948 and Chairman of the North Korean Workers' Party (**KWP**)in 1949. He created a united Communist Party ideologically similar to its Soviet counterpart, and co-operated with the USSR, though he did not try to emulate Stalin. Kim's

Korean Provisional Government

The provisional government which represented the Korean national movement in the South.

DPRK

The Democratic People's Republic of Korea (DPRK).

KWP

The Korean Workers' Party.

power was consolidated by the support of People's Committees with a membership of peasants and industrial workers. Kim based his police force locally rather than centralising them, which would have been too reminiscent of the Japanese colonial police. He also gained support from other internal Korean groups such as the Yanan faction and Pak Hon Yong, whose reputation as a resistance fighter was well established. Kim gained credibility by merging Pak Hon Yong's South Korean Worker's Party with his own, enabling infiltration across the 38th parallel. Kim Il Sung was never simply a pawn of the USSR and stood up to Stalin. He, like Syngman Rhee, felt his government should rule all of Korea. Both leaders conducted a propaganda campaign to that effect.

South Korea: How did US economic and political policies alienate the peasants?

In the South, Hodge refused to work with the nationalist, peasant-led People's Committees, and purged them from economic organisations and government posts. In an area where 70 per cent of the population was engaged in farming, land reform was the critical issue, but at first Hodge ignored Korean demands for land reform and food distribution. Instead he re-established the oppressive rice collection 'quota' system used by the Japanese-controlled government, again linking himself to their oppressive policies. In the three weeks after their surrender, before the US troops arrived in South Korea, the Japanese had looted warehouses, sold every immovable asset and ruined the economy by debasing the currency.

The US military government tried to ease the economic situation by reforms, such as improvements in conditions of land holding for the peasants. However, when they refused to hand over their rice quotas, Hodge made the mistake of creating a free market. This encouraged corruption by officials, hoarding, speculation on the black market and spiralling inflation in the price of rice: a bushel of rice rose from 9.4 yen in September 1945 to 2,800 yen just a year later. The resort to rationing caused hardship and a wave of peasant uprisings in rice-growing regions which had to be suppressed by the national police.

The national police were loyal servants of the Japanese, who had a reputation for brutality and torture. Though the 12,000 Japanese among them were sent home, 53 per cent of remaining officers were Japanese-trained, and members of the anti-Japanese resistance were banned from joining. The numbers of police doubled; the South Korean Army would later develop from this force.

Hundreds of thousands of Syngman Rhee's opponents were imprisoned. As they did not understand the principles of democracy, local tensions were based on 'haves' against 'have-nots', landlords against peasants, those with power against those with none. Political debate was no more accepted in the South than in the North, where the North Korean Communist Party was officially established in July 1946.

North Korea: How did Stalin's economic and political policies alienate the people?

In the North, first of all the Koreans themselves occupied former Japanese industries and seized their assets. They organised the distribution of food, land and property through Communist People's Committees supported by the Soviet-backed government. Stalin used the North Korean Communist Party to coordinate land reforms and reconstruct heavy industries such as shipbuilding. But he soon decided to adopt a policy similar to the one he used in the Berlin Blockade in the winter of 1948–49. Though Koreans continued to return

southwards to their homes, Soviet troops blocked mail, rail traffic and shipments of coal from crossing the 38th parallel. Power stations in the North prevented 'Soviet' electricity connections to the South. Stalin was holding the South to ransom.

However, the North was suffering too. Shortages of rice traditionally provided by the agricultural South caused demonstrations and riots in the North, which had to be suppressed by Soviet troops. Christian protest was violently crushed, newspapers censored, non-left officials purged and moderate or right-wing groups silenced.

The failure of trusteeship

By 1947, the temporary division of Korea into North and South had become a permanent feature, and it became apparent that a policy of trusteeship would never succeed. Both Rhee and Kim wished to be the one leader of a unified independent state. Civil war was becoming increasingly likely. The USA would never agree to a democratically-elected Communist Korea, though this is exactly what Stalin and Kim hoped for.

By September 1947, the US Joint Chiefs of Staff decided that there was little to gain from maintaining US forces and bases in Korea. It had become clear that an international 'trusteeship' solution to the Korean problem had been lost because of the developing Cold War. In Europe, the East–West divide was deepening, exposed by Kennan's 'Long Telegram' and Churchill's 'Iron Curtain' speech. British withdrawal from Greece and Turkey had forced the USA to grant $400 million in Marshall Aid. The Truman Doctrine had declared America's goal of global containment, but military cutbacks were causing overstretch. China had resumed its civil war in 1946, causing the US occupation forces to harden their policy of Japanese reconstruction. The USSR's influence in Manchuria and Port Arthur had given it a dangerous Far Eastern presence.

Both sides now felt civil war might lead to superpower confrontation. The USSR did not hold Kim back, but equipped the North with military advisers, weapons and T-34 tanks for their protection. In contrast, the only US troops remained in Japan and the offshore islands. The USA denied Rhee an army or military advisers, fearing he might lead an invasion of the North and provoke direct confrontation with the USSR.

Source

(A) **A State Department adviser to Lieutenant-General John Hodge explains the situation in Korea in a report sent to the government in Washington.**

South Korea can best be described as a powder keg ready to explode with a spark. There is great disappointment that there will be no immediate independence or sweeping out of the Japanese. Although Koreans have an unbelievably bitter hatred for the Japanese, they are unlikely to resort to violence while American troops control them. The removal of Japanese officials is desirable to please public opinion, but difficult to bring about quickly. There are no qualified Koreans for other than low-ranking positions, in government or public utilities or communications.

From a report by H. Merrell Benninghoff, 15 September 1945

Sources

B A US naval officer, who had been amongst the advanced party which arrived in South Korea in September 1945, described the situation there in February 1947, when he returned.

Everything had gone downhill, nothing worked. The corruption was there for all to see. A lot of genuine patriots were being seduced by the persuasions of the north. There were Koreans wearing clothes made of army blankets, orphans hanging round the railway stations, the transport system crumbling. Most of our own people hated the country, stayed a week and just got out.

Ferris Miller, naval officer, comments made in February 1947

C A North Korean Communist, who had fought in the anti-Japanese United Army, explains the importance of the Chinese Revolution as a training ground for Korean soldiers.

Korea will soon be ours. At present there is not a single unit in the communist United Democratic forces now driving the Nationalists from Manchuria that does not have my troops in it. At the end of the campaign, the troops who are at present driving the Nationalist forces out of Manchuria will be seasoned, trained veterans. When the Americans and Russians withdraw, we will be able to liberate Korea immediately. We will use our friends in the South to aid us. We will start a civil war we can win. We have many sympathisers and supporters in the South, ready to rise up, support and help us overthrow their hated rulers.

Choe Yon Dong, quoted in a US intelligence source, May 1947

D The North Korean leader states his views on trusteeship as a solution for Korea.

The decision of the three great powers at the Moscow Conference to adopt a trusteeship policy for Korea was a further development in strengthening democracy. Despite this, several individuals are attempting openly and directly to oppose this decision. They portray this friendly aid and co-operation as similar to earlier Japanese aggressive imperialism.

From a letter by Kim Il Sung to Stalin, 1947

E Extracts on Korea from a State Department report listing the weaknesses of US 'friends' in Asia.

The weaknesses of our 'friends' are:

1 The non-democratic character of governments in the area. Rhee is about as bad in this respect as anyone we have had to deal with, as was demonstrated by his recent arrest of certain Korean assemblymen and his threats to others.

2 Lack of trained personnel. In Korea, for example, there is no substitute for Rhee.

3 Corruption and inefficiency.

4 Economic and financial difficulties are a cause of basic distress. Good progress has been made concerning land in Korea. The peasants' situation is not so bad from their point of view, but unrest is starting. In Korea there is the problem of inflation.

5 Military weaknesses in dealing with Communist guerrillas. The situation in Korea is improving owing to our efforts. However, the Republic requires anti-aircraft guns and planes, having nothing new with which it could meet an air attack from the north.

From a Conference Report, 6 February 1950

3 How far did the Korean War and its origins (1950–53) change the US conduct of the Cold War in Asia?

ACTIVITY

1 Use your own knowledge to assess how far Sources A–E support the interpretation that the situation in South Korea improved between 1945 and 1950 owing to US efforts.

2 How far do you agree that Rhee and Kim were 'puppet' rulers acting for the USA and the USSR respectively?

3 A judgement exercise on the failure of trusteeship:

Prioritise the following statements as most, less, and least convincing. Explain your decisions.

■ The Cold War had made the policy of trusteeship obsolete by 1947.

■ The superpowers had been drawn into a local Korean quarrel.

■ The USA was to blame for the failure of trusteeship.

■ The USSR was to blame for the failure of trusteeship.

Examiner's advice

1   Group the Sources according to their point of view. If a source has more than one point of view then group it more than once.

2   Remember to integrate every point you make on the sources with your answer to the question. Stay focused on the question. Points to integrate should be:

■   The significance (or not) of the views in the sources to answering the question, using accurate contextual knowledge.

■   The provenance of the sources (if relevant). This might be authorship or date, nature, purpose, audience, tone. Avoid a formulaic approach.

■   A judgement on the 'value' of each source based on completeness of content or aspects deliberately ignored; reliability of content and provenance; usefulness of content and provenance.

■   Remember to use accurate knowledge of historical context in your answer to verify, qualify or evaluate the views in the sources as well as discussing their provenance.

How did the USA attempt an international solution to the Korean problem by 'collective security' in 1947?

UN involvement

The USA decided to hand over the seemingly insoluble problem of Korea to the United Nations. In November 1947, the UN General Assembly recognised Korea's right to self-determination and set up the United Nations Temporary Commission on Korea (UNTCOK) to oversee the road to independence. Democratic elections were to be held prior to the withdrawal of foreign troops. However, Stalin demanded disqualification of Rhee's supporters who had refused to co-operate with trusteeship, a condition stated at the Moscow Conference. The USA persuaded the UN to include them regardless. The USSR therefore refused to allow UNTCOK to enter North Korea. UNTCOK proceeded to supervise elections for a 'national government' only in the South.

On 15 July, Rhee was elected President and on 15 August 1948 the Republic of Korea (**ROK**) was formally declared. In April 1948, the National Security Council had voted to withdraw US troops, leaving behind a token force to maintain security in South Korea. Truman failed to make any provisions against communist advances, and the withdrawal of US troops began on 19 May 1948.

Kim Ku, the former President of the Provisional Government of Korea in Exile, had refused to take part in the 1948 elections. He chose to work with the moderates to search for a diplomatic solution to Korean disunity. The election of Syngman Rhee's corrupt, authoritarian, right-wing government to power meant that Kim Ku's influence declined. He was assassinated in 1949.

Was civil war now inevitable?

The 1948 elections were a critical turning point in Korea. Syngman Rhee realised that the US occupation armies had crushed left-wing forces in South Korea. This would ease his way to becoming President, but would make war with the North the only route to a united Korea.

Kim Il Sung had realised this from as early as 1946. In North Korea, the Korean People's Army was officially set up on 8 February 1948. Elections were held on 25 August. The Democratic People's Republic of Korea (DPRK), under Kim Il Sung, was proclaimed on 9 September 1948. Soviet forces left the North in December 1948. The last US troops had left the South by June 1949. Both Kim and Rhee prepared to defend the 38th parallel and gain support on the other side.

Rhee's contribution to local guerrilla warfare during 1948 and 1949

Violent skirmishes and guerrilla raids raged along the 38th parallel during 1948, in two main regions: the Chiri Mountains and the island of Cheju. Guerrillas opposing the ROK in the South received advice and military aid from the North. Rhee tried to undermine their activities, encouraging the right-wing governor of Cheju to take reprisals against the whole population of the island. Five regiments and 10,000 police were involved. Estimates suggest a death toll of between 27,000 and 60,000 islanders, with 40,000 fleeing to Japan.

The Cheju rebellion provoked a mutiny within the ROK army. Mutineers set up People's Committees in October 1948 to aid the Communists. Several thousand lives were lost in the ensuing fighting, won by Rhee with the help of remaining US forces. The result was Rhee's *National Security Act*, which gave a broad definition of 'subversive activities'. It allowed the ROK government a free hand in dealing with their opponents for decades. Rhee's regime became increasingly brutal and the Truman administration began to distance itself from him.

Rebel numbers grew to between 3,000 and 6,000 by the autumn of 1949. The ROK launched a series of military offensives against rebel reinforcements from north of the border, where 3,000 guerrillas remained ready to fight at the outbreak of war in 1950. Throughout 1949, thousands of troops were involved in fighting along the 38th parallel. For example, 5,000 North Koreans fought to recapture a mountain just north of the border, which had been occupied by ROK forces. In all, 100,000 Koreans died in border skirmishes before the outbreak of war in June 1950.

ROK

The South Korean People's Republic of Korea.

ACTIVITY

Class debate:

Why did the USA and USSR choose to withdraw their troops from Korea in 1948–49?

3 How far did the Korean War and its origins (1950–53) change the US conduct of the Cold War in Asia?

Why did Rhee request a change in US policy to 'rollback' communism?

Syngman Rhee's government accelerated its aggression against the North. He realised that the ROK needed its industrial strength if he was to have any chance of uniting Korea once the US forces had withdrawn. In the North, Kim's troops had swelled to 135,000 with the return of two major divisions of the Korean Volunteer Army from China. US intelligence reports suggested he also had 36 Soviet Yak-9 fighter planes. Four of his five airfields were near the 38th parallel. He was clearly preparing to invade the South.

Rhee had only 98,000 troops, of whom 33,000 were non-combat support troops. Early in 1949, he requested US aid for his plan to 'rollback' North Korea and absorb it into the South.

How realistic was the attempt to create a US 'model state' in South Korea instead?

Rhee, like Jiang, seemed to feel that the USA could not afford to abandon him. But there was no indication that the USSR would become involved. Furthermore, US aid for a military attack on mainland North Korea might lead to a similar failure as the fall of China to communism despite US support for the Nationalists under Jiang (see pages 41–45). Truman could not afford to risk the damage of further severe criticism. Therefore, the best policy seemed to be a programme of economic and military aid to create a 'model' South Korean state strong enough to contain communist expansion. In this way, South Korea was to follow the path of the Philippines and Japan.

However, Truman followed a weak and half-hearted policy in South Korea. The plan was that Rhee's government should develop a 'client–patron' relationship as part of an 'informal empire'. Only 2,000 US civilian officials were stationed in the American embassy in Seoul to ensure ROK links with the West. A further 500 US soldiers in the Military Advisory Group supervised internal security. There was not even a mention of US forces establishing a South Korean military base to defend against attack.

ACTIVITY

An interpretation and judgement exercise:

Study all four Sources on page 65.
Use your knowledge to assess how far the Sources support the interpretation that US policy towards Asia was inconsistent and indecisive in 1949–1950.

Consider the authorship, date, purpose, audience and tone of Sources A–D as evidence for US foreign policy in 1950.

1 Explain how each of these aspects helps you understand the use and reliability of each Source. For each one, discuss the:

- Date – what had happened to influence their content and tone?

- Tone – what emotions are provoked by their terminology?

- Audience – how will the audience react to their messages and tone?

- Purpose – can you take these at face value or do they have other, less obvious, purposes?

2 Prioritise these aspects in helping you group and analyse the Sources to answer the question.

Sources

(A) **President Rhee's war plans, explained in a memo by the US Secretary of the Army, during a visit to Seoul. He records a conversation he had with Rhee and the American ambassador to Korea, John Muccio, on the implications for Korea of Nationalist defeats in the Chinese Civil War.**

President Rhee said he would like the police to have enough rifles to keep 18,000–20,000 on the northern border. He said that, with enough equipment, the South Korean army could be increased by 100,000 within six weeks. He stated that if North Korea were invaded by South Korea, a large proportion of the North Korean Army would desert to the South Korean Army. He said he would like to increase the army, provide equipment and arms for it, and then in a short time move into North Korea. He saw nothing could be gained by waiting. One of the principal difficulties of the whole Korean situation was the hesitation of the US State Department. He thought this indecisiveness had played a strong part in the loss of China and might be seriously harmful to Korea.

From a memo by Kenneth Royall on President Rhee's war plans, 8 February 1949

(B) **The US Secretary of State, Acheson, gives a speech declaring his strategy in case of attack by Communist forces. He seems to suggest that the US will not back Rhee.**

What is our policy concerning the military security of the Pacific area?

Firstly, the defense and security of Japan must be maintained. The defensive perimeter runs along the Aleutians to Japan and then goes to the Ryukyus. At an appropriate time, we will offer to hold these islands under United Nations trusteeship. As they are essential parts of the defensive perimeter, they must be held. The United States would not tolerate an attack on the Philippines. So far as the military security of other areas in the Pacific is concerned, it must be clear that no person can guarantee these areas against military attack. Should such an attack occur, the initial reliance must be on the people attacked to resist it, and then upon the entire civilized world under the Charter of the United Nations. But I think it is a mistake, when considering Pacific and Far Eastern problems, to become obsessed with military considerations. Important as they are, there are other pressing problems.

From a speech to the National Press Club by Dean Acheson, 12 January 1950

(C) **A State Department report of the discussion on an increase in US funding for South Korea.**

Korea Supplemental Military Assistance.

The proposal for a program of $9.8 million to supplement the regular Military Assistance Program for Korea was discussed with Defense at the top level, with the result that Defense has advised us that 'there appears to be no military necessity for an increase in the fiscal year 1950 Program for Korea at this time'. They wish to be advised if the State Department anticipates, for political reasons, recommending the revision of existing policy to provide for increased Korean military strength. We are awaiting the return of Ambassador Muccio before proceeding further with the proposal.

From an Internal State Department report, 5 April 1950

(D) **An extract from a policy document (NSC 68) drawn up by the National Security Council in April 1950.**

- *America and its citizens at the height of their strength stand in the deepest peril.*

- *The issues that face us are momentous, involving the fulfilment or destruction not only of America but of civilisation itself.*

- *The assault on free states is world-wide now, and in the context of the present two superpowers, a defeat of freedom anywhere is a defeat everywhere.*

- *A further increase in the number and power of our atomic weapons is required for effective US retaliation.*

- *We need a huge increase in general air, ground and sea forces. The free world needs air defence and civilian defence programs if it is to survive an initial surprise atomic attack.*

- *A rapid improvement in political and economic conditions will place heavy demands on our courage and intelligence. It will be costly. It will be dangerous. But half measures will be inadequate to prevent war, and may even invite it. Budget considerations will need to be set aside. The stark fact is that our very independence as a nation may be at stake.*

From a secret statement of the National Security Council, NSC 68, 7 April 1950

3 How far did the Korean War and its origins (1950–53) change the US conduct of the Cold War in Asia?

Why did Acheson's speech in January 1950 become so controversial?

In January 1950, a landmark speech by Acheson (see Source B, page 65) seemed to suggest that the USA was beginning to look to the United Nations for military support in solving the Korean dilemma. His critics claimed his meaning was ambiguous. They felt he was sending Stalin the message that the USA would not intervene if war broke out in Korea. Acheson was speaking just weeks after Mao Zedong's victory in the Chinese Civil War on 1 October, and less than a month after Mao had travelled to meet with Stalin in Moscow. Perhaps the USA realised the potential costs and dangers of maintaining outposts beyond the defensive line, after the experience of the Berlin Crisis and the setting up of NATO. He suggested the USA would shrink from extending its defensive perimeter to the mainland, and turn to '**collective security**' through the United Nations rather than risk a war of 'superpower proxies'.

Collective security

Security through the United Nations as opposed to national security.

The President took a clearer line. Since 23 December 1949, the National Security Council had warned that South-East Asia was 'the target of a co-ordinated offensive directed by the Kremlin'. Though the USA had already stockpiled 50 atomic bombs, Truman authorised the development of a hydrogen bomb to keep ahead in the arms race. He commissioned a National Security Council review that published its findings in a document known as NSC 68.

What was the significance of NSC 68?

On 14 April 1950, a joint State–Defence Department Group issued NSC 68 (see Source D page 65, also page 49, Chapter 2). It suggested the tripling of America's defence budget to build up a massive US military presence to combat the advance of the USSR. Though its suggestions were remarkably similar to Kennan's 'Long Telegram', NSC 68 became one of the most critical planning documents of US Cold War strategy. In his memoirs, published in 1969, Dean Acheson called NSC 68 'a blunt but effective propaganda tool' to manipulate public opinion into agreeing to military funding. Unfortunately, its propaganda impact on the USSR was limited by its secrecy and by Truman's delay in seeking its approval in Congress. If Kim Il Sung and Stalin had known of its existence, South Korea might not have been invaded by the Communist North in June 1950.

Though Truman agreed with enlarging the American military, the higher taxes on which the policy depended were bound to be unpopular and might mean cuts in the welfare programme. He was aware of the strength of Republican opposition in Congress, and there was no tradition in America of retaining large armies in peacetime. The outbreak of the Korean War hastened Congress approval of the policy, but even then the USSR remained unaware of it.

Why did Stalin hesitate to aid the North in 1949 and then change his policy in 1950?

Throughout 1949, Kim Il Sung kept on urging the USSR to give him military support. He wished to attack the Ongjin Peninsula, south-west of Pyongyang, to open a path to Seoul and the South. Stalin consistently refused to support this plan. He was reluctant to become involved in a serious, costly and prolonged civil war. It might justify similar US aid to Rhee's regime, backed by a stockpile of nuclear weaponry.

Instead, Stalin suggested increasing support to guerrilla fighters to provoke a general uprising in the South. This would prepare the ground for an offensive from the North. Stalin refused to make a mutual security pact with North Korea. Europe, rather than Asia, was his first concern at this time. Kim could not go ahead until Stalin's policy changed to support an offensive. He tried every persuasion possible to change Stalin's mind, including playing the Soviets off against the Chinese. Eventually he got the go ahead from both Stalin and Mao and went to war.

Why did Stalin decide to support Kim's invasion plan?

Kim travelled secretly to Moscow to meet with Stalin in April 1950. Stalin had said in 1948:

> *'If socialism is victorious in China and our countries follow a single path, then the victory of socialism in the world will be virtually guaranteed. Nothing will threaten us.'*

Stalin did not wish to be seen to be holding back the flow of revolution by restraining Kim Il Sung. Furthermore, Mao might intervene and take the lead. Kim had told Stalin he would prefer Mao to be brought in to share the risk of starting a war.

The success of the first Soviet atomic bomb testing, at the end of August 1949, removed the US military advantage and increased Soviet confidence. Stalin's failure to force the West to back down over the Berlin Crisis led to NATO being created. This reduced Soviet chances of achieving their European ambitions through diplomatic means. They redirected their policy of expansion to Asia. It seemed to Stalin that the USA was not prepared to fight a war over Korea, and might stand aside if the North invaded the South. Acheson's speech confirmed this. If the USA should intervene, it would damage the US military presence in Japan. Soviet expansion would be helped by weakening Japan within the US global alliance system. Stalin's view that America was hesitating to help Korea was proved when the American *Korean Aid Bill* was only passed in February at the second attempt. In April 1950 Stalin agreed to support Kim with military equipment, as long as a decisive victory could be won and there would be no escalation of the war.

Although Stalin supported Kim, he would not allow Soviet troops to intervene directly. He insisted that Kim should only attack South Korea after securing Mao's agreement in person. After a secret meeting with Kim on 12 and 13 May, Mao wrote to Stalin to clarify the position of the USSR. Stalin replied:

> *'We agree to the Korean proposal. The question should be decided finally by the Chinese and the Korean comrades together.'*

In South Korea, elections on 30 May saw many of Rhee's supporters replaced by moderates. Kim assured Mao and Stalin that the war would be over in two or three weeks. He received Mao's support. A second front of the Cold War had opened in Asia.

ACTIVITY

Comparative analysis, evaluation and judgement:

1 Compare Sources B and C on page 68 as evidence for the parts played by Kim Il Sung and Stalin in the outbreak of the Korean War in 1950.

2 Use your own knowledge to assess how far Sources A–E (on page 68) support the interpretation that Mao Zedong played the main role in Kim Il Sung's decision to invade South Korea in June 1950.

Sources

A **A Soviet official reports on the appeal made by Kim Il Sung of North Korea for the support of the USSR.**

The northern army is insufficiently strong to carry out successful and rapid operations against the South. Even taking into account the help which will be rendered to the northern army by the partisans and the population of South Korea it is impossible to count on rapid victory. Moreover, a drawn-out civil war is disadvantageous for the North both militarily and politically. It is inadvisable that the North begin a civil war now. An attack on the South would only be correct if the North Koreans could count on ending the war quickly. That is not the case.

From a message by Grigorii Tunlin to the Soviet Foreign Ministry in Moscow, September 1949

B **A Russian General, the Soviet Ambassador to North Korea, reports to Foreign Minister Yshinsky a conversation he had with an intoxicated Kim Il Sung.**

Kim said that when he was in Moscow in March 1949, Comrade Stalin told him it was unnecessary to attack the South, except to retaliate against an attack on the North by Syngman Rhee's army. Kim felt that liberation of the South and the unification of Korea were being delayed by Rhee not starting an attack. Kim felt he needed to visit Comrade Stalin again, to receive an order and permission for the offensive action by the People's Army. Furthermore, Kim said that he could not begin an attack himself, because he is a communist, a disciplined person. For him the order of Stalin is law. Kim stressed that his friend Mao Zedong promised to give him assistance after the conclusion of the war in China.

General Terentii Shtykov, 19 January 1950

C **Stalin replies to Shtykov's report, giving the first indication of his change of mind, and revealing the status of Kim Il Sung as the junior partner in relations between Moscow and Pyongyang.**

1. I understand the dissatisfaction of Comrade Kim Il Sung, but he must understand that the large matter regarding South Korea that he wants to undertake needs large preparation. The plan must be organised to avoid too great

a risk. I will always be ready to discuss this with him. Let Kim Il Sung know all this and tell him I am ready to help him.

2. I have a request for Kim Il Sung. The Soviet Union is very short of lead. We would like to receive a yearly minimum of 25,000 tons of lead from Korea. I hope that Kim Il Sung will not refuse us in this. It is possible that he needs our technical assistance and a number of Soviet specialists. We are ready to give this assistance. Tell Comrade Kim Il Sung of my request and ask him to let me know his views on this matter.

From a message by Josef Stalin to General Terentii Shtykov, 30 January 1950

D **Shtykov reports a conversation between Mao, Zhou Enlai and the North Korean ambassador to China, Li Chou-yuan, about Kim Il Sung's intentions.**

Mao turned toward Li as if asking when Kim intended to begin the unification of Korea. Without waiting for an answer, he said that if Kim intended to begin military operations against the South in the near future, a meeting between Kim and Mao should be unofficial. He saw the unification of Korea by peaceful means as impossible, only military means would work. There was no need to be afraid of the Americans. They would not enter a third world war for such a small territory. Kim reported to me that he wishes to begin the operation in June.

From a telegram by General Terentii Shtykov to Moscow, 12 May 1950

E **Krushchev explains his view on Stalin's part in the outbreak of the Korean War in June 1950.**

The North Koreans wanted to give a helping hand to those under the heel of Syngman Rhee. Stalin persuaded Kim Il Sung to think it over. Kim returned to Moscow when he had worked everything out. Stalin had his doubts. He was worried that the Americans would jump in, but we thought that if the war were fought swiftly, and won quickly, then intervention by the USA could be avoided. Nevertheless, Stalin decided to ask Mao Zedong's opinion about Kim's suggestion. I must stress it wasn't Stalin's idea, but Kim was the initiator. Stalin didn't try to dissuade him. Mao also approved Kim's plan and said he believed the USA would not intervene since the war would be an internal matter which the Korean people would decide for themselves.

From: Nikita Khrushchev, *Khrushchev Remembers*, 1971

The Korean War

When the invasion took place, the USA did take immediate action. In 1949, Korea's crucial role in securing Japan and the Pacific had been recorded in this top-secret internal State Department memo: 'Korea is another area in which United States influence should show results in the social and economic life of the country. Therefore, it is important that we not let the Republic fail.' If they had known of this and of NSC 68, the USSR might have realised that the USA would actively defend Korea.

The Korean War can be considered to have four main phases:

1. Pusan and Inchon, June to September 1950.
2. 'Rollback' of communism to the Yalu River, September to October 1950.
3. Chinese involvement and escalation, October 1950–February 1951.
4. The war of attrition, January 1951–July 1953.

Phase 1: Pusan and Inchon, June to September 1950

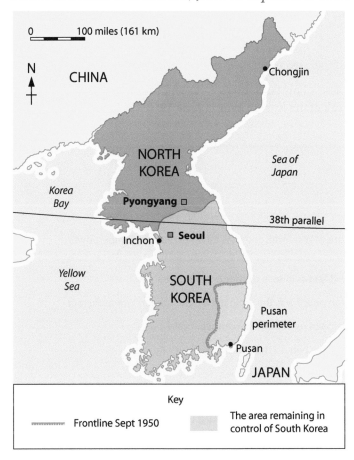

Figure 3.3 Map of Phase 1 of the Korean War, showing the Pusan perimeter in September 1950.

The 135,000-strong North Korean Army quickly advanced south. Ill-equipped and poorly trained South Korean troops could do little to stem the onrush of North Korean troops. Within three days the South Korean capital, Seoul, had fallen to the North Koreans, marking a great victory for communism. They promised political reforms and unification of the country. Though the Korean people began to feel the war might soon end, the North Koreans continued to thrust southwards, driving demoralised South Koreans before them. Some of the army of South Korea threw down its weapons and fled.

3 How far did the Korean War and its origins (1950–53) change the US conduct of the Cold War in Asia?

US ground forces were small in number and had no anti-tank artillery, so they were forced to retreat South with the ROK troops. They had been told that they would only be there for a matter of weeks and were not ready to fight a war. By the end of July, all of South Korea was overrun by the North Korean 'blitzkrieg', except for a small area around Pusan (see Figure 3.3). More US forces were hastily flown in from Japan, and deployed to Pusan. The US Seventh Fleet positioned itself off the coast of Taiwan.

Large numbers of civilians were inevitably caught up in the fighting. American air crews were ordered to fire on 'the retreating enemy', though many were civilians. A US Air Force Colonel wrote to General Timberlake, on 25 July:

> 'It is reported that large groups of civilians, either composed of or controlled by North Korean soldiers, are infiltrating US positions. The army has requested we strafe all civilian refugee parties approaching our positions. To date, we have complied with the army request in this respect.'

(see: www.heinemann.co.uk/hotlinks/)

Stretch and challenge

Answer the Sources question and then hold a debate on the topic .

Use your own knowledge to assess how far Sources A–D (opposite) support the interpretation that the outbreak of the Korean War in June 1950 was the result of aggressive Soviet expansion.

ACTIVITY

Judgement and debate

How far were the origins of the Korean War local, and how far an extension of superpower rivalry?

1 Consider the following views and find evidence to support or refute them.

- Stalin's aggressive expansion policy was the main reason the Korean War broke out.

- US neo-colonialism was the main reason the Korean War broke out.

- Kim Il Sung was the driving force behind the invasion of South Korea.

- Stalin was hesitant and cautious about helping Kim.

- Mao wished to keep Kim at a distance as his priority was to rebuild China.

- Rhee's regime provoked the outbreak of the Korean War by alienating South Koreans.

- Mao was the driving force. He feared the USA might gain control of a united Korea and try to recover China.

2 Use these ideas, and any others you can add, as the basis for a debate.

Sources

A **A Russian journal records a conversation between Stalin and Kim Il Sung, in which Stalin explains the reasons why he will support Kim's invasion of South Korea.**

■ *Firstly, the victory of the Chinese revolution, the alliance signed between the USSR and the PRC, and the USSR's own atomic bomb.*

■ *Secondly, the obvious weakness of the reactionaries. The shameful defeat of America's intervention into Chinese affairs and Western troubles in South-East Asia. The inability of the South Korean regime and its American masters to improve the social, economic, and political situation in South Korea.*

■ *Thirdly, the dishonest, untrustworthy and arrogant behaviour of the United States in Europe, the Balkans, the Middle East. Its decision to form NATO reveals that America is no longer a partner, but an enemy. The Soviet Union cannot bind itself any longer to such an enemy.*

■ *Fourthly, the aggressive designs of the South Korean regime. It is determined to launch an attack on the North, sooner or later. It is important to forestall this aggression.*

From a Russian journal, Moscow, April 1950

B **An extract from a secret policy document (NSC68) produced by the US National Security Council.**

The Soviet Union seeks to impose its absolute authority over the rest of the world. Being a totalitarian dictatorship, the Kremlin's objective in these policies is the total subjective submission of the peoples now under its control. The concentration camp is the prototype of the society which these policies are designed to achieve; a society in which the personality of the individual is so broken and perverted that he participates in his own degradation. The Kremlin seeks to bring the free world under its domination by the methods of war. We advocate an immediate and large-scale build-up in our military and general strength with the intention of righting the power balance and in the hope that through a means other than all-out war we could induce a change in the nature of the socialist system.

From: NSC 68, 7 April 1950

C **The United States Secretary of State at the time of the outbreak of the Korean War, writing later, explains the reasons for the North Korean attack on South Korea.**

It seemed close to certain that the North Korean attack had been mounted, supplied, and instigated by the Soviet Union and that it would not be stopped by anything short of force. If South Korean forces proved unequal to the job, only American military intervention could do it. Plainly, this attack was an open, undisguised challenge to our internationally accepted position as the protector of South Korea, an area of great importance to the security of American-occupied Japan. Therefore we could not accept the conquest of this important area by a Soviet puppet.

Dean Acheson, *Present at the Creation: My Years in the State Department*, 1969

D **A modern historian gives her view on the origins of the Korean War.**

The origins of the Korean War lie primarily with the division of Korea in 1945 and the polarization of Korean politics that resulted from the policies of the two occupying powers. The Soviet Union played a key role in the outbreak of the war, but it was as a means of carrying out Kim's plan, not as the originator of his plan.

Kathryn Weathersby, article, 1993

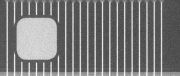

3 How far did the Korean War and its origins (1950–53) change the US conduct of the Cold War in Asia?

How did the Korean War cause disagreements between Truman and MacArthur?

The USA reaction to the North Korean attack on 25 June 1950

On 25th June 1950, ten combat divisions of the North Korean army launched its surprise attack on the South, equipped with Soviet tanks and artillery and directed by Soviet military officials. North Korean soldiers fought in what they saw as a war of national independence, to liberate and unite all Korea.

Truman, however, on the contrary, saw the attack as a direct communist challenge to the free world and to US global influence, with North Korea acting as a puppet of Soviet expansion. His immediate reaction was that 'the attack upon South Korea makes it plain beyond all doubt that communism has passed beyond the use of subversion to conquer independent nations, and will now use armed invasion and war.'

Figure 3.4 The Soviet Union's seat is conspicuously vacant as the UN Security Council votes on 27 June 1950 to use force to push North Korean troops out of South Korea.

The USA put a resolution before the United Nations Security Council on that same day, 25 June 1950. It called for a cease-fire behind the lines of the 38th parallel. Involving the United Nations made the war into one of 'collective security'. America presented the attack as one upon the United Nations itself. The UN resolution was passed by nine votes to nil, with Yugoslavia abstaining. The Soviet Union was unable to exercise its veto due to its absence in protest at the Council's refusal to let Communist China take the seat occupied by Nationalist China. The same evening, Truman ordered US air drops of supplies to South Korea and, on 29 June, MacArthur was ordered to intervene in the fighting with air and naval forces, though he was denied the use of land forces. It seemed that Washington was determined to pursue a limited war from the start. Two days later, the UN passed a resolution to create a military force to defend South Korea. MacArthur was placed in charge of UN forces, and his ego was such that he saw himself as invincible. Truman's television address to the American people stated:

> 'Korea is a small country thousands of miles away, but what is happening there is important to every American. The fact that communist forces have invaded Korea is a warning that there may be similar acts of aggression in other parts of the world.'

From the start, the USA assumed that the invasion could not have happened without Soviet involvement. The Korean War began as a very popular war amongst Americans.

HONEST, MISTER, THERE'S NOBODY HERE BUT US KOREANS

Figure 3.5 Cartoon by David Low published in the *Daily Herald*, 28 June 1950, which delivers the message that the USSR was responsible for the outbreak of the Korean War.

What part did MacArthur and United Nations Command forces play in this phase?

The UN viewed the North Korean invasion as an unprovoked act of aggression, and asked member states to give military aid and other supplies to South Korea. Troops from 15 countries aided US troops in the United Nations Command force (UNC), which organised a counter offensive in mid-September. The main UN strategic objective was to avoid a major war on the Asian continent.

MacArthur organised a massive reinforcement of the Pusan perimeter and, by end of August, had built up a troop superiority ratio of 2 to 1. He planned a counter-offensive by sea at Inchon as a diversion, so his forces could break out from Pusan and surround the North Koreans in a pincer movement. MacArthur planned a brilliant amphibious attack on Inchon, the port for Seoul, by the 'X-Corps' of 80,000 men under the command of Major General Almond. Luckily the North Koreans hadn't mined the harbour, despite Chinese advice to do so. The war at this stage seemed to be a civil war with international help, but there was some Soviet presence among the troops of the North.

The beachhead at Inchon was secured and the UNC forces advanced quickly inland, combining forces with a US infantry division which had been flown there. On 19 September, the break out from Pusan confused the North Koreans and drove them back. On 28 September, Seoul was retaken, with 50,000 casualties, and the bulk of the North Korean army found itself cut off in a pincer movement of two UNC forces. The following day MacArthur ceremonially reinstalled Syngman Rhee's government in Seoul.

Phase 2: 'Rollback' of communism to the Yalu River, September to October 1950

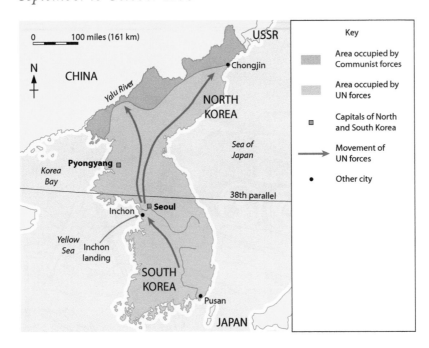

Figure 3.6 Map showing Phase 2 of the Korean War.

The hawks of the Defence Department were now driving policy and they had $15 billion annual expenditure to defend US prestige. In a memo of July they had argued that:

> *'the free world should take this opportunity to displace a communist state from the Soviet orbit.'*

In this way they presented the conflict as a war by the USA against a Soviet proxy. Despite British Foreign Office misgivings about the possibility of Chinese intervention, Foreign Secretary Ernest Bevin persuaded the Cabinet to agree to a UN offensive to advance across the 38th parallel and unify Korea under Syngman Rhee's control. However, this action was not at Rhee's request, but seen as in keeping with the US role of 'global policeman'. Truman was persuaded by Congress and by hawks, such as Rusk, Dulles and MacArthur. False intelligence suggested North Korea was weak despite Soviet aid. Elections were approaching and McCarthyists were pressing for hard line action.

The UN also played its part, but the USA was forced to use the General Assembly rather than the Security Council, to which the USSR had returned in August 1950. By declaring North Korea the aggressor, the UN reminded the world that its Charter obliged its members to defend a nation state whose territorial integrity had been violated. In practice, the UN did not recognise North Korea as a state, so the 'border' of the 38th parallel ceased to exist in its eyes. It viewed Korea as one country, and hoped a military advance would soon unify it.

On 7 October, a UN resolution proposed:

> *'all appropriate steps be taken to ensure conditions of stability throughout Korea; and elections be held, under supervision by the United Nations, to establish a unified, independent and democratic government in the sovereign state of Korea.'*

This resolution gave backing to MacArthur's advance into North Korea, but he made sure to allow South Korean forces to form the front line. This change of policy, known to the USA as 'rollback' (to roll back the advance of communism), was now authorised by the United Nations General Assembly. It also set up a commission to oversee elections in the 'soon to be liberated' country of Korea.

NSC 81 and its limitations on MacArthur's actions

Truman accepted a new policy document, NSC 81, ordering MacArthur to cross the parallel but stipulating that only Korean troops were to be used near to the Soviet and Chinese borders. MacArthur later ignored this order. If the USSR were to intervene, MacArthur was ordered to assume a defensive position and consult Washington. Later he also ignored this order. If the Chinese were to intervene, though this was not expected, MacArthur could continue the UNC offensive as long as he judged he had a good chance of success. This order proved to be sensibly cautious, as China in fact was watching events and had strong views on whether to intervene.

The following quote shows Mao's views. It was written by a British Minister in Beijing, to report a conversation between Zhou Enlai and the Indian Ambassador on 3 October:

> 'Zhou Enlai informed the Indian ambassador that if "American" forces crossed the 38th parallel the People's Government of China would send in troops to defend North Korea. Zhou said that action would not be taken if only South Korean troops were to cross the 38th parallel. He added that he would accept no settlement of the Korean problem to which China was not a party.'

MacArthur's over-confidence made him feel that there was no chance of China intervening. Two days after crossing the parallel, he ordered Kim to surrender, which Kim refused to do in a radio broadcast from Pyongyang on 10 October.

MacArthur met with Truman five days later, on Wake Island in the Pacific, and told the President that victory would be achieved in time for the Eighth Army to be home by Christmas. On 19 October, US forces took Pyongyang and on 24 October, MacArthur ordered UNC forces to move north as far as the Yalu River, violating Truman's orders to use only Korean forces in the border region. He was pursuing a 'total victory' policy. After querying his order, Washington approved this move. This decision was to lead to direct war with Chinese forces.

Why did MacArthur provoke Chinese intervention?

The CIA predicted that China would not send in troops, based on intelligence reports that Mao was worried about UN intervention in the light of his desire to take a seat on the Security Council. Mao's concern seemed to focus on the sending of the US Seventh Fleet to Taiwan. But on 27 August 1950, US planes had accidentally attacked Manchurian airfields. Mao feared the American forces would invade the Chinese mainland. Mao therefore sent 90,000 experienced troops to defend Manchuria as a precaution. This number had grown to 300,000 along the northern bank of the Yalu River during August, with orders to prepare for possible involvement in the conflict. The Chinese did not wish the Americans to confront them across the Yalu River.

PRC

The People's Republic of China.

Stalin responded to Kim's pleas for help by asking Mao to send 'volunteers' to buy time for the North Koreans to regroup. Mao quickly refused, fearing a war against the USA which might not only hinder the **PRC**'s economic reconstruction, but also escalate into a full-scale

3 How far did the Korean War and its origins (1950–53) change the US conduct of the Cold War in Asia?

confrontation between the two superpowers. Stalin argued that it was a good time to show Sino–Soviet solidarity, as the USA was not ready for a global war. Japan was disarmed and could not aid US forces. The USA would have to abandon its peace treaty with Japan, and make it a regional defensive partner instead. Mao was persuaded by secret cables from Stalin to intervene in Korea, in the hope of avoiding a two-front war with the USA in Taiwan and along the Yalu River, so he committed nine divisions of Chinese troops to support North Korea.

ACTIVITY

Analyse these two posters (Figures 3.7 and 3.8) as evidence for propaganda during the Korean War.

Figure 3.7 Not many Chinese posters have been produced that explicitly show North Koreans actively engaged in their struggle against US troops during the Korean War. In the few examples that are available today, the North Koreans are barely distinguishable from their comrades-in-arms, the Chinese People's Volunteers. In this poster the member of the Chinese Volunteers is on the right, creating the impression that the Chinese are doing the bulk of the fighting.

Figure 3.8 A completely different picture emerges when looking at North Korean sources, if only because they do not acknowledge any of the armed support they received from the Chinese.

Phase 3: Chinese involvement and escalation, October 1950–February 1951

On 14 October, 180,000 Chinese troops secretly crossed the Yalu River into Korea. The fighting had severely reduced the numbers of both the North and South Korean armies. On 19 October, Pyongyang, capital of North Korea, fell to UN and South Korean forces. The lightly-equipped Chinese were more used to the bitter North Korean winter weather as it set in. They sheltered in caves and drew on their experiences of guerrilla action in the Chinese Civil War. The US forces, who had reached their target as they approached the Yalu River, were looking forward to returning home for Christmas. They had been told that no Chinese forces had been detected in the area, although some sightings had been rumoured. Unknown to them, on 25 November 1950, the entire US Eighth Army was encircled.

US troops celebrated Thanksgiving on 23 November, but on 27 November the eerie noise of Chinese bugles sounded a sudden attack. PRC forces annihilated them at Kunu-ri and the entire UNC Army was forced south in a disorganised rout. Acheson declared that 'giving up the part of Korea we do not yet occupy would at this time be interpreted as a sign of weakness.' Then, two days later, the First US Marine Division and elements of the US Seventh Division were surrounded and scattered by 300,000 Chinese Communist forces at the Chosin Reservoir. Many US troops were taken prisoner, and they abandoned vehicles and equipment as they hastily retreated. Shockwaves resounded through the US army and public, undermining morale, as the impact of an unthinkable defeat of the strongest superpower by Chinese 'volunteers' struck home.

> ### Source
>
> **Captain Charles Bussey of the 77th US Engineer Combat Company described the US retreat in the face of the Chinese attack at Chosin.**
>
> *We'd been humiliated, debased, overwhelmed, routed. The news writers would slant it all to sound like a minor setback. Take it from me, however, it was carnage. Intelligence said* *they'd hit us with a million men. I believe it. They turned our army into a leaderless horde, running headlong for Pusan. Our soldiers had lost every bit of confidence in all of their leaders, from the commander-in-chief down to the platoon leaders.*
>
> C.M. Bussey, *Firefight at Yechon: Courage and Racism in the Korean War*, 1991

The UNC general HQ went into a state of total panic at this humiliating defeat. On 30 November, in a press conference, Truman said he would take 'any steps necessary to meet the military situation' and admitted that the USA might be considering using the atom bomb.

Figure 3.9 The marine and army retreat from the Changjin (Chosin) reservoir in December 1950 occurred in temperatures of around zero degrees Fahrenheit (minus 17 degrees Celsius). These are some of the 385 able-bodied survivors of the 2,500 Seventh Division men caught in a series of Chinese ambushes along the eastern shore of the Changjin (Chosin) reservoir in late November, 1950.

How did US allies react to the escalation of the war?

- NATO allies of the USA feared being drawn into an escalated war between the superpowers that might affect Europe. To break with American policy in Asia would threaten US support in Europe.
- France also feared Chinese intervention in Indochina, where they were fighting insurgency led by Vietnamese Communist, Ho Chi Minh.
- British Prime Minister Attlee met with Truman and won the concession that the USA would inform Britain and Canada before using the atom bomb. However, this was not a written agreement and involved no requirement to consult them.

By 5 December, the US Eighth Army was 25 miles south of Pyongyang and by the end of the month had reached the 38th parallel, losing all their gains in North Korea. Chinese forces crossed the 38th parallel and took Seoul on 4 January 1951. General Ridgway now led the Eighth Army and was the new Field Commander. (His predecessor, General Walker, had been killed in a car accident north of Seoul.) Ridgway evacuated Seoul and withdrew from Inchon. UN forces adopted a 'scorched earth policy', blowing up ports as they retreated. The war was about to turn into a dangerous **war of attrition**.

War of attrition

The military strategy of wearing down the enemy by continual losses in personnel and materials.

How did the USA react to the shock of defeat in North Korea?

- General MacArthur's response was to put forward a list of targets in China and Korea, which he said required the use of 26 atomic bombs!
- Right-wing Republican Senator Joseph McCarthy called for the impeachment of Truman and the resignation of Secretaries of State Acheson and Marshall.
- Truman declared a state of national emergency on 15 December 1950. The Third World War seemed imminent.

Phase 4: stalemate – the war of attrition, January 1951–July 1953

The US forces had air superiority, using similar tactics to those used in the two World Wars. Stalin now sent Russian MiG fighters with well-trained and experienced Soviet pilots to the war zone, posing a serious challenge to US air supremacy. They were originally intended to train North Korean pilots, but soon found themselves directly involved in war. Stalin demanded complete secrecy, so that the Americans would never know they were fighting Russians, in case direct confrontation between the two superpowers resulted. US F86 Sabre and F9F Panther aircraft were introduced to restore US air supremacy and to keep up consistent bombing of ground targets. They carried 100 gallon **napalm** tanks as well as conventional 1,000-pound bombs, and used them on occasions.

Napalm

A jellied gasoline that burns deeply into the skin.

Seoul became the target of the North Korean allies, and it fell to them on 4 January. Soon UN troops were forced to abandon Inchon and withdraw even further south. The USA began the 'Operation Thunderbolt' counter offensive on 25 January. News of a general withdrawal of Northern forces along the border led General Ridgway to adopt a war of attrition, beginning with 'Operation Killer'. He hoped to bring the Communists to the negotiating table in February 1951. This was followed in March by 'Operation Ripper' and in April by 'Operation Rugged'. In the meantime, on 15 March, combined forces of the USA, UN and ROK recaptured Seoul and the North Koreans were driven back across the 38th parallel. The front stabilised once more. Many UNC troops were captured and subjected to systematic brainwashing by their Chinese and North Korean capturers.

By mid-March, Washington began to recognise that the war had entered a stalemate phase, and refused to recommend any more major military surges across the 38th parallel. The Truman administration now thought in terms of restoring the pre-war situation. The President privately prepared for a limited peace initiative with the Communists. However, he had no intention of allowing the PRC to take a seat on the UN Security Council.

How acceptable were Mao's pre-conditions for a ceasefire?

Mao had hoped to gain a seat on the Security Council, as well as weakening US power in Asia, which he had already achieved. He informed the UN Secretary General, Trygvie Lie, of his pre-conditions for a ceasefire:

- withdrawal of UN troops from Korea;
- agreement that only Koreans should resolve the conflict;
- a UN Security Council seat for the PRC;
- the expulsion of Taiwan;
- a conference to be set up to prepare a Japanese peace treaty.

The reaction of the UN, under US influence, was to table a resolution in the General Assembly to declare China an 'aggressor'. However, debate on the resolution was delayed by 48 hours due to the opposition of 27 states, including Britain, France and Canada. In this 'cooling-off' period, the Americans made some limited changes to the resolution which delayed further measures against China, and on 1 February it was passed by a vote of 44 in favour to 7 against, with 9 abstentions. The opportunity for cease-fire negotiations had been lost. But MacArthur's personal methods of 'delaying further measures against China' meant demanding their unconditional surrender.

How did MacArthur bring about his own downfall?

MacArthur's popularity in the press and with the American people who regarded him as a war hero, made it very difficult for Truman to remove MacArthur from his position, in spite of several incidences of openly defying Truman's orders. The following table describes MacArthur's eventual downfall.

Date	Action
October 1950	MacArthur refused to salute Truman
December 1950	In an interview with a journalist MacArthur publicly questioned Truman's political decisions and blamed his defeats on the restraints imposed by European pressure on the President (that he was not allowed to bomb China's Manchurian bases). He was told not to repeat such an indiscretion.
15 March 1951	MacArthur, in a press statement, stated his intention to unify the two Koreas and requested permission to bomb the Manchurian bases and poison the Yalu river with radioactivity.
20 March 1951	Truman informed MacArthur of his intention to order a ceasefire on the 38th parallel
24 March 1951	MacArthur made a public statement threatening China with war on their own territory. He was reprimanded by Truman.
5 April 1951	MacArthur wrote a letter to the Republican leader arguing against Truman's policy. The letter was read out in the House of Representatives. He criticised the European priority and argued for total victory in Korea with the use of Taiwanese Nation Forces. This would lead to war with China and alienation of American allies in Europe.
11 April 1951	MacArthur was sacked.

Given MacArthur's popularity, the removal of MacArthur could have been disastrous for Truman but he had the backing of some like-minded Republicans who recognised the necessity to replace MacArthur with someone who was prepared to follow the administration's foreign policy. Also, the Joint Chiefs of Staff were offended by MacArthur's military inconsistencies and felt it was time for him to be replaced.

Sources

(A) In a book serialised in a popular American magazine, MacArthur's military secretary at the time of the Korean War explains MacArthur's frustrations at the limitations placed upon him in November and December 1950.

MacArthur ordered bombing of bridges over the Yalu River, ignoring instructions to stay well clear of Soviet and Manchurian borders. He hotly disagreed when the Joint Chiefs of Staff suggested he hold his line short of the Yalu, because of Chinese intervention. Their suggestion was prompted by the views of other U.N. countries involved and British fears that MacArthur might involve the west in a large-scale war with Communist China. Angry about his forces' defeat by the Chinese, MacArthur defended himself sharply, blaming the enormous limitations on his operations caused by selfish European interests. He criticised both the U.N.'s 'limited war' policy and Truman's administration, who were trying hard to reassure uneasy allies.

Major General Courtney-Whitney (1956). *MacArthur: His Rendezvous with History*

(Sources continue on page 80.)

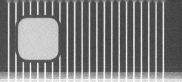

> **B** On the day he relieved General MacArthur of his command, the President addresses the American public on television.
>
> *I believe we should limit the war to Korea for these vital reasons:*
>
> ■ *to make sure that the precious lives of our fighting men are not wasted*
>
> ■ *to see that the security of our country and the free world is not needlessly jeopardised*
>
> ■ *and to prevent a Third World War.*
>
> *A number of events have made it evident that General MacArthur did not agree with that policy. I have therefore considered it essential to relieve General MacArthur so that there would be no doubt or confusion as to the real aim of our policy.*
>
> From a speech by Harry S. Truman broadcast to the nation, 11 April 1951

ACTIVITY

1 Compare Sources A and B as evidence of reasons for a 'limited' or 'total' war strategy.

2 Use Sources A and B to plan and hold a debate between the supporters of Rhee and the supporters of Truman. Decide who has the better strategy for the future course of the Korean War.

Attempts to break the stalemate

Congress strengthened NATO's military structure and sent General Eisenhower to head a unified NATO command. General James Van Fleet assumed tactical command of the Eighth Army in Korea. Offensives and counter offensives continued under his command, with little land changing hands.

On 18 May 1952, members of the United Nations Organisation (UNO) started a military goods boycott of the People's Republic of China. The war of attrition resumed on 30 May, when 'Operation Piledriver' began, leading to Ridgway broadcasting the first American request for peace talks at the end of June. Then Washington authorised the bombing of Korean power plants on the Yalu River. A month later Pyongyang was attacked by the US air force. It was to take two more years of stalemate before an armistice could be signed.

How did President Eisenhower finally bring the war to an end?

On 5 August, Syngman Rhee won another clearly rigged election in South Korea. This was in contrast to the landslide Presidential election victory for Republican **Dwight D. Eisenhower** on 4 November. Eisenhower had promised to go to Korea in person, and go he did. At the end of the month, he secretly travelled to Korea on a fact-finding mission and by February had replaced the frustrated General Van Fleet with Lieutenant General Maxwell Taylor.

Eisenhower, a Second World War General with an immense reputation, newly-elected as president, brought extra impetus to the peace negotiations. He did not shrink from threatening the use of nuclear weapons, a policy which Richard Nixon was later to copy in trying to end the Vietnam War. Both had learned lessons from Joseph McCarthy's damaging 'commie' allegations at the time of the 'Red Scare'.

BIOGRAPHY

Dwight David 'Ike' Eisenhower (1890–1969)

Eisenhower was President of the United States from 1953 until 1961 and a five-star general in the US Army. During the Second World War, he served as Supreme Commander of the Allied forces in Europe, with responsibility for planning and supervising the successful invasion of France and Germany in 1944–45. In 1951, he became the first Supreme Commander of NATO. As US President, he oversaw the cease-fire of the Korean War, kept up the pressure on the Soviet Union during the Cold War, made nuclear weapons a higher defence priority, launched the Space Race, enlarged the Social Security programme, and began the Interstate Highway System. He was the last First World War veteran to serve as US president.

Why did it take so long to reach a peace settlement?

The sticking point was a symbol of Cold War ideological tensions: the question of prisoners of war. Both sides mistreated their prisoners of war, using severe beatings and bayoneting those who did not keep up on marches. Others died from dysentery or malnutrition. One in three Americans POWS died during the first winter of the war, and those who survived were often indoctrinated by communist propaganda.

> **Source**
>
> **A UN soldier captured by the Chinese records the speech of a Chinese senior officer after the Battle at Imjin, showing communist views on indoctrinating prisoners of war.**
>
> *You have been tricked by the American imperialists. You are tools of the reactionary warmongers, hired by the barbarous Rhee puppet-government. You will be given the chance to learn the truth through study, and correct your mistakes. Do not be afraid, we shall not harm you. At home your loved ones await you. Obey our rules and you will not be shot.*

There were approximately 130,000 communist prisoners of war. The Americans insisted that no prisoners should be repatriated against their will, suggesting the attraction of democratic values might make them unwilling to go home. Violent protests dogged the POW camps. The Chinese, supported by Stalin, requested that all Chinese and North Korean prisoners must be returned. This question was not resolved until June 1953, when 75,000 were handed over.

Kim Il Sung had tried without success to get Stalin to make peace, because of the devastation of North Korea from US bombing, which had continued during the talks. Most of the big cities in North Korea were flattened. As many as 2 million North Korean civilians were killed and Pyongyang was totally destroyed. But Stalin wished to keep the USA tied down in Korea, to distract them from other theatres of the Cold War. Only after his death, on 5 March 1953, did Soviet participation in talks become possible. On 23 June, the Soviet representative at the UN delivered a radio speech declaring that the USSR was prepared to negotiate.

On 27 July 1953, the final *Peace Treaty* was signed at Panmunjom. The point of contact close to the 38th parallel became the boundary between the communist North and the anti-communist South. China and the USA were relieved to end hostilities, though Eisenhower warned that any breach of the terms would bring a nuclear reprisal from

3 How far did the Korean War and its origins (1950–53) change the US conduct of the Cold War in Asia?

America. Cold War tensions continued unabated. South Korea refused to sign the treaty. Rhee would not admit that his hopes of leading a united Korea were over.

General Mark W. Clark wrote that he had 'the unenviable distinction of being the first US Army commander to sign an armistice without victory.' More than a million Koreans died in the War, the neglected victims of a conflict that saw raids continue well into 1954. Serious long-term tensions remained, which have intensified with the recent development of nuclear capability by North Korea.

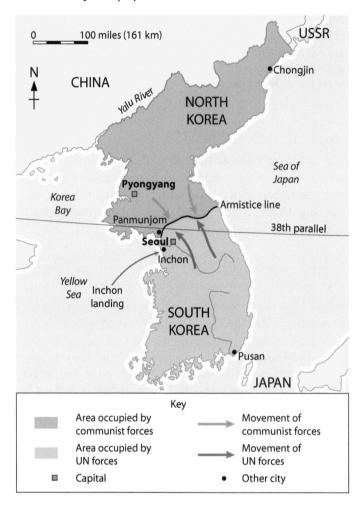

Figure 3.10 Map showing the armistice line at the end of the Korean War, 1953

ANALYSIS

What was the significance of the Korean War?

- **'Proxy war' between the Cold War superpowers?**

  The way in which the Korean War has been seen has changed over time. Primarily, it was interpreted as an example of the Cold War in practice, as a superpower 'proxy war' between North Korea, as a proxy of the Soviet Communist expansion on one side, and the forces of defensive Western liberal democracy on the other. Alternatively, the USA was seen as acting provocatively with its superpower allies to extend and confirm its global power. The fundamental 'Cold War' argument was that any gain by one side would be to the detriment of the other anywhere in the world. The Korean War was seen as a turning point, an intensification of existing rivalries, which confirmed military and diplomatic alliances and consolidated the political power of the USA and USSR.

ANALYSIS cont.

■ Collective security in practice?

More recent interpretations have suggested the Korean War was a practical application of the principle of 'collective security', part of a wider global peace effort by the United Nations to avoid a Third World War. Truman stressed the importance of learning the lesson of appeasement and the weakness of the League of Nations in the 1920s and 1930s, which many felt contributed to the outbreak of the Second World War. However, critics of this view have pointed out that the United Nations Command (**UNC**) forces were far from neutral or objective, and were largely led and funded by the USA.

■ US containment of communism?

The Korean War has been seen as consistent with the USA's own 'containment' objectives, reinforcing its role as 'global policeman' with the added claim to legitimacy within a United Nations peace-keeping force. However, the War also marked an important turning point in US strategy, with a shift from the Defensive Perimeter Strategy to a 'forward' war on mainland Asia itself. It was also the first test of whether the USA would settle for a 'limited' rather than 'total' victory to avoid direct confrontation with the USSR. Under MacArthur, as Supreme Commander of the UN forces, the outcome of this test was never predictable and you can see hints of later '**brinkmanship**'.

■ A limited, local war?

Most recently, the origins of the War have been seen as local to the Korean peninsula itself, as a revolutionary nationalist struggle against corruption and foreign domination. Both North and South claimed that their aim was to achieve national independence for a united Korea. Historians of the 1980s viewed it as a civil war, with Korean civilians themselves as the primary actors in the events leading to the War, and the impact of the War viewed as limited and local rather than global.

■ A multi-causal war?

There are certainly elements of a national, local civil war, but set in the context of the bi-polar world dominated by the USSR and USA. No conflict anywhere in the world could remain of only local concern. For the USSR, Korea had always been the launch pad for foreign attacks on Russia. It could also be seen as an ex-colony of Japan, the satellite now at the heart of US strategy in Asia. The USSR publicly condemned South Korea for provoking civil war between the two Korean states. It also sought to justify North Korea's 1950 offensive as 'responding to unprovoked South Korean aggression' instigated by the USA. However, documents released in the 1990s show that the 1950 offensive was planned jointly by the USSR and North Korea, but also that Chinese approval played an important role, indicating that North Korea was far from a Soviet pawn. As far as the UN forces were concerned, Britain and France had colonial interests in South-East Asia, and the French needed US help in Indochina. Turkey sent UN forces to gain acceptance into NATO. Pacific interests motivated the Australians and New Zealanders who joined the Canadians in the first ever Commonwealth division of UN forces.

UNC

United Nations Command; US Generals MacArthur, Ridgway and Van Fleet were commanders of the UN forces as well as the US Eighth Army.

Brinkmanship

The practice of pushing a dangerous situation to the verge of disaster in order to achieve the most advantageous outcome.

ACTIVITY

Discuss the analysis on the interpretation of the Korean War, and reach a supported judgement on which interpretation is most convincing.

What were the military, strategic and financial consequences of the Korean War?

Military

The USA created a 'fortress America' as a result of NSC 68, which had for the first time advocated the funding of US troops in peacetime. Serving members of the US armed forces more than doubled, to over 3.2 million, as a result of the Korean War. Army divisions rose

3 How far did the Korean War and its origins (1950–53) change the US conduct of the Cold War in Asia?

from 10 to 18, air force wing groups from 42 to 72, and US Navy ships from 600 to more than 1,000. By 1952, there were 6,000 CIA personnel in the Office of Policy Co-ordination, marking a huge rise on the 302 employed in 1949. The 7 foreign CIA branches in 1951 had grown to 47 by early 1953.

The Korean War proved Mao right in his view that US nuclear capability was a 'paper tiger', unusable for fear of global destruction. Subsequent administrations felt restrained in their objectives and forced to fight a 'limited war' of air-strikes, attrition and nuclear threats. From 1954, the USA was to try to save face after the humiliation in Korea, by protecting Taiwan and its offshore islands, and becoming increasingly embroiled in an immensely more costly war in Vietnam. There the USA shrank from liberating a communist state by a military invasion, fearing another thrashing by the Chinese and Soviets who had collaborated in aiding North Korea. Indeed, Chinese and Soviet veterans of the Korean War became involved later in Vietnam.

The Korean War proved to be a turning point in global rearmament. It increased global security due to fears of 'Mutually Assured Destruction' (MAD). Policy was seen starkly in context of potential confrontation between two balanced superpowers. The War changed the attitudes of America's NATO allies from that of reluctance to contribute to defence spending to a willingness to see even West Germany rearmed. Averell Harriman is quoted as having said that it took the Korean War to 'put the "O" in NATO'. The War made NATO seem inadequate on its own, making America's European allies agree to discuss the creation of a European Defence Community revised into the Western European Union. Agreement was also obtained for moving the defensive line of the strengthened NATO further eastward into Europe.

There was significant opposition in Congress to the policies that pushed China to intervene in Korea. This reined in the freedom of future administrations to pursue an interventionist foreign policy. The US public pressurised governments to ensure Congress played a major role in formulating policy. In future, their approval was required before US troops could even be sent to NATO in Europe.

The War cost an estimated four million Korean casualties, 10 per cent of the population. There were ghastly atrocities on both sides, including Rhee's mass executions of those suspected of being communists. Innocent civilians were often the victims. The Chinese suffered an estimated one million casualties; the US lost 33,600 men killed and 103,200 wounded. 75,000 of the 130,000 Communist prisoners of war were handed over after the signing of the treaty, and 12,000 UN prisoners of war were also set free.

The US disarmament policy for occupied Japan was reversed as an effect of the Korean War, so that it could take its place at the heart of the Defensive Perimeter Strategy of US military bases in the Pacific chain. The *US–Japan Security Treaty* enabled the long-term stationing of formidable US ground, air and naval forces in Japan and the Pacific island chain. American strategy would not neglect Asia in future. The War delayed the US peace treaty with Japan until September 1951. A separate treaty was signed between Japan and Taiwan (see Chapter 2). The USSR and China were isolated from that treaty process.

Financial

The financial impact of implementing NSC 68 meant that American military spending more than quadrupled between 1950 and 1953. Before the Korean War, US annual military expenditure was anticipated at about $13 billion, but the estimates for programmes planned in September 1950 rose to $287 billion over five years. In the USA, a trade-off was necessary between military spending and social reform costs, which allowed Republican Congressmen to block Truman's 'Fair Deal' programme.

Increased military costs aggravated existing balance of payments deficits in Britain and France, causing the USA to increase its spending to help them pay for the expensive military build-up associated with the proliferation of nuclear weaponry. The increased costs of defence contributed to de-colonisation by powers such as Britain and France, which left significant power vacuums in some parts of the world.

Japanese business gained a major impetus from arms-related contracts which boosted the Japanese economy. Toyota was one company which was declining before the war, producing only 300 trucks in June 1950, but 5,000 for the US market in the following year. Its shipyards refitted US ships and its electronics industry began to dominate global production. By 1954, the Japanese defence industry had earned the country $3 billion worth of goods. By the late 1950s, the Japanese economy exceeded pre-war levels for the first time, producing textiles, construction materials, motor vehicles, communications, short-band radios and chemicals for the US market.

The Korean War had proven very costly in undermining China's economic reconstruction after the damaging Civil War. The USSR found the costs of financing the War and supplying North Korea were not worth the minimal improvement in bargaining position, so compromise and *détente* (easing of tensions between countries) were more likely choices for Stalin's successors.

Strategic

Korea failed to gain national unification and sovereignty. It remained divided at point of contact at the end of the War, not at the 38th parallel itself. North and South Korea faced each other across a de-militarised zone, at the cutting edge of the Cold War, in a similar way to divided Germany across the 'Iron Curtain'. The lesson of Korea was that the Cold War might at any time erupt into open fighting, but without direct confrontation between the USA and USSR it remained a limited, local war. There was, though, an element of a 'proxy war': Korea marked the one Cold War conflict where Soviet and US fighter pilots engaged in dogfights and Chinese ground forces confronted American infantry in open combat.

South Korea

- South Korea was militarily secure with an army of 600,000 men who could potentially face North Korea or the Chinese. It gave the USA a considerable number of troops for the Vietnam War.
- Rhee gained a mutual defence treaty from the USA, long-term economic aid and the presence of the US Eighth Army for the rest of the Cold War period.
- South Korea emerged from the war domestically unstable with frequent student protests and authoritarian governments. Rhee himself was overthrown in a *coup d'état* in 1961.

North Korea

- North Korea remained a powerful military state with close links to the USSR and China. Re-indoctrination in communism was necessary to raise money for its successful economic reconstruction by the late 1950s.
- Kim Il Sung followed Stalin's lead in executing his opponents and creating a myth of personality which allowed him to retain power and later pass it to his son, Kim Jong Il, who rules Communist North Korea today.

The USA, USSR, People's Republic of China and the UN

- The Korean War could be seen as a loss for the USA, which had to be content with limited power in Asia. However, if the USA had not intervened, the USSR and PRC might have extended their power on the Asian mainland. The USA learned the lesson never again to try to liberate a state by invasion, though George W. Bush later ignored this lesson in Iraq with disastrous consequences.

- The USSR and PRC defended their existing positions, but failed to dislodge the USA from the Asian mainland. Stalin's death was followed by a power struggle which brought a breathing space in Cold War tensions. The economic costs to China meant it had to resort to guerrilla tactics during the rest of the Cold War period. Mao's support for the USSR strengthened Sino–Soviet relations in the short term, making the USA stubbornly refuse the PRC a seat on the UN Security Council until Nixon's presidency in 1971. However, China had fought largely alone, and Soviet requests that China pay for all the military equipment the USSR had supplied led to a rift in their relations with the USSR. The PRC increased its influence in Asia and the Third World, and its veterans became advisers to the Vietnamese liberation movement.

- The UN could claim a victory for 'limited war' and fulfilment of its demands with only minor concessions in the peace treaties. The failure to resort to using nuclear weapons raised questions about their value as a deterrent, despite the nuclear threat tactics used by MacArthur, Truman and Eisenhower. Unfortunately, although the UN acted decisively in intervening, unlike its predecessor the League of Nations, its action was only made possible by the chance of the USSR's absence from the Security Council. The tactic of attrition had enabled 'limited war', preventing escalation, and was used in later wars.

US policy

- The USA no longer relied solely on economic aid and the creation of model democratic states in Asia.

- It strengthened the defensive perimeter of Pacific offshore islands.

- It accepted that military action on the mainland might be the only way to prevent the 'domino effect' of neighbouring states falling to Communism one after the other.

- It recognised an escalation in the intensity of the Cold War by strengthening NATO, with increased interest in Europe and Asia.

- There was a tactical shift away from the objective of total victory to 'limited war' and the maintenance of the status quo.

- The influence of Congress on policy increased, thanks to MacArthur's insubordination.

- Public opinion began to have greater influence on policy. Administrations could not afford to ignore the electorate. For example, a father disgusted by his son's fate in Korea sent his 'purple heart' medal back to Truman with a bitter letter which generated enormous public interest.

US status – propaganda and reputation

The Korean War was to an extent a propaganda success for US 'containment' policy. America wished to win a propaganda victory, implying that some communist prisoners of war would be forced home against their will. The propaganda war had also involved communist accusations that the USA was involved in germ warfare, with claims that swarms of infected insects had been dropped on North Korea. On a visit to Paris in 1952, after his appointment as NATO Supreme Commander, General Ridgway was greeted with

SUMMARY ACTIVITY

To what extent did the Korean War mark a major turning point in US policy and status? Draw a mind map to represent the key issues.

protestors calling him 'Ridgway La Peste' (Ridgway the Plague). However, this claim was less credible than the charge that napalm had been used by the Americans, building on Japanese experiments with chemical warfare.

The USSR and China publicly denounced the dependence of South Korea and Japan on the USA. They also published propaganda exposing the differences between British and American views on China to drive a wedge into the 'special relationship' on which the United Nations was founded (see Figure 3.11).

Figure 3.11 Cartoon by Leslie Illingworth published on 29 January 1951. Stalin drives Korea as a wedge between the USA and Britain to destroy the special relationship of the two countries on which the United Nations had been founded. The mallets represent the views of the USA and Britain on whether China should be allowed to take its seat on the UN Security Council.

Conclusion

This chapter has focused on a shift in US policy. No longer did the Americans rely on the Defensive Perimeter Strategy to establish democratic, capitalist model states across the Pacific islands to contain communism. In 1950, the USA found itself drawn, against its will, into a three-year war on the Asian mainland between North and South Korea. This necessitated rapid rearmament by the USA to try to maintain the global balance of power. It had to face not only the Soviet threat in Eastern Europe, exemplified by the Berlin Blockade in 1948–49, but perceived Soviet expansion into Asia backed by a Sino-Soviet alliance.

The Korean War marked a significant turning point in US Cold War strategy. Previous plans for economic reconstruction, in line with Marshall Aid and the reconstruction of Germany and Japan, now gave way to the defence of democracy by open but conventional warfare on the Asian mainland. However, though the USSR backed Communist North Korea and China intervened on its behalf and UN forces from 15 countries fought alongside US troops, this remained a limited, local war. There was no direct military confrontation between the two superpowers, both of which had nuclear capability by 1950.

3 How far did the Korean War and its origins (1950–53) change the US conduct of the Cold War in Asia?

Some historians have called the Korean War a 'forgotten war', as US public opinion felt deeply humiliated by its outcome: limited victory and maintenance of the status quo. At the time, General Marshall, the pre-eminent US military historian, called the Korean War 'the century's nastiest little war'. It seemed at the time that this claim was unlikely to be surpassed. However, accounts written later about the 'forgotten' war in Korea distorted its nature and significance. By the 1970s, Americans were swamped by a wave of despondency in the wake of the US retreat from Vietnam.

What was the role of the UN, USA, USSR and China in the course of the Korean War?

North and South Korea – a local war

The war can be seen as a local war of independence. Both North and South wished to see Korea united and independent of foreign control, and approximately 4 million of them died in this cause.

Kim Il Sung was the driving force in playing off Stalin and Mao to gain the support and military advice he needed before invading South Korea in June 1950. He refused to surrender to MacArthur, when UN forces advanced over the 38th parallel. His forces were determined and well led. He negotiated continued Chinese and Soviet military aid, yet kept the independence of North Korea after the War. He was willing to accept the peace terms in order to maintain North Korea and continue to push for the eventual unification of the country by more peaceful means.

Syngman Rhee played his part in the 'local war', appealing for US aid against the wishes of Truman's administration, and building good relations with successive military commanders. However, his corrupt regime hindered the US policy of attempting to create a model democratic state, and so he may be seen as contributing to the outbreak of the war. The USA refused to arm South Korea for fear that he would provoke superpower confrontation, so again mistrust of him contributed to the start of the war. He was hampered by lack of US military aid and advice in the run up to the war and its early stages. He sided with MacArthur in wishing to extend the war into China, so cannot be seen as acting in Korean interests in the same way as Kim. His military forces played a limited part in the war, and generally proved weak and unpopular.

UN – collective security

Through their attempt at trusteeship, but the willingness to accept elections in South Korea alone, the United Nations played a part in the divisions which began the war. The flexibility of its organisation allowed the USA to direct the war through the General Assembly when the USSR returned to the Security Council. However, it acted decisively and collectively in condemning the North and raising military forces to aid the USA and the South. It raised troops from 15 other countries so that the USA would not be seen as acting unilaterally, as imperialist or aggressive, so containing the threat of superpower confrontation. It was the United Nations' authority which allowed UNC forces to cross the 38th parallel into North Korea, due to its Charter and its resolution to work for a united Korea. Unrest within the UN, and NATO, restrained the USA from using nuclear weapons and it oversaw the peace treaty which ended the war in 1953.

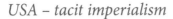

USA – tacit imperialism

US backing for the puppet Rhee regime in South Korea might be interpreted as immoral, as it was neither liberal nor democratic. Successive Presidents backed Rhee due to the defensive policy of containment, but laid themselves open to communist criticisms of neo-colonialism by setting up a regime without popular or national support. Negatively, the USA provoked the war by sending out the message, in January 1950, that it would not intervene in Korea as there were more pressing concerns in Europe. Together with its unwillingness to arm South Korea, this encouraged communist powers to view Korea as a potential **sphere of influence**. The Defensive Perimeter Strategy had been a half measure, publicly announced and based on military cutbacks, whereas NSC 68 was not openly stated. Therefore the change of policy to one of military intervention on mainland Asia came as a surprise to Mao and Stalin, after Kim's invasion had already taken place. Had NSC 68 been stated clearly the communist forces may have restrained Kim. US troops made up the bulk of UNC forces, leading some commentators to see the war as US action under a veil of collective security. MacArthur played a dominant role in military events, during his tenure of command, with both positive and negative effects. His troops defended the Pusan perimeter heroically and the landing at Inchon was a military inspiration. However, his advance to the Yalu River using US troops, against Truman's orders, brought China into the war and came close to provoking a nuclear war. Truman acted wisely in restraining and sacking him in the face of the many McCarthyist jibes against his action. The USA played a major part in the aerial bombing campaign and held out for the rights of prisoners of war (POWs) in negotiating peace terms. It adjusted to a mindset of 'limited war' after a history of gaining total victory in past wars. Unfortunately, it did not learn the lesson of Korea and avoid involving itself in Vietnam.

Sphere of influence

A geographical, and also political, area that can be influenced by either the USA or the USSR, or another superpower.

USSR – a 'proxy' war

The USSR co-operated in halting at the 38th parallel in 1945, to avoid confrontation with a stronger USA, and acted in a very restrained way during the Korean War, even though it had its own nuclear capability by then. It gave Kim military advisers, supplies, tanks, MiG fighters and pilots, but tried to back the North without causing confrontation. It co-operated with the Chinese and encouraged their involvement in the war so that it could give its attention to Europe, hoping that the USA would find itself overstretched and Eastern Europe could be consolidated within the Soviet sphere of influence. Mao and Kim might be seen as 'proxy' clients of the USSR. Stalin proved a block to peace negotiations, especially concerning the return of **POWs**, and this could also be seen as a delaying tactic to aid Soviet strength in other theatres of the Cold War. A change of regime in Moscow was the most significant factor in speeding up the peace talks.

POWs

Prisoners of war

China – defence or imperialism?

The fall of China to communism encouraged Kim and humiliated the USA. This made the USA show its strength to maintain its superpower status, hence NSC 68. China was the trigger for Kim's invasion, as Stalin had insisted Mao had to give the go-ahead before he would sanction Kim's invasion of South Korea. Chinese 'volunteers' prevented North Korea from falling under UN/US control and America from extending its influence over the whole of Korea to threaten the rest of the Asian mainland. China established itself as a major power as a result of the war, and was encouraged to aid the North Vietnamese communists. The War strengthened relations between China and the USSR in some ways, but Chinese resentment at the lack of Soviet help started it on the slippery slope to a Sino–Soviet dispute.

3 How far did the Korean War and its origins (1950–53) change the US conduct of the Cold War in Asia?

Limited war – rather than total victory

None of the international participants wished to see the war become a global confrontation between superpowers. Truman had realised that the use of nuclear weapons for 'total victory' was unacceptable to the rest of the international community. In future, maintaining the status quo proved the most realistic action in the face of communist expansion. Eisenhower backed 'limited war' with the threat of using nuclear weapons and there was a shift to the more limited aim of maintaining the US reputation. The Cold War had developed a 'psychological' dimension, when all the participants wished to win the 'media war' and claim victory.

Skills practised

In this chapter you have:

- learned and practised the skills of source analysis, comparison and evaluation
- linked four or five sources to a question in order to evaluate an interpretation to answer it
- studied the contextual information to understand these sources and use their provenance
- gained knowledge of the origins, causes, course and consequences of the Korean War.

Bibliography

Bragg, C. (2006). *Vietnam, Korea and US Foreign Policy 1945–75* (Heinemann Advanced History). Oxford: Heinemann.

Halberstam, D. (2007) *The Coldest Winter: America and the Korean War*. New York: Hyperion.

Hastings, M. (1987). *The Korean War*. London: Pan.

Hickey, M. (1999). *The Korean War: the West confronts Communism, 1950–1953*. London: John Murray.

Kaufman, B. I. (1996). *The Korean War: Challenges in Crisis, Credibility and Command (America in Crisis)* 2nd edn. xxxMcGraw Hill.

Lee, S. H. (2001). *The Korean War, 1950–1954*. Harlow: Longman.

Malkasian, C. (2001). *The Korean War (Essential Histories)*. Oxford: Osprey Publishing.

Manchester, W. (1978). *American Caesar: Douglas MacArthur 1880–1964*. Boston: Little, Brown

Meernik, J. D. (2004). *The Political Use of Military Force in US Foreign Policy*. Farnham: Ashgate.

Articles

Wingrove, P. 'Who Started Korea?' *History Today*, July 2000 Volume: 50 Issue: 7

Websites

See www.heinemann.co.uk/hotlinks

Videos/DVDs

CNN video: Korea Ch. 9

Why and with what results did the USA become involved in Vietnam to 1968?

4

91

This chapter deals with the most disastrous episode in the story of US policy in South-East Asia, the Vietnam War. We will look at Eisenhower and the end of French control in Indochina 1954; the rise of the Viet Minh; the *Geneva Agreement*; the influence of the 'domino theory'; the impact on the USA of the fall of Diem's regime; the emergence of the NLF in 1960; the impact of Kennedy's aid, military advisors and interventions 1961–63, and Johnson's Gulf of Tonkin Resolution. We will evaluate the results of US intervention up to 1968.

In this chapter you will build up more experience in the skills of source analysis, interpretation and evaluation. You will gain more knowledge of the developing strategies used by the USA in Asia to maintain its reputation as a global superpower. You will practise analysing sources, grouping them for argument and using your knowledge to evaluate their content and provenance to answer a question.

Key questions

The key questions for evaluation are:

- What were the reasons for the rise of the Viet Minh?
- Why was there controversy over the Geneva Agreement?
- What policy did Eisenhower follow concerning the end of French control in Indochina in 1954?
- Why and how did the NLF emerge in 1960?
- What policy did the US follow in the lead up to the fall of Diem's regime?
- What effects did Kennedy's policies have (1961–63)?
- Was Johnson's policy concerning the Gulf of Tonkin incident a miscalculation?
- What were the results of intervention to 1968?

French Indochina and the origins of conflict

One of Truman's aims had been to reinstate old colonial European powers in South-East Asia in order to spread the costs of defending the area from Soviet expansion. This ran counter to US anti-imperialist rhetoric and, after the fall of China to communism, proved a difficult task. When France failed to control nationalist and communist forces in Indochina, the USA found itself obliged to fill the power vacuum. The integrity of Japan and the trading sphere of the southern Pacific were in jeopardy, but successive American Presidents found themselves trapped in what had begun as a war of national independence on the border of Communist China.

Timeline 1930–1966

1930	Ho Chi Minh founds the Indochinese Communist Party (ICP).
1941	ICP organises a guerrilla force, the Viet Minh, in response to invasion by Japan during Second World War.
1945	The Viet Minh seizes power. Ho Chi Minh announces Vietnam's independence.
1946	French forces attack the Viet Minh in Haiphong in November, sparking the war of resistance against the colonial power.
1950	Democratic Republic of Vietnam (DRV) is recognised by China and USSR.
1954	The Viet Minh forces attack an isolated French military outpost at Dien Bien Phu. The attempt to take the outpost lasts two months, during which time the French government agrees to peace talks in Geneva. At the Geneva conference, Vietnam is split into North and South at the 17th Parallel.
1956	South Vietnamese President Ngo Dinh Diem begins campaign against political dissidents.
1957	Beginning of communist insurgency in the South.
1959	Weapons and men from North Vietnam begin infiltrating the South.
1960	American aid to Diem increases.
1962	Number of US military advisors in South Vietnam rises to 12,000.
1963	• The Viet Cong, the communist guerrillas operating in South Vietnam, defeat units of the ARVN, the South Vietnamese Army. • President Diem is overthrown. • The USA enters the war.
1964	US destroyer allegedly attacked by North Vietnamese patrol boats. This triggers start of pre-planned American bombing raids on North Vietnam.
1965	200,000 American combat troops arrive in South Vietnam.
1966	US troop numbers in Vietnam rise to 400,000, then to 500,000 the following year.

Eisenhower, Kennedy and Johnson all tried to save face as they embarked on the tricky task of securing the south-west corner of the Pacific Rim to contain the spread of communism and prevent 'domino' states falling. Indochina was the key domino which might set the others rolling. They tried similar tactics to those used in the Philippines and Korea: supporting a puppet regime with economic aid and military advisers, attempting to secure democratic reforms and a prosperous economy. But Vietnam had a much stronger, more united nationalist spirit than Korea, with a popular communist leader who used Mao's revolutionary tactics and drew inspiration from the USSR. In the 1960s, the USA prioritised the Cold War distractions of Berlin and Cuba, and domestic reform policies. However, the evolving disaster of involvement in Vietnam made the war there a national obsession.

Figure 4.1
A map showing the main regions of French Indochina before the Vietnam War.

Indochina held key strategic significance for the security and trade of South-East Asia (see Figure 4.1). Vietnam's traditional enemy was China, which had dominated it for more than a thousand years from 111 B.C. to 938 A.D. In the fifteenth century, Vietnam expanded southwards and took the Mekong delta from Cambodia. Its first contacts with the West came through Jesuits and merchants more than a century later. Its people were fiercely independent and had developed effective warrior techniques to hold off the persistent ambitions of their vast Chinese neighbour.

After France had defeated Siam and China in brief wars in the 1860s and 1880s, it sought to compete with the empires of other European powers and took over much of Indochina. Internal quarrels enabled it to divide the region into five provinces:

- the territory of Cochinchina;
- the protectorates of Tonkin and Annam (which together form modern Vietnam);
- Laos;
- Cambodia.

This federation, based on the principle of 'divide and rule', continued until 1954. Formal power remained in the hands of local rulers, such as the Emperors of Vietnam and the Kings of Cambodia. In practical terms, however, they were merely figureheads and the real power lay in the hands of the French imperialists.

Fertile Cochinchina in the south became the area to which French settlers flocked. Economic exploitation of the land took place, with rubber plantations established along the border with Cambodia and productive rice-fields in the virgin lands and drained marshes of the Mekong delta. The capital of Cochinchina, Saigon, became known as 'the Paris of the Orient', full of prosperous Vietnamese traders and absentee landlords. The region was transformed culturally with French education, food and clothing. The French-educated Vietnamese professional classes desired peaceful, moderate reform through the Constitutional Party, but even this was denied by the colonisers.

What were the reasons for the rise of the Viet Minh?

More revolutionary national movements began resistance almost immediately the French took control. Early revolts aimed to restore the local mandarin class, but once they failed, it was only a matter of time until French policies stifled further opportunities. The colonial power prevented the emergence of an educated middle class, leaving resistance in the hands of peasant national movements. Indochina had strong rural communities and resistance, under early nationalist leaders such as Phan Boi Chau, focused on demonstrations, violence and propaganda. In the 1920s these fledgling nationalists were suppressed by the French and their remnants forced into exile in China.

Ho Chi Minh and the ICP

ICP

The Indochinese Communist Party

The **ICP** emerged as the most resilient nationalist movement. Their leader, renowned in history as Ho Chi Minh (1890–1969, see Figure 4.2), was born Nguyen Sinh Cung at Hue, the son of a mandarin, or local official. His father was away on business when Ho's mother died in childbirth when he was 11 years old. Ho detested the French, even though his father paid for his French education. His father criticised the government for accepting French rule, and was demoted from the status of mandarin because of his nationalist activities. He wandered the countryside as a teacher and doctor. Ho was expelled from his prestigious academy at the age of 17 for helping a nationalist protest. Ho left Indochina after enlisting as a seaman on a French merchant ship in 1911 and spent 30 years travelling the world. He experienced the impact of colonialism on many other countries, but while in France, applied, but was turned down, as a trainee colonial official. He spent some time in America, taking menial jobs in hotels in New York and Boston, and may have been influenced by Korean Nationalists in exile there. He continued on to London during the the First World War, and worked under the famous French chef Escoffier at the Carlton Hotel.

Figure 4.2 Ho Chi Minh

Ho ended up in Paris in 1919, at the time of the Versailles Peace conference, and became inspired by post-war views of anti-colonialism and national self-determination. He admired Maurice Chevalier, a popular singer, and reviewed films for a French newspaper. He published anti-colonial news sheets for French Vietnamese and smuggled his views back to Vietnam. He was condemned to death by the French Vietnamese regime should he ever set foot in Vietnam again. He became one of the founders of the French Communist Party in 1920, at a time when the Bolshevik Revolution was transforming Russia, calling himself 'Nguyen the Patriot'. Under this pseudonym he presented a petition to Woodrow Wilson for Vietnamese civil rights, but it was ignored.

In 1923, he left Paris to study in Moscow, where he took the name *Ho Chi Minh* ('Bringer of Light') and was invited to join the Comintern (Communist International Organisation). He made Soviet links that were to continue and strengthen throughout his life. He was sent to China the following year to form communist groups, met up with other nationalists and formed the Indochinese Communist Party (ICP). By 1927 he could speak several languages and saw himself as a professional revolutionary. In 1930, hoping to emulate the events of 1917, he led his party in organising peasant revolts against French rule. In 1931, Ho began two years' imprisonment in a British jail in Hong Kong before returning to Moscow. He had a wife or concubine in Hong Kong at this time, though later propaganda claimed he was celibate. He joined the Chinese Communists during their civil war and was imprisoned by Jiang Jieshi's local authorities. His ideas were smuggled into Indochina. He changed his name several times to avoid capture. After a time in Thailand, disguised as a Buddhist monk, he deliberately disappeared and was reported dead.

In 1941, Ho Chi Minh returned to the jungles of North Vietnam after 30 years' absence, and formed the **Viet Minh** by merging the ICP with more moderate groups, with the dual objectives of national independence and social reform. The majority of the peasants knew nothing of him, so he presented himself to them as their 'Uncle'. He appealed to the issues the people cared about: social change, land reform and better working conditions. He did not talk of communism and the movement began to gain momentum. Two years later, he suggested to the US forces in southern China that they train his Viet Minh forces against the Japanese, but was turned down. By that time, French weakness had been exposed by their humiliating surrender to Hitler. They had been forced to concede Indochina to Japanese imperial control under nominal French administration.

Ho returned to Vietnam and attempted to lead an uprising in the south. This time, not only was the uprising crushed but several important leaders were executed and he was imprisoned. He was released in 1943 after persuading his captors to use him as a spy against the Japanese. He walked to North Vietnam and resumed the leadership of the ICP at the age of 53. He managed to gain some aid from the American secret service in return for spying on the Japanese and rescuing downed US pilots. He considered the Americans his allies, smoking American cigarettes and gaining their help in setting up the Viet Minh. He received radios, weapons and training from them.

In March 1945 the Japanese overthrew the French colonial system and placed the figurehead Emperor **Bao Dai** (see page 96) at the head of a collaborative government. There was a power vacuum, especially in the countryside. It was the intensity of the Vietnamese national identity which gave the Viet Minh its unity and domination. It led a resistance movement against the Japanese during the Second World War. Other national movements in Vietnam and South-East Asia were splintered and quarrelled amongst themselves.

Viet Minh or 'League for the Independence of Vietnam'

Was a national liberation movement which dated its foundation to 19 May 1941 in South China. The Viet Minh initially formed to seek Vietnamese independence from France and later to oppose the Japanese occupation.

4 Why and with what results did the US become involved in Vietnam to 1968?

BIOGRAPHY

Emperor Bao Dai (1913–1997)

He was born in Hue (ancient capital of Indochina); the son of Emperor Khai Dinh (a puppet of the French colonial regime) and a concubine of peasant ancestry, Nguyen Vinh Thuy. He was educated in France and spent little of his youth in his homeland. He succeeded to the throne in 1926 and assumed the title Bao Dai ('Keeper of Greatness'). He initially sought to reform and modernise Vietnam but was unable to win French co-operation.

During the Second World War the French colonial regime exercised a firm control over Bao Dai until the Japanese swept away French administration in Indochina in March 1945. The Japanese considered bringing back the aging Prince Cuong De from Japan to head a new semi-independent Vietnamese state, but they finally allowed Bao Dai to remain as an essentially powerless ruler. When the Viet Minh seized power in the August revolution of 1945, Ho Chi Minh and his colleagues judged that there was symbolic value to be gained by having Bao Dai linked to them. The Viet Minh asked Bao Dai to resign and offered him an advisory role as 'Citizen Prince Nguyen Vinh Thuy.' Finding that the Viet Minh accorded him no role, and distrustful of the French, Bao Dai fled to Hong Kong in 1946. There he led a largely frivolous life, making appeals against French rule.

In 1949 the French accepted the principle of an independent Vietnam but retained control of its defence and finance. Bao Dai agreed to return to Vietnam, in these circumstances, in May 1949, and in July he became temporary premier of a tenuously unified and nominally independent Vietnam. Reinstalled as sovereign, Bao Dai continued his pleasure-seeking ways and became generally known as the 'Playboy Emperor.' He left the affairs of state to his various pro-French Vietnamese appointees, until the French defeat at Dien Bien Phu in May 1954, when it was agreed that South Vietnam would be ruled by Ngo Dinh Diem, a strong opponent of communism. In October 1955 a national referendum called for the country to become a republic. The South Vietnamese people were asked to choose between Bao Dai and Ngo Dinh Diem for the leadership of the country. US Colonel Edward Lansdale helped Diem rig the vote. Bao Dai retired to France and died in Paris in 1997.

When Japan surrendered, Bao Dai abdicated. The French were in no position to continue ruling after four years of occupation and collaboration with the Nazis, so the Communist Viet Minh seized the government headquarters in Hanoi in the north (see Sources A–C, opposite).

To live down public criticism for the fall of China, Truman supported France in Indochina, exaggerating the Soviet threat to get $15 million annually. Eisenhower, frustrated by limited victory in Korea, refused to accept the Geneva Accords. His increase in US involvement, with military advisers in South Vietnam, cost $100 million, provoking the USSR and China. The Christian Secretary of State, Dulles supported Catholic Diem who was overthrown with Kennedy's acquiescence in 1963. Kennedy attempted 'flexible response' to please 'hawks' and 'doves', sending 16,000 US combat troops to prop up weak South Vietnamese military regimes. Secretary of Defense McNamara's counter-insurgency policy, under Kennedy, escalated to Johnson's bombing campaigns with half a million troops deployed.

Sources

The first two sources, describing events of 1945 in the countryside, are oral accounts recorded in Stanley Karnow, *Vietnam: a History*, **published in 1984.**

(A) A villager from Thai Binh province, in the Red River Delta of north-east Vietnam, recalls the 'August Revolution' when the Viet Minh seized power.

The village marketplace was jammed. A man in brown pants and a cloth shirt climbed onto a chair, and guards armed with machetes, spears and sticks surrounded him. He delivered a speech, saying that the Japanese had surrendered to the Allies, and that the time had come for the Viet Minh to seize power. I was just a teenager in ragged clothes and I asked a schoolmate, 'Now that we've seized power, who will be the mandarin?' He replied 'Get this. The mandarin is just a peasant - really ordinary.'

(B) An eyewitness recalls the trial of a village official, conducted by the Viet Minh in front of the whole village.

They read out the charges. The official had been an accomplice of the Japanese but said he was just carrying out orders. He had forced the peasants to pull up their rice to plant jute and peanuts, enriching himself, though the peasants were miserable and dying. The Viet Minh announced that his crime was very serious because he had opposed the revolution and helped the enemy. So they sentenced him to death and shot him right there. This really fired up the people. They dragged Japanese accomplices out of their houses, making them lower their heads and beating them.

(C) Ho Chi Minh declares the Independent Democratic Republic of Vietnam (DRV) in Hanoi on 2 September 1945. Wearing his trademark faded khaki suit and rubber sandals, he reads out his statement to half a million people in front of the French governor's mansion. His comments are based on the American Declaration of Independence.

All the peoples on the earth are equal from birth, all the peoples have a right to live, to be happy and free. For more than eighty years, the French imperialists, abusing Liberty, Equality and Fraternity, have violated our Fatherland and have oppressed our fellow citizens. They have acted contrary to the ideals of humanity and justice. In politics, they have deprived our people of every democratic liberty. They have wrecked our national unity. They have drowned our uprisings in rivers of blood. They have impoverished our people and devastated our land. By their taxes, they have reduced our people to a state of extreme poverty. The French imperialists went down on their bended knee and handed over our country to the Japanese Fascists who had violated Indochina's territory. Our people have broken their chains. We represent the whole Vietnamese people in declaring that we are determined to fight to the bitter end against any attempt by the French to reconquer our country. The entire Vietnamese people will use all their physical and mental strength; sacrifice their lives and property to safeguard their independence and liberty.

ANALYSIS

It is debatable how far Ho was sincere in his admiration for the American constitution (see Source C above) and how far he was making a bid for US support for his regime. Ho was flattering the USA by likening his struggle to their War of Independence, and disarming their hostility by stressing that free Vietnam was a nationalist state, not a communist one. He knew that Roosevelt had expressed support for Vietnamese independence and disliked de Gaulle, so perhaps it was a genuine gesture of solidarity. He had wanted a trusteeship solution in Indochina, similar to the one attempted in Korea. However, US attitudes had begun to shift since Roosevelt's death. The pro-European lobby in Washington sought British and French support to share the costs of containing communism. Truman was less interested in Asia and less anti-colonial in his views.

ACTIVITY

Use these three Sources (A–C) to evaluate the view that the Viet Minh seizure of power was a 'people's revolution'.

4 Why and with what results did the US become involved in Vietnam to 1968?

BIOGRAPHY

General Vo Nguyen Giap (c.1911– present)

Giap was from an educated gentry family, attended the University of Hanoi and became a history teacher. He was brought up with anti-colonial views and joined the communist movement in 1926. He educated himself in guerrilla tactics and developed a patient approach to winning a people's war. Equipped with a Law degree, and with experience as a journalist, he became Minister of the Interior in the newly created Democratic Republic of Vietnam (DRV) in 1945. He also served as Politburo member of the Lao Dong Party. He became President Ho Chi Minh's defence minister, Viet Minh military commander during the First Indochina War (1946–1954) and defeated French forces at Dien Bien Phu in 1954. After this success he was made Deputy Prime Minister of North Vietnam. He was commander of the People's Army of Vietnam (PAVN) during the Vietnam War (1960–1975) and was responsible for major offensives and inspiring leadership until the war ended. He retired from politics in 1982.

After Ho's speech (Source C), a Vietnamese band played The Star Spangled Banner as General **Giap** was joined by US Army officers for his parade of troops and American aircraft flew overhead.

In September 1945, the **Independent Democratic Republic of Vietnam** (DRV) claimed control over Tonkin, Annam and Cochinchina, but they faced not only internal challenges, such as other nationalist and religious groups, but also foreign challenges to their legitimacy:

Independent Democratic Republic of Vietnam (DRV)

The Independent Vietnamese state declared by Ho Chi Minh on 2 September 1945.

- During the Second World War it had been agreed that Jiang's Chinese Nationalists should receive the surrender of the Japanese in northern Indochina, and there might have been a danger of annexation. But though they ransacked the area, the Chinese could not afford to be distracted, as they were preparing to resume their civil war. Chinese forces moved in to occupy and disarm the Japanese, but did not interfere with the new government.

- Under an allied plan, the British took control of southern Indochina, but soon had to deal with internal unrest fomented by the Viet Minh. The British had to use surrendered Japanese forces to get some semblance of order in Saigon.

- In October 1945, General LeClerc and 5000 French forces arrived in Saigon and, together, they and the British drove Viet Minh forces out of Saigon. The French had re-established control over the whole of South Vietnam by the end of the year. De Gaulle was determined to retain the French empire intact to restore his country's prestige. He wished to restore control in the form of a French Union. Truman tried to help re-establish French control by negotiation with Ho during 1946, but Ho was satisfied with nothing less than total independence.

A succession of weak, short-lived ministries in France hesitated on whether to copy the British in their 1947 withdrawal from India or make a larger financial commitment to keep control of Indochina. Ho went to Paris to find a basis for negotiations, offering to integrate smaller nationalist parties into a National Assembly to govern the north. In March 1946, a preliminary agreement was drawn up to make the DRV a free state within the French Union. But without strong direction from Paris, local French officials followed an independent line and fighting resumed.

Franco-Viet Minh hostilities, 1946–50

The French launched a bombardment of Haiphong, the main port in northern Vietnam, and mounted an **amphibious assault** on the north which resulted in the capture of Hanoi, capital of Vietnam, in February 1946. The French then set up garrisons throughout the northern provinces. They publicly claimed they were seeking independence for the region by setting up a Vietnamese state under Bao Dai in 1949. With no prospect of colonial rule French troops lost the will to fight, giving confidence to the Viet Minh. The French were not used to the Viet Minh habit of retreating to more remote areas and launching guerrilla attacks.

Viet Minh tactics copied those used by Mao in the Chinese Civil War:

> 'When the enemy advances, we retreat. When the enemy halts and encamps, we harass him. When the enemy seeks to avoid battle, we attack. Whenever the enemy retreats, we pursue.'

Mao's forces attacked quickly with a sudden concentration of force and then quickly dispersed when the attack was over. They avoided, at all costs, pitched battles against forces that outnumbered them. Communists in unfriendly territory operated underground and through a united front. When a military operation was mounted, it aimed to follow classic Maoist insurgency theory: overrun police outposts and remote military bases; let the state overreact with human rights abuses; capitalise on the resulting public anger over the abuses to gain support and win new recruits. Giap was able to build up his forces in the mountains and rural areas, while the French concentrated on the cities. This pattern also characterised the later Vietnam War.

> **Amphibious assault**
> Attack by land and sea.

Sources

(A) **The Military commander of the Viet Minh describes the 'people's war' he is waging.**

Our nationwide war against France, which was a people's war, was a new development; it was a truly revolutionary war, a war by the entire people, a total war. The masses were mobilised and organised with the aim of achieving national democratic revolution. Our Party's correct revolutionary line succeeded in grouping all patriotic layers of the population in a broad front, based on a strong worker-peasant alliance. We carried out a reduction of land rent, land reform, political struggle in urban centres and enemy-occupied areas, together with an economic and cultural struggle. To keep the offensive, the revolutionaries must ceaselessly develop guerrilla war into regular war. Only through regular war can the forces of the people annihilate enemy forces and liberate vast areas of land.

Vo Nguyen Giap, 1946

(B) **The President of the Democratic Republic of Vietnam (DRV) likens the Viet Minh to a tiger and the French forces to an elephant.**

If the tiger stands still, the elephant will crush him with his mighty tusks. But the tiger does not stand still. He lurks in the jungle by day and emerges by night. He will leap on the back of the elephant, tearing huge chunks from his hide, and then he will leap back into the dark jungle. And slowly the elephant will bleed to death.

Ho Chi Minh, 1946

(Sources continue on page 100.)

C **The US Secretary of State makes a blunt public statement about Ho Chi Minh's political outlook, in response to French requests for American aid.**

Questioning whether Ho is as much a nationalist as a Commie is irrelevant. All Stalinists in colonial areas are nationalists. With achievement of national independence, their objective necessarily becomes subordination of the state to Commie purposes and ruthless extermination of not only opposition groups but all elements suspected of even the slightest deviation.

Dean Acheson, May 1949

D **The US Secretary of State informs President Truman of his views on whether the USA should support French colonial control of Indochina.**

The choice confronting the USA is to support the French in Indochina or face the extension of Communism over the remainder of the continental area of South-East Asia, and, possibly farther westward. We then would be obliged to make staggering investments in those areas and in that part of South-East Asia remaining outside Communist domination or withdraw to a much-contracted Pacific line. It would seem a case of 'penny wise, pound foolish' to deny the French support in Indochina'

Dean Acheson, memorandum, 2 February 1950

ACTIVITY

How far do Sources A–D support the interpretation that the War in Indochina of 1946–49 was driven by French and American imperialism?

The impact of Mao's victory in the Chinese Civil War

The victory of Mao's CCP in China in October 1949 transformed the situation in Vietnam in three respects:

- Firstly, the Chinese sent weapons and artillery to Ho and provided him with facilities to train large numbers of guerrillas for open combat. In January 1950, Ho declared his was the only legitimate government, a claim recognised by the USSR, the CCP and the rest of the Communist bloc.

- Secondly, the French now argued that they were no longer fighting a colonial war, but had been drawn into the global war against communism. They used the excuse that the Chinese were supplying arms to the north to portray the Indochinese War as part of the global Cold War. This ensured the USA would have to become involved.

- Thirdly, the outcry in the USA following the fall of China had seriously undermined Truman's administration. They did not wish to be seen to appease communists and were not prepared to countenance further expansion of communism.

Truman was determined to stand firm to protect the trade and security of South-East Asia. In May 1950, he gained approval from Congress for $15 million dollars of aid, to supply the French with weapons, lorries and transport aircraft for the conflict in Indochina. US arms began to be shipped to Saigon (capital of the south), and the West recognised the French-sponsored Bao Dai regime. From this small beginning grew the involvement which was to lead the USA into the disaster of the Vietnam War. The US National Security Council issued policy documents **NSC 64 and 68**, arguing that Indochina was a crucial link in the defensive perimeter and tripling US military spending.

NSC 64 and 68

Two US National Security Council Documents which respectively proposed US aid for the French in Indochina and a tripling of US military expenditure.

Truman support for the French war effort, and the *Battle of Dien Bien Phu*

By the end of 1950, the Americans had sent only a few dozen men to Saigon, as a Military Advisory Group. Eisenhower supported the French with $100 million of supplies, including US aircraft, patrol boats and ground combat equipment, which was shipped to Saigon. However, there was uneasiness in Washington about propping up old colonial regimes.

Also, though anti-communist containment policy won the day, the more aid that was supplied the more the French seemed to request. The USA did not wish to repeat its mistake with Jiang in China, by 'pouring sand down a rat hole'. They had to make sure the money was used wisely. The security of the **defensive perimeter**, south-east Asian trade and democratic values were all at stake. But the US military response was half-hearted, as it had been in Korea, and the French had to fend for themselves when a period of intensive fighting followed.

The situation in 1951–1953

In 1951, the French General de Lattre de Tassigny, High Commissioner and Commander-in-Chief introduced a new strategy to secure key areas in northern Indochina, with air power to attack Viet Minh bases and the 'de Lattre line' of defences to protect Hanoi. Mobile columns supported by air power defeated Viet Minh forces, under Giap, with heavy casualties, but they regrouped in the rainy season. De Lattre reoccupied the frontier area to cut Viet Minh supply routes from China. However, French troops were out on a limb and more troops were tied down protecting lines of communication with northern outposts.

In November, de Lattre returned to France, saddened by the death of his son in Indochina, and died two months later. General Raoul Salan took his place and saw that the French needed to send more troops if they were to have a chance of crushing the Viet Minh. However, the French government refused to allow conscripts to be called up for Indochina, as the public was disillusioned with the war. By April 1953, the Viet Minh had invaded Laos, stretching French forces even further. The French tried to close this door to the Viet Minh by signing an independence treaty with Laos in 1953, which allowed a continued presence of French troops there.

The Battle of Dien Bien Phu, May 1954

An uneasy peace had at last been obtained in Korea, but the new President, Eisenhower, preferred to let ex-colonial powers deal with unrest in their states rather than deploy US troops. Supplied by $385 million of US aid and weapons, the French felt their superior fire-power would allow them to win a better bargaining position in negotiations, if they could lure Giap into the open. The French chose the village of Dien Bien Phu, on the main Viet Minh supply route from China to Laos. Unfortunately, it was a hollow, surrounded by hills. On 20 November, the French seized the village using an air attack, refortified it and supplied its garrison by air. They felt Giap would need to concentrate on it, but he would not be able to bring in heavy artillery to re-capture it due to the dense jungle terrain. Giap and the Viet Minh solved this problem by hacking a new supply route through the jungle, and brought in Chinese anti-aircraft guns and weapons in pieces and reassembled them.

At the beginning of the attack the Viet Minh had dug over 100 kilometres of trenches around the northern French strong points of Beatrice, Gabrielle, and Anne-Marie. The command post at Beatrice was destroyed in the initial artillery attack and all radio communications with the outpost ceased. The Viet Minh bombed the airfield, preventing reinforcements. Gabrielle fell to massive artillery fire and infiltration. Viet Minh anti-aircraft guns were hidden throughout the area but those in the hills around Claudine were temporarily knocked out by a French attack. The Viet Minh dug trenches approaching the strong points of Dominique and Eliane. Viet Minh infantry assaults overcame the outpost at Eliane, and Isabelle was isolated, where 1,000 French troops fought for survival. By the end of April, the French only held parts of Huguette, Dominique, and a few highpoints on

Defensive perimeter
A chain of Pacific off-shore islands with US military bases to contain the spread of Communism in Asia and defend vital resources and trade for the West.

4 Why and with what results did the US become involved in Vietnam to 1968?

Eliane. The final assault was launched by waves of Viet Minh following artillery barrages. The French would beat back one assault only to be hit with more waves. The final Viet Minh assault on 1 May reduced the French to scattered pockets of resistance, they were encircled. Plans for a breakout had been considered, but the situation became hopeless and the French commander ordered his men to surrender on 7 May, destroying what weapons and equipment they had left. Although they inflicted heavy casualties on the Viet Minh, the *Battle of Dien Bien Phu* was a tactical and operational failure for the French. It was a deep humiliation and a military turning point, as the first victory for a Third World Asian army over European ground forces in regular combat. It was a victory for Mao's theory of **communist revolutionary warfare** (see pages 99–102).

Why was there controversy over the Geneva Agreement?

Peace negotiations had already opened in Geneva before the *Battle of Dien Bien Phu* began. In mid-1953, policy makers were hoping for a quick settlement for Indochina, but Secretary of State, **John Foster Dulles**, would not agree until the tide of battle turned and France could dictate terms. Containment was a case of strategy over diplomacy. The Geneva Conference, which opened on 26 April 1954, was attended by:

- Great Britain
- the USSR
- France
- Communist China
- the Democratic Republic of Vietnam (DRV)
- Cambodia and Laos.

The USA and representatives of Bao Dai's State of South Vietnam were observers and took no part in proceedings. Dulles even refused to shake hands with Zhou Enlai, the Chinese Foreign Minister. After the defeat at Dien Bien Phu, the French government and Western public opinion gave up hope of retaining Indochina.

Communist revolutionary warfare

Phases from terrorism to open warfare, dependent on support of the local people. (See page 99.)

BIOGRAPHY

John Foster Dulles

From a military background, Dulles criticized containment which he felt should be replaced by a policy of 'liberation'. Under Eisenhower, he neutralized the Taiwan Strait during the Korean War and supervised the signing of the Japanese Peace Treaty. He built up NATO and other alliances, with a strategy to control Soviet expansion. He was architect of SEATO and strongly opposed the Anglo-French invasion of the Suez Canal in 1956. (See also page 14.)

ACTIVITY

Read the following five Sources and use them for the Role play exercise which follows.

Role Play: The 1954 Geneva negotiations to end the French Indochinese War.

- Form 7 groups. 3 groups should each represent one of the following countries: the warring sides: North Vietnam and France, and China, which backed Ho. The next 2 groups represent the USSR and Britain, the chair countries. The final 2 groups are reluctant observers with firm views: South Vietnam and the USA.

- Firstly, rate your bargaining position in relation to the other countries.

- Secondly, draw up the list of your demands on which you will negotiate terms.

- Thirdly, decide which concessions you would be willing to accept.

- Hold your 7-power discussion, write up your agreement and decide which of you will sign it. You should explain your reasons if you do not wish to sign.

Sources

A **The President of the Democratic Republic of Vietnam (DRV) expresses his views on the need for peace negotiations with France.**

The war has been forced on us by the French government. But if the French government wishes to sign an armistice, and solve the Vietnam problem through negotiations, we are ready. The people of France oppose the war because it has caused them much suffering, but it is not just the independence of Vietnam which is under severe attack, the independence of France is also seriously threatened. On the one side, American imperialism drives the French colonialists to continue and extend the war of re-conquest in Vietnam with the object of making the French weaker and weaker and overtaking her place in Vietnam. On the other side, American imperialism forces France to sign the European Defence Pact which means the rebirth of German militarism.

From: Ho Chi Minh, interview, 29 November 1953

B **The US Secretary of State appeals for a collective response to defend Indochina from Communism, in the event of a French withdrawal when the Battle of Dien Bien Phu appeared to be lost. This was within a year of the ending of the Korean War.**

The Chinese Communists have avoided the direct use of their own Red armies in open aggression against Indochina, but they promote that aggression by all means short of open invasion. The imposition on South-East Asia of the political system of Communist Russia and its Chinese Communist ally must be a grave threat to the whole free community. The United States feels that possibility should be met by united action.

John Foster Dulles, 29 March 1954

C **The British Conservative government explains its views on the need for a political settlement at Geneva.**

Any direct intervention by the armed forces of any external nation would probably result in Chinese intervention, with the danger that this would eventually lead to global war. As long as there is a hope of success, we should continue to urge the French to maintain their present policy. The provision of increased military aid and instructors appears to be the most hopeful military expedient. We should discourage any more dangerous form of US involvement. If it becomes clear that the French are determined to withdraw, we should use our influence in favour of a solution least damaging to our interests in South-East Asia.

British policy document, 31 March 1954

D **The British Foreign Secretary criticises American policy at the Geneva conference. He was a leading advocate of a peaceful solution for Vietnam.**

I am doing everything I can to bring the real Asiatic powers along but the Americans are too impatient. They like to give orders, and if they are not at once obeyed, they become huffy. They have never put their weight behind the conference or made any effort to get an agreement. I personally do not agree with the people who suggest that if Indochina were to go, Thailand, Malaya etc must be indefensible. They would obviously be much more difficult to defend, but that is not in itself a reason for intervening in Indochina, even if we could do so effectively at this stage. We do not want to bring a greater disaster upon our heads by intervening to try and avert the immediate one.

Anthony Eden, letters to Cabinet colleagues, May 1954

E **The President of the Democratic Republic of Vietnam (DRV) reports to the Party Central Committee on his meeting with the Chinese premier, Zhou Enlai at the Geneva conference.**

The Americans have used every means to sabotage the Geneva conference. Faced with our victory at Dien Bien Phu, the USA plotted to issue a 'joint declaration' with France, Britain and a number of other countries to intimidate China, charging it with intervention in the Indochina War. But due to the opposition of Britain and reluctance of the other countries, the move failed. Vietnam, China and the USSR are closely united. The friendly meetings between Comrade Zhou Enlai and the representatives of India, Burma and Vietnam have tightened solidarity among the Asian nations. This is a success for our camp. Some of you are partial to military action and make light of diplomacy, seeing the French, but not the Americans. We must not set forth excessive conditions unacceptable to the enemy.

Ho Chi Minh, 15 July 1954

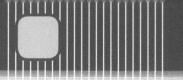

4 Why and with what results did the US become involved in Vietnam to 1968?

Terms of the Geneva Accords

Though the Viet Minh were militarily dominant, the terms did not reflect this (see also Source A opposite). The Pathet Lao, a militant communist revolutionary force, controlled more than half of Laos, and the Viet Minh had won a decisive victory at Dien Bien Phu. However, by July 1954, the final terms were:

■ A temporary 10-mile demilitarised zone (**DMZ**), fixed at the 17 parallel as a demarcation line. The Viet Minh were to withdraw north of the DMZ and French troops south of it. The French signed an agreement to evacuate Indochina at once. Many Vietnamese tried to leave with the French as they went home.

■ Elections to be held after one year of consultation, during which time no troop reinforcements, military bases or foreign military alliances were allowed. An International Supervisory Commission (**ISC**) was to oversee this. The USA had used a diplomatic 'holding action', as Dulles described it. They had used thinly veiled military threats to prevent a communist takeover of the whole of Vietnam. Britain and France were anxious that US initiatives in Europe, especially the European Defence Community (**EDC**) should go forward. The French themselves wished to retain a presence in Vietnam. Neither Britain nor France wished to see US military intervention in Indochina. The USSR saw continuing French involvement in Indochina as useful to distract it from links to the EDC. The USSR saw Indochina as of marginal interest and wished to demonstrate 'peaceful co-existence' so soon after the death of Stalin.

■ China also accepted the terms to keep a US military presence out of Indochina whilst it established the new Communist China's economy and reconstructed after the Chinese Civil War. Ho Chi Minh's Communist regime was to remain in control of the North, Bao Dai was to rule non-Communist South Vietnam, while Laos and Cambodia would be independent. The USSR and Communist China were able to persuade Ho Chi Minh to accept these terms, as the Viet Minh also did not wish to see a US presence in Vietnam. They were exhausted after defeating the French. They were confident that the country would be easy to unite. But they had lost much of their position of strength, so they were willing to abandon Laos and Cambodia.

The US would now have the problem of finding a solution that would protect the free world from Chinese- or Soviet-inspired Communist expansion in an area of vital economic resources. The Defensive Perimeter would be of no use if mainland Indochina opened a route to Communist control of Malaya, Burma and their vast resources of petrol, rubber and tin. Japan would lose its markets, and with them its propaganda value as a model democratic state, within less than two years of gaining independence.

Vietnam DMZ

In July 1954, a temporary 10-mile demilitarised zone (DMZ) was fixed at the 17 parallel as a demarcation line.

ISC

The International Supervisory Commission set up to oversee the period in 1954 when no foreign military alliances, troop reinforcements or military bases were allowed in Vietnam.

EDC

The European Defence Community, which rearmed West Germany.

Sources

(A) The Geneva Accords stated:

■ *On the cessation of hostilities in Vietnam, no foreign troops or military personnel shall be introduced into the country.*

■ *No foreign military base may be established nor do the zones become part of any military alliance.*

■ *The military demarcation line between north and south, and the demilitarised zone are provisional and in no way should be seen as a political or territorial boundary.*

■ *The Vietnamese people shall enjoy fundamental freedoms, guaranteed by democratic institutions established as a result of free general elections by secret ballot. These general elections shall be held in July 1956 under the supervision of an International Supervisory Commission.*

Terms agreed at Geneva, 21 July 1954

(B) The President of the Democratic Republic of Vietnam gives his personal view of the Geneva Accords.

The struggle of our delegation and the assistance of the Soviet Union and China have ended in a great victory for us: the French government has recognised the independence, sovereignty, unity and territorial integrity of our country; it has agreed to withdraw troops from our country. From now on, we must make every effort to consolidate peace and achieve reunification, independence and democracy throughout our country. We must endeavour to struggle for the holding of free elections throughout our country to reunify our territory. We must do our utmost to carry out social reforms in order to improve our people's livelihood and realise genuine democracy.

Ho Chi Minh, 22 July 1954

Figure 4.3   A map of Vietnam in 1954, as divided by the terms of the Geneva Accords. The DMZ is shown, as a temporary boundary between North and South.

ACTIVITY

Compare Sources A and B as evidence for Viet Minh achievements at the Geneva conference in July 1954.

The USA and State of Vietnam would not sign the Geneva Accords. To have signed alongside China would have been to recognise the PRC. Washington issued a statement saying that they agreed with the 'Accords' in principle and would not threaten to use force against them or disturb them. But Eisenhower stated that the USA 'had not been itself a party to or bound by the decisions taken by the conference'. They wished to have freedom

of action for the future. They knew Bao Dai had little popular support and that there was every chance for Hanoi to unite the country. The US National Security Council met to discuss how to fill the power vacuum left by withdrawal of France.

What policy did Eisenhower take following the end of French control in Indochina in 1954?

A new sense of urgency developed because of the '**Domino theory**', publicly declared by President Eisenhower in a press conference of 7 April 1954 to stress that any broken link in the chain would lead to the collapse of democracy in Thailand, Malaya, the Philippines, Indonesia and Burma. They had vital resources of tin, petrol and rubber, which the USA sorely needed. Truman did not wish China to establish a 'co-prosperity sphere', following the route of Japanese imperialism.

Source

President Eisenhower explains the Domino theory, with regard to South-East Asia.

'Firstly, the locality produces materials that the world needs: tin and tungsten, the rubber plantations and so on.

Then many human beings might pass under a dictatorship detrimental to the free world. Asia has already lost some 450 million of its peoples to Communist dictatorship and we simply can't afford greater losses.

Finally, broader considerations might follow the 'falling domino' principle. You have a row of dominoes set up, you knock over the first one, and the last one will certainly go over very quickly. The loss of Indochina, of Burma, of Thailand, of the Peninsula, and Indonesia would follow. It turns the island defensive chain of Japan, Taiwan and the Philippines; it moves in to threaten Australia and New Zealand. Now you are talking about millions and millions of people. The geographical position would take away the economic region that Japan must have as a trading area. Then Japan, in turn, will have only one place in the world to go: toward the Communist areas in order to live. So, the possible consequences of the loss are just incalculable to the free world.

Dwight D. Eisenhower, news conference, 7 April 1954

The setting up of SEATO

Secretary of State John Foster Dulles feared Chinese expansion into Indochina.

Restoring US prestige meant preventing further losses in South-East Asia, and this must be done through a defence system, but the Geneva conference had shown that other countries would not support the USA through the United Nations, as they had done during the Korean War. The NCS 5429/2 policy document, approved by Eisenhower on 20 August, stated:

'the US must protect its position and restore its prestige in the Far East by a new initiative in South-East Asia, where the situation must be stabilised as soon as possible to prevent further losses to communism through (1) creeping expansion and subversion, or (2) overt aggression. The recommendation is for a South-East Asia security treaty.'

The South-East Asia Treaty Organisation (SEATO) was therefore set up. The USA, Britain, France, Australia and New Zealand, Thailand, the Philippines and Pakistan chose to join. In outline it was similar to NATO, but action would be 'in accordance with constitutional practices'. Because none of the other members shared US fears of communism, its real purpose was to allow US unilateral action in Vietnam under the cloak of collective security (see Chapter 3, pages 63–72, 83 and 89). The USA could use SEATO as an excuse to increase US military intervention in Indochina in defiance of the Geneva Accords, which it considered it was not bound by, as neither the USA nor South Vietnam had signed them. They saw the loss of North Vietnam as another potential failure for the policy of containment and feared that other states would soon fall to communism.

However, some Americans doubted whether the Viet Minh were inspired by Soviet communism.

Eisenhower's support for Diem as leader of South Vietnam

Despite evidence of genuine national support for the Viet Minh, the USA now decided to try to support other nationalist movements against the Viet Minh to undermine their influence – something the French had not tried to do. Bao Dai had appointed **Ngo Dinh Diem** as Prime Minister while the Geneva conference was in session. Ngo Dinh Diem was a fanatical Catholic bachelor with messianic tendencies but virulently opposed to Communism. The USA had found a 'man rather than a movement', but this time he was not their own choice, but the legacy of a corrupt French regime.

BIOGRAPHY

Ngo Dinh Diem (1901–1963)

Diem was educated at the National Academy, and had a law degree from Hanoi University. He went into the civil service and rose quickly to become Minister of the Interior under Bao Dai. He turned down the premiership in late 1945 and travelled to Japan, Europe and the USA, spending 2 years in Maryknoll Seminary in New Jersey. He was ascetic and reclusive. He made contact with the Catholic John F. Kennedy, among others. At the time of the Geneva Accords, he raced back to Saigon and accepted the offer of the premiership. The USA was unenthusiastic about his appointment, due to his arrogance, reclusive nature and lack of popular support. A US diplomat called him a 'messiah without a message'. He distrusted advice from anyone outside his family, and meditated for long hours alone. There is no evidence that he ever had sexual relations, and he was never comfortable around women.

Figure 4.4 Ngo Dinh Diem as the new President of South Vietnam, *Time* magazine

From the start, US officials were very doubtful that Diem would be able to establish an independent South Vietnam. A US analyst said:

> 'we are prepared to accept the seemingly ridiculous prospect that this **"yogi-like mystic"** could assume the charge he is apparently about to undertake only because the standard set by his predecessors is so low.'

Large areas of South Vietnam were under the control of rival religious sects such as the Cao Dai and Hoa Hao, who had made deals with Bao Dai and recruited private armies. The Binh Xuyen gang of criminals boasted 2500 armed men. General Ba Cut led the Hoa Hao army. The USA realised Diem needed an army, and so Eisenhower gave him 78 per cent of the US total foreign aid budget between 1955 and 1961! In trying to make Vietnam a model democratic state between 1954 and 1961, Eisenhower sent military advisers to train Diem's

'Yogi-like mystic'

Diem was deeply Catholic in his beliefs and spent long periods in contemplation and spiritual retreat from everyday affairs. 'Yogi' and 'mystic' are terms used for spiritual leaders who spend long periods in contemplation.

4 Why and with what results did the US become involved in Vietnam to 1968?

ACTIVITY

1 Compare Sources A and E as evidence for US presidential attitudes to Diem.

2 Use your own knowledge to evaluate how far Sources A–E support the view that the problems faced by Diem's regime in South Vietnam were of its own making.

police, and financial aid was poured into social, economic and political reforms. Perhaps this shows that Eisenhower was responsible for beginning to escalate US involvement in South Vietnam.

US officials supported Diem's refusal to allow democratic elections, fearing Ho's communists would win. The USA was pinning its hopes of containment on another unpopular authoritarian puppet. But he was not behaving like a puppet ruler after replacing Bao Dai as head of state. Diem's regime was narrowly based on his family and deeply Catholic, though the majority of the population was Buddhist. He stubbornly refused US demands for reforms and ignored French officials, who now decided to withdraw their remaining 160,000 troops. Washington contemplated withdrawing their support from him, but was left with no alternative. He was using US aid to consolidate his own position after rigging a referendum in 1955. He suppressed the power of the sects with the help of US Colonel Lansdale, who used bribes to split up the Hoa Hao. Diem had General Ba Cut publicly beheaded, rounded up anyone suspected of opposing his regime, and 're-educated' them in special camps.

Sources

(A) **The American President writes to Ngo Dinh Diem, the President of the Republic of South Vietnam, expressing his support for the new South Vietnamese government in rescuing Catholic refugees from the North.**

I have been following with great interest the developments in Vietnam, particularly since the conclusion of the Geneva conference. The implications of the agreement concerning Vietnam have caused grave concern regarding the future of a country temporarily divided by an artificial military grouping, weakened by a long, exhausting war and faced with external enemies and internal collaborators. We have fulfilled your recent requests for aid in the formidable task of moving several hundred thousand loyal Vietnamese citizens away from areas ruled by a communist ideology they hate. I am glad that the United States is able to assist in this humanitarian effort.

Dwight Eisenhower, Letter, 23 October 1954

(B) **The US Special representative in Vietnam gives his view on problems facing South Vietnam at the time of 'the sects crisis' of 1955, in a National Security Council discussion.**

■ *There is the remote possibility of an overt attack on South Vietnam by the Viet Minh.*

■ *The South Vietnamese Army has limited loyalty to Diem, and will not support him in a civil war.*

■ *Diem's has handled the sects badly, by trying to cut down their private armies and dry up their financial resources.*

■ *The attitude of French colonial officials has generally been to sabotage Diem's government.*

■ *The personality of Diem is such that there are serious doubts about his ability to govern. His Cabinet has lost men of ability and consists of unknowns with no public standing.*

General J. Lawton Collins, 28 April 1955

(C) **The South Vietnamese government renounces any possibility of negotiations with the regime of North Vietnam.**

The government does not consider itself bound in any respect by the Geneva Agreements which it did not sign. Its aim is to achieve national unity, peace and freedom. Confronted with the partition of the country, which is contrary to the will of the entire people, we will see to it that everybody throughout the country may live free from fear and from all totalitarian oppression. As a champion of justice, of genuine democracy, the government always holds that the principle of free election is a peaceful and democratic means only if freedom to live and freedom to vote is sufficiently guaranteed. Nothing constructive can be contemplated in the present situation in the North, where the rule of the Communists denies its citizens fundamental freedoms and democratic rights.

From a South Vietnamese government statement, 9 August 1955

D An American political analyst gives his view of Diem's South Vietnamese regime in a magazine published by the Council for Foreign Affairs, a non-partisan group which provided a forum to discuss international affairs. The author firmly believed that Ho Chi Minh's movement was nationalist.

South Vietnam is today a quasi-police state characterized by arbitrary arrests and imprisonment, strict censorship of the press and the absence of an effective political opposition. All the techniques of political and psychological warfare, as well as pacification campaigns involving extensive military operations have been brought to bear against the underground [dissidents].

From: William Henderson, article in *Foreign Affairs*, January 1957

E The American President writes publicly to Diem, promising to increase American aid for the South Vietnamese regime.

Our indignation has grown at the deliberate savagery of the Communist program of assassination, kidnapping and random violence. The campaign of terror, now being waged against your people and your government, is supported and directed from outside by the authorities at Hanoi. They have thus violated the terms of the Geneva Accords to ensure peace in Vietnam. We shall promptly increase our assistance to protect your people and preserve their independence. We shall also seek to persuade the Communists to end their violence.

From: John F. Kennedy, Letter, December 1961

Why and how did the NLF emerge in 1960?

Land policies as a reason for the rise of the NLF

Ho was held back from mounting military action against Diem by his advisers in Hanoi, as they preferred political pressure. His frustrated southern supporters now took matters into their own hands, and in 1957 came into open conflict with the **ARVN** (Saigon's Army of the Republic of South Vietnam) when they launched an attack on southern communist strongholds. Diem's actions against the southern communists, whom he called the **Viet Cong**, decimated their membership.

In return, the Viet Cong assassinated hundreds of local Diem officials and in 1959 the Viet Minh began shipping supplies and personnel along the Ho Chi Minh trail to reinforce their strength. This insurgency was so effective that Diem was forced to change his policy. He ignored an assassination attempt, and set up '**agrovilles**' using a similar method to that used by the British in countering insurgents in Malaya. Peasants were uprooted from their ancestral homes, where they had shrines for the spirits of their ancestors. To deny the communists any support from the local population, southern communities were transported to isolated rural villages and fortified against infiltration. This further alienated an already negative population.

Hanoi created and directed the **NLF** (National Liberation Front) in December 1960 to co-ordinate the various nationalist groups and achieve as broad a range of support as possible within the national movement. NLF land reforms attracted peasant support, and early in 1961 those groups which existed in the south organised themselves into the **PLAF** (People's Liberation Armed Forces).

ARVN

Saigon's Army of the Republic of South Vietnam.

Viet Cong

South Vietnamese Communists, so named, disparagingly, by Diem as a corruption of '**Viet**namese **Com**munists'.

Agrovilles

Fortified settlements in South Vietnam set up by the Agroville Program (1959–60) of President Ngo Dinh Diem, which forcibly resettled peasants in remote rural areas to keep them away from communist influence.

NLF

National Liberation Front.

PLAF

People's Liberation Armed Forces.

Sources

A US columnist Joseph Alsop reports on his tour of Viet Minh-held territory in 1954.

It was difficult for me, as for any westerner, to conceive of a Communist government genuinely "serving the people". I could hardly imagine a communist government that was also a popular government and almost a democratic government. But the Viet Minh could not possibly have carried on the resistance to the French for one year, let alone nine years, without the people's strong united support.'

From: George N. Katsiaficas, *Vietnam documents: American and Vietnamese Views of the War*, page 39, originally published in the *New Yorker* magazine in 1955

B A US journalist who covered the Vietnam War for *New York Times* later expresses views which were difficult to get published at the time.

Diem's regime had become more convinced than ever that it had its ally in a corner and that it could do anything it wanted. It felt continued support would be guaranteed because of the communist threat and that the US could not suddenly admit that it had made a vast mistake.

David Halberstam, *The Making of a Quagmire: America and Vietnam during the Kennedy era*, published in 2007

ACTIVITY

Evaluate Sources A and B as evidence of US journalists' views on Vietnam.

What policy did Kennedy's administration follow in the lead up to the fall of Diem's regime?

When **John F. Kennedy** (JFK) (see page 113) replaced Eisenhower he also saw the problem in Vietnam as one of containment. Neither had wanted to see an Asian state fall to Communism for fear of the 'domino theory'. Kennedy kept John Foster Dulles as a chief foreign policy adviser and appointed a new Secretary of Defense, Robert McNamara.

In his inaugural address, on 20 January 1961, Kennedy stated:

'Let every nation know that we shall pay any price, bear any burden, meet any hardship, support any friend, oppose any foe, in order to assure the survival and success of liberty.'

(see: www.heinemann.co.uk/hotlinks/)

He perceived a united front of Soviet, Chinese and North Vietnamese Communists as part of a global Cold War scenario.

JFK's pressing dilemma was how to handle the civil war that had erupted in Laos in 1959. This issue, together with the crises in Berlin and Cuba, dominated most of his presidency (see case study). The USA and USSR supplied aid to the competing sides, and it was left to another Geneva Conference to solve the issue. This conference established in Laos a 'neutral' coalition of communist and non-communist elements working together. In practice, however, northern Vietnam's National Liberation Front (NLF) supply route through Laos into South Vietnam remained active. Kennedy responded secretly by using the CIA to support anti-communist forces without consulting Congress. Unofficially, US B52 bombers attacked communist positions in central and eastern Laos during 1962 and 1963. By the autumn of 1962, US officials in Saigon estimated that Diem controlled only 49 per cent of South Vietnam, while the NLF held 9 per cent of the rest of this unruly country.

Case study

Crises in Laos, Berlin and Cuba 1959–63

Fighting broke out all along the border between Laos and North Vietnam in 1959. Ho Chi Minh aided the communist forces of the Pathet Lao against other nationalist groups in Laos. This was seen as a violation of his agreement at Geneva, not to interfere in neighbouring countries.

Also in 1959, Fidel Castro seized power in a communist revolution in Cuba, 90 miles off the coast of Florida. This provoked Kennedy to attempt, unsuccessfully, to remove Castro by sending troops to invade Cuba at the Bay of Pigs in 1961, which were swiftly repulsed. This fiasco was a major humiliation for the USA, and led to the Cuban Missile Crisis of 1962, when the USSR came 'eyeball to eyeball' with the USA on the brink of a global nuclear war.

In 1961, Cold War tensions also flared up in Berlin, resulting in the construction of the Berlin Wall, separating the Eastern and Western sectors of the ex-German capital which lay deep inside East German Communist territory.

Sources

(A) The NLF sets out to attract the broadest possible coalition, at the time of its formation in opposition to the Diem regime.

The American imperialists, who had in the past helped the French to massacre our people, have now replaced the French in enslaving the southern part of our country through a disguised colonial regime. They have been using their stooge, the Ngo Dinh Diem administration, in their downright repression and exploitation of our compatriots, to permanently divide our country and to turn its southern part into a military base in preparation for war in south-east Asia. The aggressors and traitors have set up an extremely cruel dictatorial rule. They persecute and massacre democratic and patriotic people, and abolish all human liberties. High anger with the present tyrannical regime is boiling among our compatriots, who are determined to unite and struggle unflaggingly against the US imperialists' policy of aggression. Among workers, peasants and other toiling people, among intellectuals, students and pupils, industrialists and traders, religious sects and national minorities, patriotic activities are gaining in scope, seriously shaking the US-Diem dictatorial regime. Compatriots around the country! Let us march forward confidently and valiantly to score brilliant victories for our people and our fatherland!

From the Manifesto of the National Liberation Front, December 1960

(B) The Vietnamese People's Revolutionary Party explain their aims.

■ *We will overthrow the Ngo Dinh Diem government and form a national democratic coalition government.*

■ *We will carry out a program involving extension of democratic liberties, general amnesty for political detainees, abolition of agrovilles and resettlement centres, abolition of the special military tribunal law and other undemocratic laws.*

■ *We will abolish the economic monopoly of the US and its henchmen, protect domestically made products, promote development of the economy, and allow forced evacuees from North Vietnam to return to their place of birth.*

■ *We will reduce land rent and prepare for land reform.*

■ *We will eliminate US cultural enslavement and depravity and build a nationalistic progressive culture and education.*

■ *We will abolish the system of American military advisers and close all foreign military bases in Vietnam.*

■ *We will establish equality between men and women and among different nationalities and recognize the autonomous rights of the national minorities in the country.*

■ *We will pursue a foreign policy of peace and will establish diplomatic relations with all countries that respect the independence and sovereignty of Vietnam.*

■ *We will re-establish normal relations between North and South as a first step toward peaceful reunification of the country.*

■ *We will oppose aggressive wars and actively defend world peace.*

From the Program of the People's Revolutionary Party of Vietnam, January 1962

(Sources continue on page 112.)

4 Why and with what results did the US become involved in Vietnam to 1968?

C **A Viet Cong recruit, who opposed Diem, explains why he joined the revolution.**

In 1957, Diem gave us his own version of land reform, giving land only to peasants who could afford it. The government gave support to landowners who sabotaged the reform in the countryside and prevented land changing hands. Two facts were clear to me: firstly, the country had settled into high-handed rule and utter disregard of the welfare of the people, and secondly, subservience to foreigners was still the order of the day. We had a ruler who would prop himself up using the Americans, and they in turn used him for their own strategic purposes. We had no say in the shaping of our new nation. We established a network of people from all walks of life, some with close ties to the sects, the legal political parties and the Buddhists. We sent Nguyen Van Hieu to Hanoi to begin working out a channel of support from our northern compatriots.

From: Truong Nhu Trang, *A Viet Cong Memoir*, 1985

D **A peasant Viet Cong recruit, who later became deputy commander in the main Viet Cong forces, explains how he was persuaded to join the NLF in the 1960s.**

I was poor. We lived a very hard life and much of our rice went to the landlord. I was married. I lost my land and I didn't have enough money to take care of my four children. In 1961 propaganda **cadres** *of the NLF contacted me. They said that the rich people had always served the French and had used the authority of the French to oppress the poor. The cadres told us that if the poor people did not stand up to the rich, we would be dominated by them forever. The only way to ensure freedom and a sufficient life was to overthrow them. I knew that the rich oppressed the poor. In our village there*

were about 4300 people and maybe only ten landlords. The poor had nothing to eat and they also had no freedom. We had to get rid of a regime that allowed a few people to use their authority and money to oppress the others, so I joined the Liberation Front.

From: Nguyen Tan Thanh, *A Viet Cong Memoir*, 1986

E **A South Vietnamese peasant girl explains why she became a Viet Cong supporter in 1961.**

The first time I saw a Viet Cong fighter close up it was just about dark and I was cleaning up our kitchen. Without a sound, a half-dozen strangers scampered into teacher Manh's house next door. People began running out of his house, but Manh was the last out, led by gunpoint with his hands above his head. One of the strangers was standing just outside. I could hear Manh pleading for his life, when two rifle shots silenced him. The guard outside my window glanced over and gave me a wink. He reminded me of my brother. 'The Viet Cong just shot Manh! He was nice to us and never hurt anyone!' I cried. My father replied 'He was a Catholic and a follower of President Diem. He talked too much about how Buddhists were ruining the country. What he said endangered others.' The Republicans came back the next day, but they left weapons behind. We hid them to protect ourselves from enemy tanks. When the handsome Viet Cong cadre returned, he said, in his funny Northern accent, 'We are soldiers of liberation! We are here to fight for our land and our country! Help us win and you will keep your property and everything else you love. Down the road you will see two traitors; I trust they are the last we shall see in this village.' After he left, and when the Republicans failed to find any Viet Cong, they arrested nearby farmers, beat them or shot them on the spot. As a result, more villagers joined the Viet Cong cause.

From: Le Ly Hayslip, *When Heaven and Earth Changed Places: A Vietnamese Woman's Journey from War to Peace*, 1989

Cadres

Leaders of groups within communist communities.

ACTIVITY

Role play: Reasons for joining the NLF

- Form groups of five.

- Each plays the role of an author of one of the Sources above.

- Those playing NLF officials, Sources A and B, explain which of your views you

consider to be most persuasive in attracting recruits.

- Viet Cong recruits, Sources C, D and E, explain which of the arguments you found most persuasive and why.

You may cross-examine, question or persuade each other.

BIOGRAPHY

John Fitzgerald 'Jack' Kennedy (1917–1963)

John F. Kennedy is often referred to by his initials JFK. He was the President of the United States from 1961 until his assassination in 1963. With the encouragement of his father, Joe Kennedy, he was elected to represent Massachusetts as a Democrat in the House of Representatives 1947–53, and in the Senate 1953–60. Kennedy defeated then Vice President and Republican candidate Richard Nixon in the 1960 presidential election, one of the closest in American history, the only Catholic to become president. Events during his administration include the Bay of Pigs invasion, the Cuban Missile Crisis, the building of the Berlin Wall, the Space Race, the African American Civil Rights Movement and early events of the Vietnam War.

Kennedy was assassinated on November 22, 1963, in Dallas, Texas.

Kennedy found the situation he had inherited in Vietnam virtually impossible. The USA continued to support Diem's regime though it was becoming increasingly unpopular, and there were some voices in Washington questioning their support for Diem. There were only 800 military advisers in South Vietnam, and Kennedy was determined the USA should not find themselves in the same position as the French. He found himself between two opposing groups of advisers:

■ **The Joints Chiefs of Staff were 'hawks'**, wanting strong military support for South Vietnam. Their view was that 'any reversal of US policy could have disastrous effect, not only on our relationship with South Vietnam, but with the rest of our Asian and other allies as well.' In 1961, General Maxwell Taylor was sent to evaluate whether the situation could be improved by sending more US troops. His report suggested increasing the US presence to 8000 ground troops. He later said '*I don't recall anyone strongly against this plan except one man, the President.*' Kennedy's view was that:

'The troops will march in, the bands will play; the crowds will cheer, and in four days everyone will have forgotten. Then we will be told we have to send in more troops. It's like taking a drink. The effect wears off, and you have to take another.'

(From Vivienne Sanders, *The USA and Vietnam*, page 66.)

■ **On the other side were the 'doves'**, such as J.K. Galbraith, US ambassador to India, who wanted a phased withdrawal from Vietnam using a strategy similar to that used in Laos. In 1962, **William Averell Harriman** (page 114), US envoy to the USSR, was responsible for gaining Soviet agreement to the policy of neutralisation of Laos, where a coalition of communist and non-communist forces had been set up, and Kennedy wished to achieve something similar. However, the communist guerrillas in the south would have to be defeated first, so Kennedy never seriously considered the 'neutralisation' policy.

'Domino theory' was shifting to the '**doctrine of credibility**'. This prioritised limiting the psychological effect of newly created communist states on America's international reputation, rather than attempting to contain the loss of territory. Vietnam became a 'testing ground' for new strategies to prove that the USA was strong, and willing to use its power in world affairs to actively counter the communist threat rather than to appease it.

'Doctrine of credibility'
Keeping up the credibility of the USA's reputation as a global superpower.

BIOGRAPHY

William Averell Harriman (1891–1986)

Harriman was a candidate for the Democratic Presidential Nomination in 1952, and again in 1956 endorsed by Truman. He lost to the less liberal Adlai Stevenson. His presidential ambitions over, Harriman became a widely-respected elder statesman of the party. After holding the post of Ambassador at Large, in November 1961 he became Assistant Secretary of State for Far Eastern Affairs. In December 1961, a defector from the Soviet Union named Harriman as a Soviet spy, but he remained in this post until April 1963, when he became Under Secretary of State for Political Affairs. He resumed his post as Ambassador at Large in Johnson's presidency. Harriman was the chief US negotiator at the Paris peace talks on Vietnam. On behalf of the State Department, Harriman supported the coup against President Ngo Dinh Diem in 1963. Alongside Kennedy, Johnson confessed to involvement in the assassination of Diem which could indicate some complicity by Harriman.

Counter insurgency

A strategy of combat against an insurgency, i.e. infiltration by enemies.

'Green Berets'

The United States Army Special Forces, also known as Green Berets, is a Special Operations Force (SOF) of the United States Army tasked with five primary missions: unconventional warfare, foreign internal defence, special reconnaissance, direct action and counter-terrorism.

CIDGs

Civilian Irregular Defense Groups, recruited from mountain tribes (montagnards) who carried out search actions.

Kennedy's testing ground for New Strategies

Kennedy's administration spent $500 million on aid for South Vietnam. The new US strategy was one of **counter insurgency**. It had two elements. The first saw an increase in military advisers from 800 to 3000 by December 1961, to 10,000 in 1962 and 16,000 by Kennedy's death in November 1963. Kennedy was prepared to do anything to prevent a Viet Cong victory. These advisers included '**Green Berets**', an elite group of Army Special Forces trained in guerrilla warfare. The plan was to face the Viet Cong on their own terms. The Green Berets were helped by Civilian Irregular Defense Groups (**CIDGs**), recruited from mountain tribes (montagnards) who carried out search actions. The **Strategic Hamlets Program** was the other element of the policy, started in 1962. Similar to the British policy in Malaya that had solved the problem of communist insurgency in the 1950s, and to an extent like the earlier 'agrovilles', Strategic Hamlets were villages surrounded by barbed wire and fortified against insurgency and infiltration. Within the year, there were 3000 of such villages. Unfortunately, Diem's corrupt regime established them in areas where it could gain more political support, rather than where they might hold off the communist threat. Congress agreed to further aid to prop up Diem's regime, convinced that it would otherwise fall. They sent economic aid, aircraft, ARVN training advisers and intelligence equipment to South Vietnam. The Kennedy administration constantly portrayed Diem in the media as the 'strong man' of Vietnam, though they knew this was far from reality.

Strategic Hamlets Program

This was a plan by the governments of South Vietnam and the United States during the Vietnam War to combat the Communist insurgency by means of population transfer. In 1961, US advisors in South Vietnam, along with the Diem regime, began the implementation of a plan which attempted to isolate rural peasants from contact with and influence by the National Liberation Front. The Strategic Hamlets Program, along with its predecessor, the Rural Community Development Program, played an important role in the shaping of events in South Vietnam during the late 1950s and early 1960s. Both of these programs attempted to separate rural peasants from communist insurgents by creating 'fortified villages'. The program backfired drastically and ultimately led to a decrease in support for Diem's regime and an increase in sympathy for the communists.

In May 1961, Vice President Lyndon B. Johnson visited Saigon and enthusiastically declared Diem the 'Winston Churchill of Asia'. Diem himself believed in this image and became over-confident as a result. The inefficiency and corruption of his regime allowed a rise in insurgency. His brother Ngo Dinh Nhu, South Vietnam's Head of Secret Police, was very unpopular and arrogant, as was his obnoxious and insensitive wife, Madame Nhu. Military advisers found Diem and Nhu reluctant to become involved in military action, so they aided the deployment of ARVN forces by using helicopters to leapfrog and surround NLF positions. US advisers also suggested the use of herbicides to clear the jungle in areas open to insurgency. The idea was to cut off the Viet Cong from access to food and cover. '**Agent Orange**' and **napalm** had some effect, leading General Paul Harkins to write that napalm 'really puts the fear of God into the Viet Cong, and that is what counts.'

'Agent Orange'
Code name for a herbicide and defoliant used by the U.S. military in its Herbicidal Warfare program during the Vietnam War. It was transported in orange coloured canisters.

Napalm
A jellied gasoline that burns deeply into the skin.

Figure 4.5   The dropping of napalm in 1966 to destroy jungle areas of South Vietnam.

However, innocent villagers were often the ones to suffer. It was almost impossible to identify insurgents or locate them in the dense forests and swampy paddy fields of South Vietnam. Even if they were located and cleared, as soon as the US forces were airlifted back to their bases, the insurgents returned. The Strategic Hamlets Program alienated rural peasants, who refused to pay land taxes and often chose to back the NLF. Hanoi wished to prevent US military intervention by emphasising their political agenda to unite the country. They hoped the Saigon regime would collapse on its own. Neither China nor the USSR wished the conflict to escalate.

Sources

A Senator John F. Kennedy comments on the Cold War at Salt Lake City Mormon tabernacle, during his presidential campaign.

The enemy is the communist system itself, implacable, insatiable, unceasing in its drive for world domination. The Kremlin rules a ruthless empire stretching in a great half circle from East Berlin to Vietnam. The prestige of this once-feared and hated nation now weaves a glittering web entrapping neutralists and nationalists in all corners of the globe. In military, diplomatic, economic, scientific and educational areas, the Communists can now compete with the United States on nearly equal terms. But they can never overcome us in the one area of spiritual values: moral strength and the strength of our will and our purpose. These qualities and traditions make this Nation a shining example to all who yearn to be free. This is not a struggle for supremacy of arms alone. It is also a struggle for supremacy between two conflicting ideologies: freedom under God versus ruthless, godless tyranny.

From a campaign speech, 23 September 1960

B A statement of the goals of the NLF, the united front that brought together Communists and non-Communists to liberate Vietnam from foreign control.

The present South Vietnamese regime is a camouflaged colonial regime dominated by the Yankees, and the South Vietnamese government is a servile government, implementing faithfully all the policies of the American imperialists. Therefore, this regime must be overthrown, and a government of national and democratic union put in its place. It must be composed of representatives of all social classes, of all nationalities, of various political parties, of all religions. Patriotic, eminent citizens must take over for the people the control of economic, political, social, and cultural interests. Thus we will bring about independence, democracy, well-being, peace, neutrality, and efforts toward the peaceful unification of the country.

From a program of the National Liberation Front of South Vietnam, January, 1962

ACTIVITY

Compare Sources A and B as evidence of the views of the opposing sides.

Examiner's advice

When comparing sources:

■ first consider provenance: who wrote the sources, when, why and to whom;

■ give attention to the details of their content, cross-referencing ideas by similarity and difference;

■ link your ideas to answering the question.

Diem mistrusted those of his Generals who might gain reputation, so did not promote on ability, and his forces soon gained a name for their inefficiency. General Cao, for example, had been promoted because he was a loyal Catholic crony of Diem. On 2 January 1963, at the Battle at Ap Bac, he ordered his 2000 ARVN troops not to advance or attack the 350 lightly-armed Viet Cong. They also refused to recover US helicopter pilots who had been shot down. The small band of communist forces declared the resulting battle a turning point, their first victory against a much larger and better-equipped South Vietnamese force. Though the ARVN also claimed to have won, the US media took a negative view. The NLF followed up this victory by making considerable gains, destroying 2600 of the 3700 Strategic Hamlets. By the summer of 1963 they were planning a major offensive. It seemed that it would be impossible to hold South Vietnam militarily using only Diem's armed forces.

Religious unrest and nationalism in South Vietnam

Diem was a fanatically Catholic ruler of a predominantly Buddhist country. The USA had funded Catholics living in the north to return to the south to swell his support, which further alienated the sects and in fact narrowed Diem's support base. The Buddhist population were seen by some US analysts as the key to creating a Vietnamese nation state, but Diem's fanatical Catholic belief made him the wrong man to gain their support. In May 1963, Diem's troops fired into a crowd of Buddhists celebrating Buddha's birthday and waving flags. All banners, other than those of the government, were prohibited. A full-scale Buddhist revolt broke out at Hue, and government troops killed several thousand protestors. One Buddhist monk (Figure 4.6) made the front pages of international newspapers by burning himself to death at a Saigon intersection. The glamorous Madame Nhu told the press 'Let them burn and we shall clap our hands'. She called the burnings 'Buddhist barbecues' and delighted in offering gasoline and matches to others who wished to do the same.

Figure 4.6 After the riots in Hue, Thich Quang Duc, a 73-year-old Buddhist priest, burned himself to death at a busy Saigon road intersection on 11 June 1963. Thich Quang Duc was protesting at the persecution of Buddhists by South Vietnam's Diem regime.

A group of generals of the Army of the Republic of Vietnam had asked Diem to give them extra powers to fight the Viet Cong because they secretly plotted to overthrow Diem's regime. Diem agreed. On 21 August, after martial law had been declared, midnight raids were made on Buddhist pagodas across South Vietnam. The pagodas were extensively vandalised, hundreds of Buddhists were killed and more than a thousand monks and nuns were arrested. Nhu had taken advantage of martial law to attack Buddhist pagodas while disguised as regular ARVN forces. His Special Forces and Secret Police were responsible for the raids.

US officials were becoming increasingly angry at Diem's oppressive regime, and, to make matters worse, he openly called for a reduction by half in the number of US advisers in South Vietnam. The Kennedy administration was particularly worried about reports that Diem was seeking a settlement with Hanoi. Nhu admitted to negotiating with representatives of the North for national Vietnamese independence. The French leader, de Gaulle was outspoken in his support for a reunified Vietnam, free of 'outside interference'. He told Kennedy in May 1961:

> *'the more you become involved out there against Communism, the more the Communists will appear as the champions of national independence. You will sink step by step into a bottomless military and political quagmire, however much you spend in men and money.'*

But de Gaulle made no concrete proposals.

4 Why and with what results did the US become involved in Vietnam to 1968?

Soviet and British observers were sceptical of US chances of solving the problem, but adopted a 'wait and see' approach. There was also a deepening split between the USSR and China in 1963. This led Soviet officials to fear that escalation of the conflict in Vietnam would increase American or Chinese domination in the area. If Moscow tried to reach 'peaceful co-existence' with the West, China would claim leadership of the global communist movement. However, as the Diem regime crumbled, a high-level Chinese delegation visited Hanoi and offered support to the northern regime.

China did not rule out a negotiated settlement, unlike the USA, which stood firm on the view that no diplomacy would take place until the insurgency had been defeated. The USA wished to dictate terms, fearing that an agreement, though a viable solution, would favour North Vietnam. This was against the 'doctrine of credibility'.

Kennedy could have claimed that Diem and Nhu had broken the conditions of their economic aid, in failing to carry out the reforms required and refusing to compromise with the Buddhists. Instead, Kennedy stated in a press conference, on 17 July 1963,

> *'We are not going to withdraw from this effort. In my opinion, for us to withdraw would mean a collapse not only of South Vietnam, but of South-East Asia. So we are going to stay there.'*

This comment contradicts the argument of those who suggest that Kennedy would have withdrawn from Vietnam, had he not been assassinated in November 1963.

Henry Cabot Lodge and the coup of the Generals

However, Nhu's brutality was undermining US policy. There was a severe crisis throughout the rural and urban areas of South Vietnam during the summer of 1963. It became clear that the Generals were planning a **military coup**, and the US government knew about it.

Military coup

Sudden seizure of political power.

> **BIOGRAPHY**
>
> **Henry Cabot Lodge (1902–1985)**
>
> Henry Cabot Lodge was an experienced and ambitious Republican politician from Massachusetts, who had run for Vice-President to Richard Nixon when Kennedy was elected. In 1963 Kennedy appointed Lodge as Ambassador to South Vietnam. Lodge's main task was to improve relations with the press, which was highly critical of support for Diem.

In January 1963, a State Department report had stated that there was no overall planning about the kind of country to be created by a victory in Vietnam. It proposed giving authority to a single, strong executive - a man perhaps with a military background but who understood the war as essentially a struggle to build a nation out of the chaos of revolution. Consequently, Henry Cabot Lodge was chosen as the new Ambassador. A CIA agent, General Tran Van Don, communicated to him that Nhu had framed the ARVN for the Buddhist raids in order to increase dissent among its lower ranks to weaken support for the generals' plans for a coup. He informed Washington, while Kennedy and McNamara were on vacation, and received a telegram of reply from Dean Rusk, the Secretary of State that seemed to give informal US approval for the coup. Lodge agreed in a telegram (Source A page opposite).

The State Department, authorised by Kennedy when he returned to Washington, replied to Lodge's telegram, agreeing that Diem should be persuaded to remove Nhu and the embarrassing Madame Nhu. If he refused, 'we must face the possibility that Diem himself cannot be preserved.' On 9 September, Kennedy told Walter Cronkite on CBS that 'in the final analysis, it is their war [the South Vietnamese]. They are the ones who are going to have to win it or lose it.'

Sources

A The new Ambassador to Vietnam soon realised that Diem was inept and politically corrupt. In this telegram to the Secretary of State he shows his support for General Minh's coup to remove Diem and Nhu and seize power.

We are launched on a course from which there is no respectable turning back: the overthrow of the Diem government. US prestige is already publicly committed to ending the war, and the war cannot be won under a Diem administration. The regime has alienated the educated class, both civil and military, not to mention the American people. I am personally in full agreement with the policy I was instructed to carry out by Sunday's telegram.

We should make an all-out effort to get Generals to move promptly.

We must press on for several reasons. Some of these are:

- *the explosiveness of the situation: if issue of discontent with regime is not met, riots and violence may lead to pro-Communist or neutralist set of politicians*

- *war cannot be won with the present regime*

- *our own reputation for steadfastness*

- *if we do not take this action, a body blow will be dealt to our reputation. We must not let down those who expect us to fulfil our responsibility*

I realise this course involves a very substantial risk of losing Vietnam. It also involves some additional risk to American lives. I would never propose it if I felt we had a reasonable chance of holding Vietnam with Diem.

General Harkins thinks I should ask Diem to get rid of the Nhus before starting the Generals' action. I think this would be seen as American indecision and delay. The Generals distrust us already. Diem would ask for time to consider and this would give the ball to Nhu.

From: Henry Cabot Lodge, telegram to Dean Rusk, 29 August 1963

B A representative of the Kennedy administration expresses his view to the US Ambassador in South Vietnam, concerning a planned coup by rebel generals there.

President today approved recommendation that no initiative should now be taken to give any active encouragement to a coup. Ambassador to identify and build contacts with possible alternative leadership as and when it appears. Essential that this effort be totally secure and fully deniable. We repeat that this effort is not to be aimed at active promotion of a coup, but only at observation and readiness. In order to make denial credible, suggest only you, and no-one else in Embassy, issue these instructions and make those acting for you responsible to you alone.

From: McGeorge Bundy, telegram to Henry Cabot Lodge, 5 October 1963

C This cartoon suggests that the Americans' claim to fight for freedom and democracy is a sham, as their actions will bring a military dictatorship to Vietnam.

'If there's a general election tomorrow, which General would you vote for?'

Cartoon by Abu Abrahams, first published in the *Observer*, 17 April 1966

ACTIVITY

How far was the USA to blame for the assassinations of Diem and the Nhus?

Use Sources A–C, and your own knowledge to help you evaluate the answer to this question.

The coup did not take place until three months later, and some critics of Kennedy have suggested that he should have taken the option of withdrawal from Vietnam at this stage. It has been suggested that Kennedy may have withdrawn, had he lived, but the evidence suggests otherwise. He tried to silence de Gaulle's demands for US withdrawal, and publicly attacked Walter Lippmann in the *New York Times*, when he asked for a political rather than a military solution.

Kennedy revived the coup plan. On 1 November 1963, ARVN Generals carried out the coup and murdered Diem, and the Nhus the following morning. The plotters knew that Lodge was aware of their action and he did nothing to impede them. Kennedy admitted American complicity in the coup on 6 November.

Kennedy's defenders suggest he may have felt that a change of regime in Vietnam would hasten the reforms needed to build the 'model nation state', and attract support from the Viet Cong, so that the USA could withdraw with their reputation intact at a later date. After Diem's death, General Minh tried to form a government, followed soon after by General Khahn, setting off a succession of coups. It seemed unlikely that the new regime could stabilise the situation in South Vietnam on its own.

When Kennedy was assassinated in Dallas on 22 November 1963, he had in his pocket a speech which included this statement:

> 'We in this country in this generation are the watchmen on the walls of freedom. Our assistance to nations can be painful, risky and costly, as is true in South-East Asia today. But we dare not weary of the task.'

(see: www.heinemann.co.uk/hotlinks/)

The repressive government of South Vietnam that he had supported did not live up to his lofty ideals. His presidency marked a major increase in American involvement in Vietnam, but he had tried to steer a moderate course and keep the options open. His successor, Lyndon B. Johnson (LBJ), was to pursue a wholly different course. But that was because Kennedy's legacy was one of major instability and had given Johnson no option to withdraw.

What effects did Kennedy's policies have (1961–63)?

Economic aid and military advisers

There is therefore a case for holding John F. Kennedy responsible for US intervention in the Vietnam War. During the 3 years of the Kennedy administration the number of US military advisers in Vietnam increased from 800 to 17,000. Because the State Department, under Dean Rusk, was more interested in Europe and Cuba, Vietnam was left to the Defence Department. Therefore an increase in expenditure was bound to happen, even though Kennedy held out against a full scale military presence. This gave rise to 'quagmire theory', that the USA was sucked into giving Diem increasing amounts of military aid. The total US aid commitment ran to an estimated $1.2 to $1.3 billion dollars a year during Kennedy's presidency. However, it is difficult for us today to put ourselves in Kennedy's position and understand the impact of the Cold War on American attitudes. The Geneva Agreements had been seen as a failure of containment, and he tried hard to heal the rifts between his advisers to keep his options open.

Kennedy was a victim of 'the commitment trap', locked into a policy of containment and unable to escape. The Truman administration had lost China to communism, and no subsequent president wished to repeat the humiliation. In compensation, Truman had created a Japanese model state as a beacon of democracy and capitalist values. Subsequent presidents had to protect South-East Asia from Soviet and Chinese encroachment. In attempting to defend Indochina, Kennedy aided an imposed, undemocratic, repressive Catholic oligarchy followed by a military clique. He stifled criticism from the 'doves' and from the influential press.

Kennedy also inherited a firm belief in the reality of Domino theory. This also was inextricably linked with the defence of trade and the South-East Asian economy. The fall of Indochina would damage South-East Asian supply routes, protected by US bases on the Pacific offshore islands, with the vital satellite of Japan at its centre. The US commitment to defend Vietnam was based on the fear that Cambodia, Laos, Malaya and Burma would fall to communism if Vietnam were lost. Vital commodities such as tin, rubber and oil were at stake.

Interventions

Kennedy tried a range of experimental strategies and interventions in Vietnam. He placed high hopes on the Green Berets and counter-insurgency, proposing to extend this approach elsewhere world-wide. But the Strategic Hamlets policy, the use of napalm and Agent Orange were all ineffective and counter-productive. While the ARVN were not willing to adopt a forward policy and were deployed to protect Diem's regime, counter insurgency was doomed to fail. The intervention of Henry Cabot Lodge sealed Diem's fate. A historian writing in 1999 argues that 'Kennedy and his advisers had charted a course that step-by-step involved the United States inextricably deeper in the Vietnam tragedy.'

Containment was no longer seen in merely physical, territorial terms by the Kennedy administration. The 'doctrine of credibility' gave containment a psychological dimension. Unfortunately, Kennedy did not heed the mistake in Taiwan and Korea of 'going for the man rather than the movement'. In Vietnam, he had no non-communist alternative to Diem. But Ho Chi Minh embodied the Vietnamese nation and was their genuine 'strong man', however much Eisenhower and Kennedy tried to present Diem as such. In reality he was arrogant, corrupt and wayward. He followed the pattern of Jiang Jieshi and Syngman Rhee but his abuses were greater and his unpopularity deeper. Kennedy's administration failed to make Diem deal effectively with the heartfelt resentments of Vietnamese Buddhists and Nationalists.

A State Department expert on Vietnam wrote of a meeting he attended with **Robert McNamara**, Bobby Kennedy, Dean Rusk, Lyndon Johnson and Maxwell Taylor:

> *'They did not know Vietnam. They did not know the past. They simply did not understand the identification of nationalism and communism. The more the meeting went on, the more I sat there and thought, "God, we're walking into a major disaster".'*

BIOGRAPHY

Robert Strange McNamara (1916–2009)

Robert Strange McNamara was born 1916, in Oakland, California. He was an American business executive and the eighth United States Secretary of Defence. 'Strange' is his mother's maiden name. McNamara served as Defence Secretary during the Vietnam War from 1961 to 1968. McNamara grew more and more controversial after 1966. His differences with the President and the Joint Chiefs of Staff over Vietnam strategy became the subject of public speculation, and frequent rumours surfaced that he would leave office. In early November 1967, McNamara's recommendations to freeze troop levels, stop bombing North Vietnam and for the US to hand over ground fighting to South Vietnam were rejected outright by President Lyndon B. Johnson. McNamara's recommendations amounted to his saying that the strategy of the United States in Vietnam, which had been pursued to date, had failed. Largely as a result, on November 29 of that year, McNamara announced his resignation. He served as President of the World Bank from 1968 until 1981.

Diem's corrupt regime had to be removed, damaging America's reputation irretrievably. His murder locked the USA into a moral commitment to the new regime. Lodge's replacement, Ambassador Maxwell Taylor, later recalled:

> *'Diem's overthrow set in motion a sequence of crises, political and military, over the next two years. These eventually forced President Johnson to choose between accepting defeat or introducing US combat troops.'*

From W.H. Chafe, *The Unfinished Journey*, p. 264

If we accept this, it would seem Kennedy had left **Johnson** an impossible legacy in Vietnam. In Saigon, military coups quickly followed Diem's assassination, showing how powerless the USA were to end the chaos. The US 'More Flags' campaign failed to attract international support for South Vietnam. The USA was on its own.

Johnson's attitude to the situation in Vietnam

Johnson was a down-to-earth and forceful personality, who demanded total loyalty from his staff. He retained McNamara and Rusk, so locking himself into the 'commitment trap'.

BIOGRAPHY

LBJ – Lyndon Baynes Johnson (1908–1973)

Johnson was the US Vice-President who found himself automatically President on the day of Kennedy's assassination. He was born into a poor Texas ranching family and had been director of a New Deal agency in the 1930s. He was more interested in solving domestic welfare problems, but had to limit his 'Great Society' programme to pay for the US commitment to Vietnam. He also found the US obsession with the war made him neglect other foreign policy issues, such as Latin America, Europe and the Middle East. It also delayed détente with the USSR. His decision to deploy US ground forces in Vietnam made him increasingly unpopular, and although elected as President in his own right in 1964 with an unprecedented majority, he announced he would not stand for re-election in 1968. He retired to a Texas ranch in 1969, disillusioned and in favour of peace talks to end the Vietnam War. He died in 1973, when the war was still going on.

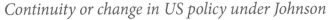

Continuity or change in US policy under Johnson

Johnson stated openly that he would continue Kennedy's policy in Vietnam:

> *'I am not going to lose Vietnam… I am not going to be the president who saw South East Asia go the way China went.'*

He felt the USSR and the Chinese would be watching his administration and confided in Bill Moyers, a young aide,

> *'I told [Lodge] to go back and tell those generals in Saigon that Lyndon Johnson intends to stand by our word, but by God I want something for our money. I want 'em to get off their butts and get out in those jungles and whip hell out of some Communists.*

(see: www.heinemann.co.uk/hotlinks)

The 'doves', led by senior Democrat Mike Mansfield, continued to warn that the only way to win the war was to gain popular support amongst the Vietnamese people by creating a united and neutralised state. Johnson and his advisers dismissed this view, saying that this would be unnecessary if Diem's successors introduced the political, economic and social reforms that were long overdue. But the new government was military-based and right wing. They were unlikely to meet the requirements of democracy and liberal change. Unlike America, the people of Vietnam did not desire the suppression of communism. Like Kennedy before him, Johnson stifled debate by demanding absolute solidarity in support of his policy.

Stretch and challenge: A 'contra-factual history' exercise

Discuss the following question using the ideas which follow.

What if . . . Johnson negotiated for a neutral Vietnam in a new Geneva agreement?

- Johnson might have persuaded the US public that the regime in Saigon would never accept the democratic reforms demanded by his administration. The influential journalist Walter Lipmann argued for a negotiated settlement in the New York Times.

- Johnson might have convinced the public that war in Vietnam had become a civil war.

- The public might have been persuaded by the view that creating his 'Great Society' in America would be the best beacon of freedom for the world.

- The DRV, especially the peasantry, were likely to have accepted a neutral, independent government for Vietnam with representation for the NLF.

- France and Britain thought the chances of military success for the USA were so slim, that they would have supported another Geneva conference.

- Détente with the USSR would be hastened if there were negotiations. The Soviet view was that escalation would lead to '**the wrong war in the wrong place at the wrong time**'. They had been restraining Hanoi from provoking superpower confrontation, but continued to offer support. If the USA saved face by disengagement, Hanoi should be strong enough to unite Vietnam as a friendly Communist state. They did not wish the Chinese to use the Sino-Soviet treaty as an excuse to drag the USSR into direct confrontation with the USA over Vietnam.

- China viewed potential US escalation of the war not as a threat to them, but as an opportunity for them to send military aid to Hanoi. Beijing looked on with delight as the USA struggled and faltered in Vietnam. The memory of Korea lingered.

4 Why and with what results did the US become involved in Vietnam to 1968?

Sources

(A) **At his tenth press conference in Paris, the French President expresses his views on American policy in Vietnam.**

Vietnam was shocked by the withdrawal of French administration and forces. The south was exposed to new perils by the existence of a communist State in Tonkin, from where our troops withdrew. It tried to find, in itself, a solid national government. It was then that the Americans arrived, bringing their aid, their policy and their authority. The United States considered itself the worldwide defender against communism. The regime established in the north aimed to impose itself also in South Vietnam, and America wanted to help this state to protect itself. Also, without intending to criticise, the American conviction of fulfilling a sort of vocation, their disapproval of other countries' colonialism, and the natural desire among such a powerful people to expand, made the Americans determined to take our place in Indochina.

From a statement of President de Gaulle, 23 July 1964

(B) **An informal comment made by the Chinese communist leader, offering military support for the North Vietnamese cause:**

It would be best to turn it into a bigger war. I'm afraid you really ought to send more troops to the South. Don't be afraid of US intervention, at most it's no worse than having another Korean War. The Chinese army is prepared, and if America takes the risk of attacking North Vietnam, the Chinese army will march in at once. Our troops want a war now.'

Mao Zedong, 1964

(C) **A report of an informal discussion between President Johnson and his advisers on the situation in Vietnam.**

We tell Moscow, Beijing and Hanoi that we'll get out of there if they will just quit raiding their neighbours, and they say 'Screw you!' All the senators are saying, 'Let's move, let's go into the North.' They'd impeach a president that would run out, wouldn't they? I stayed awake last night, thinking of this. It looks to me like we are getting into another Korea. I don't think we can fight them 10,000 miles away from home. I don't think it's worth fighting for and I don't think we can get out. It's just the biggest damned mess. Of course, if you start running from the Communists, they may just chase you into your own kitchen.

Lyndon B. Johnson, May 1964

ACTIVITY

1 Evaluate Sources A–C as evidence for the views on US problems in ending the Vietnam War.

2 Hold a class debate on whether or not Kennedy's legacy was certain to make withdrawal from Vietnam impossible under Johnson.

Was Johnson's policy concerning the Gulf of Tonkin incident a miscalculation?

An incident in the Gulf of Tonkin in August 1964 seemed a godsend to Johnson, allowing him not only to take a firmer line in Vietnam, but helping him to a landslide election victory in November (see Source B opposite).

By the summer of 1964, only 200 Americans had died in Vietnam and Johnson had only increased the US presence by 2500. The weak military rulers in Saigon, led by General Khanh, struggled to gain recognition. This was despite their command of 215,000 ARVN troops and nearly a quarter of a million support troops. The CIA estimated the strength of the Viet Cong at below 25,000 with perhaps 70,000 additional volunteers. The increase in Viet Cong air attacks led Khanh to request US military help for an expansion of the war. General Maxwell Taylor had replaced Lodge as Ambassador to Saigon, and he rebuffed their requests. In Washington it was expected that there would eventually be escalation of the war, but the time was not yet felt to be right. Khanh became increasingly desperate, aware that the people of Vietnam were war weary and felt the cause was hopeless. Johnson knew that he could not escalate US involvement without approval and funding from Congress.

An incident in the Gulf of Tonkin was to persuade US policy makers that August 1964 was the right time for increased military action after all. The South Vietnamese had recently attacked DRV territory to pressure Hanoi into withholding support from insurgents. US destroyers were sent on secret espionage missions, to support CIA approved sabotage raids on the North Vietnamese coast.

On 2 August, the US destroyer *Maddox* came under attack from North Vietnamese patrol boats in the Gulf of Tonkin. None of the three torpedoes hit their mark, but Johnson issued a stern warning to Hanoi of 'grave consequences' should any further attacks follow. Two nights later a second destroyer, the *C. Turner Joy* reported that it had come under attack and had returned fire but hit nothing. Other vessels were unaware of any such incident of North Vietnamese patrol boats in the area, and the commander of the *Maddox* urged that no retaliatory action should be made before a thorough investigation had taken place. Almost certainly, the report of the attack was unfounded.

Since 1963, Robert McNamara had been conducting the war, but Johnson now handed the responsibility to Congress 'in a stampede of misinformation and misconception' as Arthur M. Schlesinger calls it, in *The Imperial Presidency* (1973). On 7 August, Congress gave Johnson authority to 'take all necessary measures' and 'all necessary steps' to stop aggression and defend US forces in South-East Asia. As a result, Johnson ordered attacks on North Vietnamese naval bases under US SEATO obligations.

ACTIVITY

Use Source A and cartoon Source B to aid a discussion of the morality of the US action concerning the Gulf of Tonkin Incident.

Sources

(A) **Resolution passed by the US Senate, five days after the US destroyer *Maddox* had been fired upon by the North Vietnamese. President Johnson asserted that there had been two unprovoked attacks.**

Naval units of the Communist regime in Vietnam, in violation of the principles of the Charter of the United Nations and of international law, have deliberately and repeatedly attacked United States naval vessels lawfully present in international waters, and have thereby created a serious threat to international peace. These attacks are part of a deliberate and systematic campaign of aggression that the Communist regime in North Vietnam has been waging against its neighbours and the nations joined with them in the collective defense of their freedom. The United States is assisting the peoples of South-East Asia to protect their freedom and has no territorial, military or political ambitions in that area, but desires only that these peoples should be left in peace to work out their own destinies in their own way. The United States regards as vital to its national interest and world peace the maintenance of international peace and security in south-east Asia. The Constitution of the United States, the Charter of the United Nations and its obligations under the Southeast Asia Collective Defense Treaty compel the United States, as the President determines, to take all necessary steps to defend the freedom of member states requesting assistance. Therefore, the Congress approves and supports the determination of the President, as Commander

in Chief, to take all necessary measures to repel any armed attack against the forces of the United States and to prevent further aggression.

From: The Gulf of Tonkin Resolution, 7 August 1964

(B) **A recent cartoon draws a parallel between the claim of an attack on US ships in the Gulf of Tonkin in 1964 leading to Johnson's escalation of the Vietnam War, and George W. Bush's claim that Saddam Hussein had weapons of mass destruction in 2003, leading to US intervention in Iraq.**

4 Why and with what results did the US become involved in Vietnam to 1968?

Though later seen as an excuse for escalation, Johnson's main motive may have been to prop up the weak South Vietnamese regime or even to intimidate the North and China. There were dissenting voices in the Senate, which was two-thirds empty for the vote, one senator even stating that 'all Vietnam is not worth the life of a single American boy'. However, the Resolution was passed by 88 votes to 2. During the summer presidential campaign, the Republican candidate, Barry Goldwater, had accused Johnson of being soft on communism. Now Johnson's approval rating soared from 42 to 72 per cent. He publicly promised:

> 'We are not going to send American boys nine or ten thousand miles away from home to do what Asian boys should be doing for themselves.'

It seemed that he hoped the South Vietnamese could win their own war. But to the Joint Chiefs of Staff he said 'Just let me get elected and then you can have your war.' Johnson was elected in his own right, with the largest majority ever recorded. When Saigon proved unequal to the task, he felt he had a public mandate to escalate military action without a formal declaration of war in Vietnam.

Johnson set up a Working Group, known as the 'Wise Men', to consider possible strategies for ending the war. The chairman was William P. Bundy, brother of McGeorge Bundy, National Security Adviser to Kennedy and Johnson. Its members came from the Defence Department, the CIA, the State Department and Joint Chiefs of Staff. They reported back with the recommendation that North Vietnam should be bombed to take pressure off the weak government of the South.

What were the results of US intervention in Vietnam to 1968

In February 1965, after a Viet Cong attack on a US air base at Pleiku, a strategic strongpoint in South Vietnam. The attack killed nine soldiers, wounded more than 120 and damaged 22 aircraft. This event sparked the start of a major bombing campaign.

Operation Rolling Thunder, US military escalation, and its first use of ground troops

The first step in the escalation of operations took place in February 1965. *Operation Rolling Thunder* extended Johnson's policy into a systematic bombardment of the routes supplying the Viet Cong from the North. Intense air strikes began, targeting the Ho Chi Minh Trail through Laos, hoping to demoralise Hanoi and bring the North to the negotiating table. They were intended to end the war quickly and cheaply to avoid deploying substantial land forces. But more bombing took place in the South than the North, and northern industrial and military targets were not prioritised. The campaign failed to have much impact on the military capability of the NLF, because targets were largely agricultural, and China and the USSR quickly replaced damaged equipment. Supplies to the Viet Cong in the South increased during the campaign, while Soviet MiG fighters helped the North shoot down more than 700 planes.

Robert McNamara advised Johnson to send significant numbers of troops, while George Ball warned that this would lead to a humiliating defeat. In March 1965, 3500 Marines were sent to Vietnam at the request of General Westmoreland, commander of the military advisers in Saigon, to protect the bomber base at Danang. Ground troops pursued 'enclave strategy' to protect US aircraft and pilots by surrounding air bases. Later in March, the Viet Cong bombed the US Embassy in Saigon. In May, the Viet Cong overran ARVN troops in Phuoc Long Province north of Saigon.

'The wrong war in the wrong place at the wrong time'

This statement was first made by General Bradley in relation to MacArthur extending the Korean War into China. It was repeated by Kennedy regarding escalation of the Vietnam military commitment in 1960, and has been used more recently in relation to the Iraq War.

ACTIVITY

Discuss the message of this cartoon, in the context of Johnson's promise to implement a 'Great Society' social welfare programme in the USA, which he had to shelve because of the Vietnam War.

Figure 4.7 *'Let this session of Congress be known as the session which declares all-out war on human poverty'*, President Johnson, 8 January 1964. Cartoon by Victor Weisz, published in the *Evening Standard*, 1 December 1965.

Johnson initially kept the bombing campaign away from Hanoi and Haiphong, keeping them for bargaining, and focused instead on communications and ports. US B52 bombers targeted the main routes taking men and materials to the South, hoping to demoralise Hanoi. In the North, air-raid precautions were highly organised with sirens and concrete bunkers, and 2 million members of 'Shock Brigades' repaired the damage caused to roads and railways. Lack of initial success, and a deteriorating situation in the South, led to a massive increase in air attacks on North Vietnam. Hanoi was bombed even during a visit to Hanoi by Kosygin, the Soviet premier. The air campaign killed an estimated 50,000 people in the North.

McNamara's advice seemed to be the best solution. Congress granted $700 million for military operations, and by the end of May, 99,000 US soldiers were in Vietnam. This was to grow to 268,000 in 1966, 449,000 the following year and reach a peak at 539,000 in 1969 (see Figure 4.8). The conscription of young men into the US army, known as 'the draft', brought TV news of the War into every American household. Johnson had been President for 18 months before he decided to escalate the Vietnam War. Now the President was forced to justify 'Johnson's War', which seemed to have become his personal obsession.

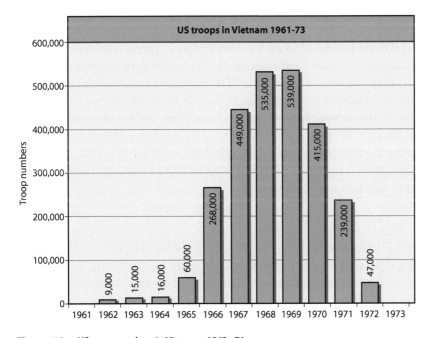

Figure 4.8 US troop numbers in Vietnam, 1963–71.

4 Why and with what results did the US become involved in Vietnam to 1968?

ACTIVITY

1 Find the following ideas in the Source below:

- the policies of previous administrations

- national self-determination

- action as a 'global policeman' for the 'free world'

- 'Domino' theory

- the 'doctrine of credibility'

- limited war rather than superpower confrontation

- fear of appearing to be an appeaser

- defensive perimeter strategy.

2 Evaluate how far US involvement in the Vietnam war was inevitable in the light of previous US policy in Asia.

Source

The President explains, on television, why American soldiers are in Vietnam.

Why are we in South Vietnam?

We are there because we have a promise to keep. Since 1954, every American President has offered support to the people of South Vietnam. We have helped to build, and we have helped to defend its independence. And I intend to keep that promise.

To dishonour that pledge, to abandon this small and brave nation to its enemies, and to the terror that must follow, would be an unforgivable wrong. We are also there to strengthen world order. Around the globe from Berlin to Thailand are people whose well-being rests in part on the belief that they can count on us if they are attacked.

To leave Vietnam to its fate would shake the confidence of all these people in the value of an American commitment and in the value of America's word. The result would be increased unrest and instability, and even wider war.

We are also there because there are great stakes in the balance. Let no one think for a moment that retreat from Vietnam would bring an end to conflict. The battle would be renewed in one country and then another. The central lesson of our time is that the appetite of aggression is never satisfied. To withdraw from one battlefield means only to prepare for the next. We must say in South-East Asia as we did in Europe in the words of the Bible: 'Hitherto shalt thou come, but no further'.

Lyndon Johnson, speech to the nation, 1965

By June 1965, the 'small brave nation' of South Vietnam had as its prime minister a flamboyant, cunning, corrupt drunkard and womaniser who wore purple jumpsuits, carried a pearl-handled revolver and idolised Hitler. Described by one US official as 'absolutely the bottom of the barrel', he was to scheme his way to the presidency to replace General Thieu in 1967. His name was Nguyen Cao Ky. Both Thieu and Ky were deeply unpopular and inept. Despite US opinion polls in 1965 showing that the US public were behind Johnson, McNamara thought victory unlikely, and Ambassador Maxwell Taylor was among others who opposed escalation. Taylor was replaced by hard-liner Henry Cabot Lodge as ambassador to Vietnam in July 1965.

Westmoreland's military strategies

US commander General Westmoreland now ran the conduct of the war in South Vietnam. Apart from air attacks, there were a variety of other tactics. 'Search and destroy' missions were organised using ARVN troops, montagnards (CIDGs) and US forces dropped by helicopter with air support. Source A, opposite, records such a 'search and destroy' exercise, carried out to mop up NVA forces (North Vietnamese Army Regulars) after the 34-day Battle of Ia Drang Valley in November 1965. 305 US troops and 3561 North Vietnamese were killed after venturing south to the Ho Chi Minh Trail. Though both sides claimed they had won the battle, the NVA was eventually proved correct and soon made good its losses. This battle first saw US soldiers directly dropped at the battle zone by helicopter, with B52s in support.

Large areas of South Vietnam were designated 'free bombing zones', where rockets, bombs and napalm were dropped indiscriminately. *Operation Ranch Hand* applied herbicides to strip 3 million acres of vegetation using Agent Orange, so named from the colour of its containers. Afterwards, these chemicals were found to cause cancer and other health problems.

B52 bombers flew high above battlefields to destroy enemy supply lines and bases. Unfortunately, helicopters not only dropped ground forces at the site of battles, they also airlifted victorious troops away from the battlefield, allowing Viet Cong reinforcements to recover the area won.

> **ACTIVITY**
>
> How far do Sources A and B support the view that US forces were hindered by Viet Cong tactics?

Sources

(A) **A US soldier describes the mopping up which took place after the NVA defeat at Ia Drang valley.**

It was agreed that, due to the increased build-up of enemy troops, key points for the defence of vital areas within each province were to be held at all costs. The airborne was alerted to prevent the North Vietnamese regiments defeated in the Ia Drang Valley from escaping back into Cambodia. From the minute we stepped off our helicopters we were involved in skirmishes and fire-fights. The valley was about twelve miles wide at the point where the Ia Drang flowed westward into Cambodia – and somewhere in those miles of dense jungle the main body of the enemy was on the move. We shelled the area below us for a half hour. Then the ARVN commander ordered his two remaining battalions to attack down the hill; there was a hell of a lot of shooting as we followed them in. Now, he didn't see a damn thing! All the action had been hidden by jungle. But we stayed in a clearing for the remainder of the day, and his troops brought in armful after armful of weapons and piled them in front of us. I was excited – we'd scored a decisive victory!

From: General Norman Schwarzkopf, *It Doesn't Take A Hero*, 1992

(B) **The Hanoi Politburo writes to the Communist Party in the South, outlining the Party's commitment to a protracted war strategy.**

Dear brothers,

Militarily, destroying the puppet government's troops is easier than American troops who have not fought us much, so are optimistic, proud of their weapons and keep their nationalist pride. The puppet troops, after many defeats, have low morale and little enthusiasm to fight. Therefore, we must strengthen our resolve to wipe out the puppet troops as fast as possible. However, our propaganda must emphasize the slogan 'Find Americans to kill.' We must thoroughly research suitable methods to destroy American troops in particular battlegrounds. Our guerrilla forces encircle the American troops' bases. Brothers and sisters must be encouraged and praised, so as to heighten their resolve to kill American troops.

From: Le Duan, *Thu Vao Nam*, Letter, November 1965

The Viet Cong followed Mao's army code, carrying out land reforms in areas where they gained control. Though some attempt was made to set up schools and improve land holding in areas of pacification, generally the US view was that the only solution to the Vietnam problem was to win a military victory, and that was impossible. American troops had been trained for conventional battle along the lines of Second World War. They were not suited to the jungle terrain, the climate or the guerrilla tactics of their enemy. There was never a measurable success using Search and Destroy tactics in isolated rural areas from which US forces retreated after victory. It was impossible to distinguish Viet Cong dead

4 Why and with what results did the US become involved in Vietnam to 1968?

from innocent Vietnamese civilians. US soldiers took the view 'If they were dead, they were Viet Cong', distorting statistics. The price paid for undermining the Viet Cong was the alienation of the civilian population.

In January 1967, Westmoreland followed up a victory that had cost 3000 PLAF troops. He began *Operation Cedar Falls*, focusing on NLF stronghold of the Iron Triangle outside of Saigon. The surrounding villages and jungle vegetation were cleared and 12 miles of underground tunnels flattened. However, there were never any clear territorial gains. The level of desertion from the ARVN was reminiscent of Jiang Jieshi's army. US troops were drawn into inconclusive battles in rural areas allowing the PLAF to win control of the cities.

The Draft and the Anti-War Movement

Over 26 million American men came of draft age during the Vietnam War and 2.15 million were sent to Vietnam, of whom 1.6 million went into combat. Those who fought were disproportionately poor, badly educated and black. It was also a teenaged army. Over 60 per cent of those who died in Vietnam were between the ages of seventeen and twenty-one. Their average age was nineteen. Tens of thousands of fit Americans managed to find excuses to avoid the military draft because they did not wish to fight. The resultant army was less efficient than a volunteer army, as conscripts lacked enthusiasm. The draft took no account of religious or philosophical objections although college students were exempt. In the spring of 1967, student rallies of 200,000 in New York and 50,000 in San Francisco demonstrated against the war. Draft cards of those defying the government were ceremoniously burned.

The Anti-War Movement grew out of a range of forces, among them local and national civil rights, anti-nuclear campaigns and pacifist movements. The political left resented Soviet human rights violations, but equally objected to supporting corrupt regimes in Saigon. Civil disobedience campaigns demanded immediate withdrawal from Vietnam. One of the most influential was the National Coordinating Committee (NCC) to 'End the War in Vietnam', where Dr Martin Luther King Jr spoke out against Johnson's policy.

Sources

(A) **Dr Martin Luther King Jr delivers a speech in New York in 1967, exposing the hidden reality of the Vietnam War on American society as well as on the Vietnamese.**

Since I am a preacher by trade, I suppose it is not surprising that I have seven major reasons for bringing Vietnam into the field of my moral vision. There is at the outset a very obvious and almost facile connection between the war in Vietnam and the struggle I, and others, have been waging in America. A few years ago there was a shining moment in that struggle. It seemed as if there was a real promise of hope for the poor -- both black and white -- through the poverty program. There were experiments, hopes, new beginnings. Then came the buildup in Vietnam and I watched the program broken and eviscerated as if it were some idle political plaything of a society gone mad on war, and I knew that America would never invest the necessary funds or energies in rehabilitation of its poor so long as adventures like Vietnam continued to draw men and skills and money like some demonic destructive suction tube. So I was increasingly compelled to see the war as an enemy of the poor and to attack it as such.

Perhaps the more tragic recognition of reality took place when it became clear to me that the war was doing far more than devastating the hopes of the poor at home. It was sending their sons and their brothers and their husbands to fight and to die in extraordinarily high proportions relative to the rest of the population. We were taking the black young men who had been crippled by our society and sending them eight thousand miles away to guarantee liberties in Southeast Asia which they had not found in southwest Georgia and East Harlem. So we have been repeatedly faced with the cruel irony of watching Negro and white boys on TV screens as they kill and die together for a nation that has been unable to seat them together in the same schools. So we watch them in brutal solidarity burning the huts of a poor village, but we realize that they would never live on the same block in Detroit. I could not be silent in the face of such cruel manipulation of the poor.

B The Proclamation of the Anti-draft Resistance 1967

To the young men of America, to the whole of the American people and to all men of goodwill everywhere:

- *An ever growing number of young American men are finding that the American war in Vietnam so outrages their deepest moral and religious sense that they cannot contribute to it in any way. We share their moral outrage.*

- *We believe that the war is unconstitutional and illegal.*

- *This war violates the Geneva Accords which our government pledged to support but has since undermined. The slaughter of peasants who dare shake their fists at American helicopters is a crime against humanity.*

- *We believe it is an unconstitutional denial of religious liberty to withhold draft exemption from those whose deep beliefs are against unjust wars.*

- *We support those who resist this war, and call on all men of good will to join us.*

In 1967, US troops in Vietnam were being killed at the rate of over 1000 a month. On 21 October 1967, 100,000 people listened to speakers at the Lincoln Memorial who demanded an end to the bombing, a negotiated settlement and US withdrawal from Vietnam. However, American public opinion remained divided. The Anti-War movement never gained widespread support, partly because of the government's misleading attacks on it.

Sources

A A controversial American journalist reports how small groups of soldiers were reviled and tormented unmercifully during the 50,000-strong demonstration outside the Pentagon.

Taste and decency had left the scene a long time before. All that remained were these lines of troops and packs of nondescript kids who taunted the soldiers. The kids went to the bathroom on the side of the Pentagon building. They threw a couple of rocks through the first floor windows. The soldiers faced them silently. There was no humor to it. These were not the kind of kids who were funny. These were the small core of dropouts and drifters who came to the front of what had started out as a beautiful day, one that would have bad meaning to it. They turned a demonstration for peace, these drifters in raggedy clothes, into a sickening, club-swinging mess. At the end of the day, the only concern anybody could have was for the soldiers who were taking the abuse.

James Breslin, October 1967

B A writer reports his account of the March on the Pentagon in the radical left wing newspaper, the National Guardian.

The Military Police tried to clear the demonstrators who ran behind them. A youth refused to be moved. A rifle butt landed in his stomach. Several youths grabbed rifles. Four helmets were stolen. The federal marshals moved forward, clubs swinging – it seemed they aimed particularly at women. Each time the action stopped in a particular spot, demonstrators sought to speak with the soldiers, who were under orders not to respond. 'Why are you doing this?' a demonstrator asked, adding 'Join us.' It was obvious that some of the troops were weakening. A few soldiers seemed ready to faint. 'Hold your lines, hold your lines,' a captain repeated harshly, over and over, to the soldiers. A girl confronted a soldier 'Why, why, why?' she asked. 'We're just like you. You're just like us. It's them,' she said, pointing to the Pentagon. She brought her two fingers to her mouth, kissed them and touched the soldier's lips. Four soldiers grabbed her and dragged her away, under arrest. The soldier she had spoken to tried to tell them that she hadn't hurt him.

Gerald Long, October 1967

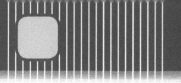

4 Why and with what results did the US become involved in Vietnam to 1968?

ACTIVITY

Compare Sources A and B on page 131 as evidence for the anti-war March on the Pentagon in October 1967.

The CIA reported their assessment of the US Peace movement in October 1967. They saw its most striking feature as its diversity, with activists from the student world, from militant elements of the minority communities, from the labour movement and the intellectual sphere. They saw its co-ordinating action as impressive. They were not thought to be interested in 'pre-packaged ideology' or excessive Communist guidance. The CIA saw 'no significant evidence that would prove communist control or direction'. Johnson increased his harassment and surveillance of anti-war opponents, encouraged by opinion polls that showed 45 per cent of Americans favoured increased military pressure in Vietnam, while only 41 per cent favoured withdrawal.

There was conflicting advice for Johnson in Washington: Vice -President Hubert Humphrey said 'America is throwing lives and money down a corrupt rat-hole.' The JCS called for 200,000 additional troops, causing George Ball and Bill Moyers to resign. Johnson granted an increase of 55,000 troops and widened Rolling Thunder. McGeorge Bundy's advice was for the President to change the commander in the field, General Westmoreland. Towards the end of 1967, 16 advisers known as the 'Wise Men' suggested 'Vietnamisation' – using more South Vietnamese troops to win a decisive victory. This might silence the outrage at home over American casualties.

The resignation of McNamara

Robert McNamara, Secretary of Defence, was blamed for limiting the bombing. In a hearing before the Senate, McNamara testified that bombing the Ho Chi Minh trail would never succeed in ending the insurgency. The Demilitarised Zone had been nicknamed 'the McNamara Line' after him. He felt increased bombing might provoke open confrontation with the USSR and was becoming increasingly stressed, even tearful, about the conduct of the war. He told Johnson:

> 'The picture of the world's greatest superpower killing or seriously injuring 1000 civilians a week, while trying to pound a tiny, backward nation into submission on an issue whose merits are hotly disputed, is not a pretty one.'

McNamara's resignation in November 1967 has been seen as a major turning point in the Vietnam War, starting the process of de-escalation. In January 1968, he was replaced as Secretary of Defence by Clark Clifford. After an unsuccessful attempt to gain more troops from countries already involved with the US in Vietnam, Clifford formed the opinion that there was little risk of dominoes falling if the USA withdrew troops from Vietnam. Just at this point, Hanoi embarked on a much more forceful policy with the Tet Offensive. Whether it was McNamara's resignation or the Tet Offensive itself is a matter of debate, but what is sure is that a turning point occurred in the War as the year 1967 ended.

In Washington the question was continually asked: are we winning the Vietnam War? The only way to answer this was to ask statisticians to report on enemy casualties; bombs dropped; forces deployed. Statistics suggested the US operations were going well, and that escalation was the right policy. However, the huge number of support staff needed to back up superior US military technology, and the impossibility of defending such a long border with Cambodia were signs of disaster that should have been heeded. However, rather than regretting having committed half a million US troops to the Vietnam War, Johnson wished that he had taken the decision to send in ground troops earlier. This, he felt, had been his only miscalculation.

ACTIVITY

The Vietnam War 1954–68

- Compare Sources C and D on page 133 as evidence for the problems faced by South Vietnam.

- Using your own knowledge, assess how far Sources A–D on page 133 support the interpretation that the main reason the USA began and continued its involvement in Vietnam until 1968 was to defend democracy.

Sources

(A) **The American President writes to Ngo Dinh Diem, the President of the Republic of South Vietnam, expressing his support for the new South Vietnamese government.**

I have been following with great interest the developments in Vietnam, particularly since the conclusion of the Geneva conference. The implications of the agreement concerning Vietnam have caused grave concern regarding the future of a country temporarily divided by an artificial military grouping, weakened by a long, exhausting war and faced with external enemies and internal collaborators. We have fulfilled your recent requests for aid in the formidable task of moving several hundred thousand loyal Vietnamese citizens away from areas ruled by a communist ideology they hate. I am glad that the United States is able to assist in this humanitarian effort.

Dwight Eisenhower, Letter, 23 October 1954

(B) **A statement of the goals of the NLF, the united front that brought together Communists and non-Communists to liberate Vietnam from foreign control.**

The present South Vietnamese regime is a camouflaged colonial regime dominated by the Yankees, and the South Vietnamese government is a servile government, implementing faithfully all the policies of the American imperialists. Therefore, this regime must be overthrown and a government of national and democratic union put in its place composed of representatives of all social classes, of all nationalities, of various political parties, of all religions; patriotic, eminent citizens must take over for the people the control of economic, political, social, and cultural interests and thus bring about independence, democracy, well-being, peace, neutrality, and efforts toward the peaceful unification of the country.

From the Program of the National Liberation Front of South Vietnam, January 1962

(C) **At his tenth press conference in Paris, the French President expresses his views on American policy in Vietnam.**

Vietnam was shocked by the withdrawal of French administration and forces. The south was exposed to new perils by the existence of a communist State in Tonkin, from where our troops withdrew. It tried to find, in itself, a solid national government. It was then that the Americans arrived, bringing their aid, their policy and their authority. The United States considered itself the worldwide defender against communism. The regime established in the north aimed to impose itself also in South Vietnam, and America wanted to help this state to protect itself. Also, without intending to criticise, the American conviction of fulfilling a sort of vocation, their disapproval of other countries' colonialism, and the natural desire among such a powerful people to expand, made the Americans determined to take our place in Indochina.

From a statement of President de Gaulle, 23 July 1964

(D) **US President Johnson explains why the USA continued to be involved in Vietnam.**

We have a promise to keep. Since 1954 every American President has offered support to the people of South Vietnam. We have helped to build and defend its independence. To dishonour that promise and abandon this small, brave nation to its enemies, and the terror that must follow, would be an unforgivable wrong. We are also there to strengthen world order. Around the globe are people whose well-being rests partly on believing they can count on us if attacked. To leave Vietnam to its fate would shake these people's confidence in the value of America's word. Let no one think for a moment that retreat from Vietnam would bring an end to conflict. The battle would be renewed in one country and then another. The appetite of aggression is never satisfied. In Southeast Asia, as we did in Europe, we must follow the words of the Bible: 'Hitherto shalt thou come, but no further.'

Lyndon Johnson, speech, 1965

Skills practised

In this chapter you have:

- learned and practised the skills of source analysis, comparison and evaluation
- had to link four sources to a question and use them in order to evaluate an interpretation
- studied the contextual information, on US intervention and growing involvement in Vietnam, to help you understand these sources and use their provenance
- gained knowledge of the origins of the French War in Indochina, and the causes and consequences of US involvement in Vietnam until the start of 1968.

Bibliography

Beschloss, M. (1999). *Taking Charge: The Johnson White House Tapes, 1963–1964*. Pocket Books.

Ferguson, N. (2003). *Virtual History: Alternatives and Counterfactuals*. London: Pan.

Gettleman M. E. et al. (1995). *Vietnam and America: The Most Comprehensive Documented History of the Vietnam War*. New York: Grove Press.

Hall, M.K. (2008). *The Vietnam War (Seminar Studies in History)* revised 2nd edn. Harlow: Longman.

Lacouture, J. (2001). *Vietnam: Between Two Truces*. London: Secker & Warburg.

Levy, D. (2004). *The Vietnam War (Chronicle of America's Wars)*. Minneapolis: Lerner Publishing Group.

Logevall, F. (2001). *The Origins of the Vietnam War (Seminar Studies in History)*. Harlow: Longman.

McMahon, R. J. (2002). *Major Problems in the History of the Vietnam War: Documents and Essays* 3rd edn. Houghton Mifflin.

Moyar, M. (2009). *Triumph Forsaken: The Vietnam War 1954–1965*. Cambridge: Cambridge University Press.

Nalty B. C. (1998). *The Vietnam War: The History of America's Conflict in South East Asia (Classic Conflicts)*. Salamander Books.

Ruane, K. (2000). *The Vietnam Wars*. Manchester: Manchester University Press.

Sanders, V. (2007). *The USA and Vietnam* 3rd edn. London: Hodder Education.

Serewicz L. W. *America at the Brink of Empire: Rusk, Kissinger, and the Vietnam War (Political Traditions in Foreign Policy*. Louisiana: Louisiana State University Press.

Wiest, A. (2002). *The Vietnam War 1956–1975*. Oxford: Osprey Publishing.

Articles

Abouzahr, S. 'The Tangled Web: America, France and Indochina 1947-50'

History Today October 2004 Volume: 54 Issue: 10

Billings-Yun, M. 'Ike and Vietnam' *History Today* November 1988 Volume: 38 Issue: 11

Websites

See www.heinemann.co.uk/hotlinks

This chapter continues the analysis of US policy concerning the Vietnam War which we began to study in Chapter 4. Its main purpose is to evaluate reasons why the USA failed to win the War. In doing so, we will look at the part played by the US military; the Viet Cong and guerrilla warfare; the Tet Offensive of 1968; the media and opposition to the War in the USA; the Draft, Nixon and the bombing campaign; the Paris peace talks 1968–73; the Northern victory and the fall of Saigon 1975.

In this chapter you will further develop the skills of source analysis, interpretation, evaluation and synthesis. Synthesis is a high level skill by which you integrate your ideas with source evaluation and knowledge to reach balanced, supported judgements.

Key question:

The key questions for evaluation are:

- What part did the US military play in Johnson's failure to win the war?
- What part did the Viet Cong and guerrilla warfare play in the US failure to win the war?
- How did the corruption of the South Vietnamese regime contribute to the US failure to win the war?
- What part did the Tet Offensive play in the US failure to win the War?
- What part did opposition to the war within the US play?
- What was the impact of the Draft, Nixon and the bombing campaign?

Synthesis

At the end of this chapter there is a special section that will help you synthesise the key issues of the whole book:

- How far had American foreign policy in Asia changed between 1945 and 1975?
- Why did US foreign policy fail in China and Vietnam, yet have more success in Japan and South Korea?

Johnson never openly declared war on North Vietnam because he feared bringing China into the War. He aimed to win a swift, limited war by conventional strategies, steering clear of Cold War confrontation with the USSR. However, this merely encouraged the communists and added to their popularity. A pacification strategy might have worked better than a war of attrition. There were no fixed or identifiable military front lines; instead they were everywhere and nowhere. The North treated Laos, Cambodia and South Vietnam as one, though treaty arrangements had made them three separate states. Kennedy's attempt to cut off the supply route through Laos had already proved ineffective. South Vietnam's long border with Laos and Cambodia gave the enemy a vast supply line, the Ho Chi Minh Trail, which was difficult to close.

It would be a near impossible task to contain communism by creating a democratic nation state of South Vietnam. A corrupt military dictatorship took charge there after the assassination of Diem, but US complicity in this murder gave it a moral obligation to support the Generals who replaced him.

Timeline 1968–1975

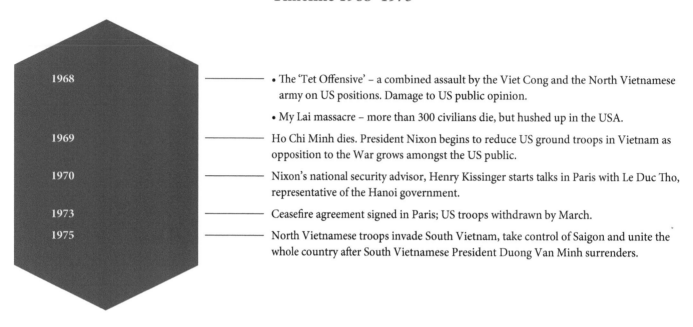

1968	• The 'Tet Offensive' – a combined assault by the Viet Cong and the North Vietnamese army on US positions. Damage to US public opinion.
	• My Lai massacre – more than 300 civilians die, but hushed up in the USA.
1969	Ho Chi Minh dies. President Nixon begins to reduce US ground troops in Vietnam as opposition to the War grows amongst the US public.
1970	Nixon's national security advisor, Henry Kissinger starts talks in Paris with Le Duc Tho, representative of the Hanoi government.
1973	Ceasefire agreement signed in Paris; US troops withdrawn by March.
1975	North Vietnamese troops invade South Vietnam, take control of Saigon and unite the whole country after South Vietnamese President Duong Van Minh surrenders.

What part did the US military play in Johnson's failure to win the war?

The US military leadership despised the ARVN, whose commanders were appointed for their loyalty to Thieu and Ky. Few of their officers had the respect even of their own men, and few were Buddhists who made up 85 per cent of the total population. The American forces were themselves disunited. US Marines had a naval loyalty and were reluctant to obey Westmoreland's military orders. In January 1968, Westmoreland himself said,

> 'The military professionalism of the Marines falls far short of the standards that should be demanded of our Armed Forces. Indeed, they are brave and proud, but their standards, tactics and lack of command supervision throughout their ranks require improvement in the national interest.'

Black soldiers fought alongside whites in mixed battalions, but blacks formed a much higher proportion of combat troops than did whites. Non-combat, deskbound or support troops made up a large proportion of the US troop numbers, distorting Washington's perception of its military strength. It was realised that, for **Operation Rolling Thunder** to be effective, bomber bases, such as Khe Sanh just south of the demilitarised zone, had to be protected, together with their personnel. Non-combat troops such as engineers, signallers, logistics, intelligence and support staff also needed protection.

B52 bombers, and Huey helicopters for troop transport, were the backbones of strategy. F-4 Phantom fighters were used in combat against Soviet MiG attack fighters. F-4s also dropped loads of radar-reflecting fibres, known as 'chaff', to scramble enemy radar. M-48 tanks were of use only in set-piece battles. US troops were trained for a conventional war strategy, similar to that used in the Second World War. This depended on superior tactical weapons and mechanised technological warfare, which was impossible in remote jungle areas. US troops found themselves fighting the terrain as well as enemy guerrillas. In these circumstances, their training was of little use against the Viet Cong. The 'teeth' of the US forces amounted to about 80,000 front line combat troops, with a tail of '**grunts**'.

Grunts
Ordinary foot soldiers.

Many US soldiers lost limbs to land mines, were impaled by the poisoned spikes of booby-traps or caught dysentery from wading through water dirtied by the human sewage used to fertilise rice-fields. They had to spray themselves with DDT to kill biting insects and take malaria tablets every day. By 1971 disobedience was rife in the US armed forces. Unwilling conscripts lacked skills, leading to war wounds and bad service records. More disturbing was the persistence of symptoms of acute distress, flashbacks, severe sleep problems, depression and rage. Estimates suggest that more than 700,000 veterans suffer from **post-traumatic stress disorder**.

> **Post-traumatic stress disorder**
>
> A psychological reaction that occurs after highly stressed event(s) (such as wartime combat). It is usually characterised by depression, anxiety, flashbacks, recurrent nightmares, and avoidance of reminders of the event(s).

Operation Rolling Thunder

This was the title of a gradual and sustained US 2nd Air Division, US Navy, and Republic of Vietnam Air Force (VNAF) aerial bombardment campaign conducted against the Democratic Republic of Vietnam (North Vietnam) from 2 March 1965 until 1 November 1968, during the Vietnam War.

The operation had four objectives, which evolved over time:

- to increase the sagging morale of the Saigon regime in South Vietnam;
- to make North Vietnam cease its support for the Communist insurgency in South Vietnam;
- to destroy North Vietnam's transport system, industrial base and air defences, and
- to impede the flow of men and material into South Vietnam.

Attaining these objectives was made difficult by international restraints imposed upon the US and its allies by the circumstances of the Cold War, and by the military aid and assistance received by North Vietnam from the Soviet Union and the People's Republic of China (PRC).

The operation became the most intense air/ground battle waged during the Cold War period. Thanks to the efforts of its allies, North Vietnam was able to create one of the most effective air defense environments ever faced by American military aviators. The North Vietnamese were successful to such a degree that, after one of the longest aerial campaigns ever conducted by any nation, *Rolling Thunder* was terminated as a strategic failure in late 1968 having achieved none of its objectives.

Sources

(A) **A US Corporal sent this letter home from hospital after he was wounded in the Tet Offensive. His platoon was situated fourteen miles south of the city of Hue.**

Well, here I am in the US Air Force Hospital in beautiful Cam Ranh Bay. I've got lacerations of the scalp, a ringing in my ears, a bullet hole in my right arm, wounds all over my lower body and my left leg looks like the surface of the moon. At 4 a.m. four hundred VC attacked with mortars, rockets, ground assault and gas. We suffered five dead and every Marine in the compound was wounded. I heard over the radio that the grunts sweeping across the tracks had found 25 PAVN bodies hastily abandoned. At two o'clock in the afternoon, the grunts had killed 12 fleeing gooks and were still in heavy contact. The gooks held part of our compound, there

were about 75–100 actually in there with us. They put over 200 rounds into our little area. I truly believed I would die. I have never fought so hard in my life. I caught a big whiff of their gas and was staggering around crying and throwing up. I was leaning over the bunker choking when a big grenade bounced off my head and hit at my feet. I saw it lying there, its fuse sparkling. I tried to run but it exploded, filling the backs of my legs with hundreds of fragments of stone, dirt, sand, wood and grenade fragments. Gooks started shooting at me from the road and paddies. They were coming across the paddy on bamboo mats, cutting the wire and crawling through. I stuck the rifle out of the door without looking, and blew the whole magazine on automatic.

Corporal Cottrell Fox, Letter, February 1968 (From Bill Adler, *Letters from Vietnam*, pp. 60–63)

(Sources continue on page 138.)

B Kien, a character in a novel written by a member of a Youth Brigade who served in Vietnam, recalls the sacrifices of North Vietnamese soldiers in early 1969 during the fighting in the Central Highlands. American air superiority led to many North Vietnamese units being completely destroyed.

During the dry season the sun burned harshly, the wind blew fiercely, and the enemy sent napalm spraying through the jungle. A sea of fire enveloped them, spreading like the fires of hell. Troops were blown out of their shelters, became disorientated and threw themselves into nets of bullets, dying in the inferno. Above them, the helicopters flew at tree-top height and shot them almost one by one, the blood spreading out, spraying from their backs, flowing like red mud. The grass clearing was piled high with bodies killed by helicopter gunships. Broken bodies, bodies blown apart, bodies vaporised. No jungle grew again in this clearing. No grass. No plants. 'Better to die than to surrender, my brothers! Better to die!' The Battalion Commander shouted insanely. Waving his pistol in front of Kien, he blew his own brains out. The Americans attacked with sub-machine guns, sending bullets buzzing like deadly bees around Kien. Hot blood trailed after him as he rolled down the slope. In the days that followed, bloated human corpses floated and drifted into the stinking marsh. Snakes and centipedes crawled over him. From then on the place was called the Jungle of the Screaming Souls.

From: Bao Dinh, *The Sorrow of War*, 1994

ACTIVITY

Compare Sources A and B as evidence for the soldier's experience of war in Vietnam.

To motivate the US troops to continue fighting, they were flown to Japan at the end of their year-long tour of duty, where they experienced a comfortable period of recreation and recuperation. The experience of the comforts of home, such as sport, girls, cigarettes, movies and American food and drink made them reluctant to return to the battlefield. Many caught STDs or became addicted to drugs, seriously undermining overall army discipline and their use for future combat. The US media sometimes placed a price on the head of an officer responsible for a defeat, and 'grunts', aware of anti-war feelings back home, showed indiscipline in view of the TV cameras.

How did statistics contribute to a false impression of imminent victory?

The Pentagon employed statisticians who advised on military strategy using computers that calculated success by output and body count. They used the same method of calculation used in the war against Germany, in order to give Washington statistical assurance that they were 'winning the war'. Output included tons of bombs dropped, sorties made, ammunition used. However, in Vietnam there were no 'set-piece' battles. If local peasants could avoid the land mines, then they were the enemy. Soldiers sometimes gained military promotion by exaggerating numbers of enemy they had killed. US authorities recognised these inaccuracies, but still estimated enemy casualties at 200,000. **Crossover point** was their aim, where more enemy soldiers were being killed than could be replaced, but this was never reached. The North managed to keep apace of US reinforcements by recruiting in the South, and equipping forces via the **Ho Chi Minh Trail**, a journey of between two and six months.

Crossover point

A US term for when more enemy soldiers were being killed than could be replaced.

The Ho Chi Minh Trail

The Ho Chi Minh Trail was a network of jungle paths that snaked from North to South Vietnam via Laos and Cambodia. Food, supplies and later trucks full of men and arms travelled along it. There were military staging posts at about 20 to 30 kilometres apart with cemeteries for those killed along the way. Travellers, often on bicycles in the early part of the war, died from a variety of causes. Some died from starvation or disease, others from attacks by tigers or bears, from snakebites or eating poisonous mushrooms. Despite incessant US bombing, the trail was kept open by repair teams who camouflaged it, and any vehicles along its route, using the local vegetation.

What part did the Viet Cong and guerrilla warfare play in the US failure to win the war?

The USSR and China equipped the North Vietnamese, under the command of Giap, with T-54 tanks and MiG fighters. However, Soviet weapons and ammunition had to be transported through Chinese territory, and often disappeared en route, failing to reach their intended target. Giap, a brilliant strategist, used the main North Vietnamese force, the PAVN (or NVA), only for conventional battles. He depended instead on Viet Cong guerrillas. He said:

> 'We were not strong enough to drive out half a million American troops, but that was not our aim. Our intention was to break the will of the Americans to continue the war.'

The Viet Cong used Mao's tactics of a 'people's war', mobilising everyone in the community to fight or give aid. Communist insurgents required local aid, shelter and food, and their aim was to lure US troops into the jungle. Territorial gain was impossible, as US troops were airlifted back to base after victorious battles, so allowing the Viet Cong to regroup and regain the land lost. They laid land mines and placed sharpened bamboo sticks in disguised hollows as booby traps to impale unsuspecting US troops.

The US military gave more attention to force than to attempting to win the hearts and minds of the South Vietnamese. Though there were American doctors, teachers, accountants and engineers able to instruct the local people, officers used brutality and compulsion rather than attempting to improve society, health or education. On the other hand, Communist **cadres** were fair, communal and hardworking. Though they could be ruthless and repressive, they won hearts and minds by redistributing land and inspiring loyalty amongst whole peasant communities. Communist informants and social organisations kept up local morale.

The US Strategic Hamlets policy had shattered ancestral homes and food-harvesting communities, so the US occupation force was very much resented. The Vietnamese lived near shrines that housed the spirits of their ancestors, in ancient communities with strong social support. Houses were made of wood and thatch with dirt floors, the rice paddies were fertilised with human and animal excrement. US soldiers saw the Vietnamese rural peasant as sub-human and alien, so they treated innocent civilians as though they were 'all Viet Cong'. Helicopters dropped and picked up US troops for battle, limiting their contact with peasants. Vietnamese peasants resented them as another occupying force who burned their homes, mistreated and brutalised them.

Operation Phoenix, which began in 1968, tried to destroy NLF structure by identifying local cadres. It involved US troops in using interrogation and very violent methods of torture, such as electric shock treatment to genitals. It had an effect in weakening the NLF, killing 26,000 people. However, its methods provoked a new wave of support for insurgency. The CIA commented that it was 'thought of by geniuses and implemented by idiots.' US bombs, napalm and herbicides were used to destroy peasant homes, livelihoods and vegetation throughout South Vietnam. The use of superior weaponry, such as heat-seeking devices, inflicted immense and indiscriminate suffering on innocent women and children. They also killed the animals on which peasants depended for food.

The Viet Cong (VC) constructed a very sophisticated network of underground tunnels north of Saigon, in which they could hide, shelter and regroup. It developed into almost a city underground with offices, cookers, furniture and clothing. Viet Cong guerrillas continued to fight, despite malaria, infections, snake-bites or ear-drums burst by continuous US bombing.

Cadres

Leaders of groups within Communist societies.

Operation Phoenix

A military, intelligence, and internal security program designed by the United States Central Intelligence Agency (CIA) to identify and "neutralize" (via infiltration, capture, terrorism or assassination) the civilian infrastructure supporting the Viet Cong. It was carried out by Republic of Vietnam's (South Vietnam) security apparatus and US Special Operations Forces. The Program was in operation between 1967 and 1972.

The Viet Cong Cu Chi Tunnels

The Cu Chi tunnels are 45 miles from Saigon. They formed an underground village used by the Viet Cong and became one of the most famous battlegrounds during the Vietnam War. They were an underground city with living areas, kitchens, storage, weapons factories, field hospitals, and command centres. In places, it was even three stories deep and housed up to 10,000 people who virtually lived underground for years: getting married, giving birth and going to school. They only came out at night to tend their crops. Parts of the tunnels have been renovated and restored. Today it is a major tourist attraction.

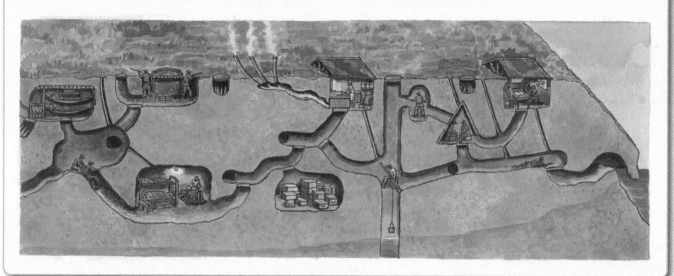

How did the corruption of the South Vietnamese regime contribute to the US failure to win the war?

The influx of half a million US troops into an already dislocated South Vietnamese society added to the instability already apparent under the regime of Ky and Thieu. Brothels sprang up around military bases; prostitution and drugs were rife in Saigon. What had been 'the Paris of the East, full of tree-lined squares bright with bougainvillea, jasmine and mimosa turned into a sleazy, downtrodden vice-trap crawling with disabled soldiers and homeless orphans. An estimated four million Vietnamese, about 25 per cent of the population, were refugees from the countryside, stretching the resources of urban areas to crisis point. They lived in squalid conditions on the outskirts of towns. Sanitation and rubbish collection was often very basic, causing the spread of disease. An influx of US goods also damaged local industries and caused price rises. A black market came into being and officials routinely demanded bribes. Vast sums of American aid were diverted into the pockets of corrupt officials. The Vietnamese urban middle class stashed it away in Zurich bank accounts, supporting the view that the USA was using dollar imperialism to prevent a united Communist state emerging in Vietnam.

The Generals suppressed public protests, tortured political prisoners and attacked Buddhist pagodas. Their attempt to fulfil their promises of constitutional reform allowed opposition parties little chance to gain support and they reserved for themselves dictatorial powers for times of emergency. The American attempt to build a nation state in South Vietnam had failed miserably. One official likened the strategy to 'trying to build a house with a bulldozer and a wrecking crane.'

What part did the Tet Offensive play in the US failure to win the War?

In January 1968, the ceasefire period for the Tet New Year celebrations marked the start of a major offensive – a series of bold, well-co-ordinated attacks by North Vietnamese and Viet Cong throughout the country.

The North Vietnamese Objectives:

■ to lure US troops away from cities into rural areas, using diversionary attacks on remote outposts;

■ to focus on locations south of the Demilitarised Zone and along South Vietnam's western border;

■ to open talks with the US as a distraction, while PLAF (the People's Liberation Armed Forces in Vietnam) and PAVN (thePeople's Army of Vietnam) launched simultaneous attacks on major cities in the south to incite a broad popular uprising.

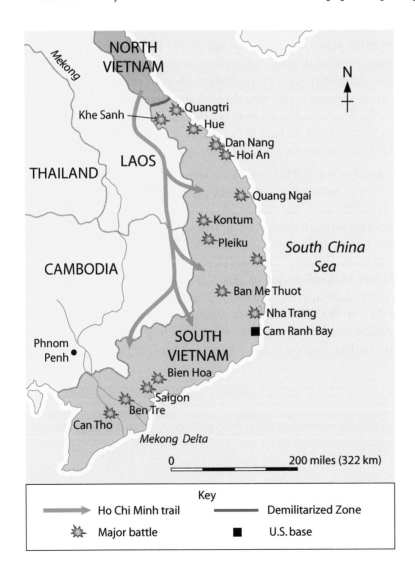

Figure 5.1 Map showing the main battles of the Tet Offensive 1968.

Source

Local communist cadres received this directive on 1 November 1967, explaining General Pham Hung's goals and strategy for the long-awaited general offensive and uprising:

This is to notify you that an offensive and uprising will take place in the very near future. Our victory is close at hand. The conditions are ripe. Our Party has carefully judged the situation. We must act and act fast. This is an opportunity to fulfil the aspirations of the entire people.

There are two fundamental steps:
First, annihilate the enemy's power. Capture all tyrant officials and spies from the villages and hamlets. We cannot act without success in this area.

Second, organise our political control of districts, hamlets and villages.

Identify all tyrants and spies and use suicide cells to annihilate them by any means. Hold 10 to 15 minute meetings to give information about the current situation. Use the populace in sabotage and support activities and raids. Encourage the masses to go on strike. Dig trenches and make spikes during night-time to transform the terrain. Encourage all people in each family to take part, regardless of their age.

ACTIVITY

Use the source above to analyse the Strategy behind the Tet Offensive 1968.

Present your analysis as a mind map.

Late in 1967 the first stage of the plan was put into operation. The PAVN attacks on isolated villages were heavily defeated by Westmoreland's forces. In their absence, NLF forces infiltrated urban areas. The communists used propaganda to broaden the rift between Saigon and Washington. Hanoi offered to talk with the USA if it stopped bombing the North. Giap then besieged the Khe Sanh Marine base as a diversionary tactic. Johnson, fearing another Dien Bien Phu, ordered the base to be secured at all costs. B52s pounded the enemy with over 100,000 tons of bombs over a five mile area.

The Tet Lunar New Year ceasefire marked the start of the second stage of the attack, and was a complete surprise. The Central Intelligence Agency (CIA) had found some enemy plans but were convinced that Khe Sanh was the key target and that the North was not capable of mounting a broad offensive. However, on 30 January, 84,000 PLAF and PAVN soldiers attacked 36 of the 44 provincial capitals in the South. This was a new forward phase in Communist military and political strategy, and was effective in inflicting heavy casualties on American forces. In Saigon 35 battalions under Tran Van Tra attacked the presidential palace, the General Staff HQ and the airport. Meanwhile 20 guerrillas of the Viet Cong C-10 Sapper Battalion broke into the US embassy compound, and fought a six-hour battle with US military police. All the attackers were killed without entering the embassy, but Communist forces had driven deep into the heart of American-held territory.

Examiner's advice

- Analyse the content and provenance of the Sources within their historical context.

- Use your own knowledge to group the Sources according to their views on success or failure.

- Make a supported judgement to answer the question.

Stretch and challenge

Use your own knowledge to evaluate how far Sources A, B and C support the US military interpretation that the Tet Offensive was 'an act of desperation by the North Vietnamese Communists which failed'. (See also pages 144–45.)

Sources

The US military interpretation

The war of attrition in 1967 took its toll on the leadership in Hanoi. Ho Chi Minh and Giap were afraid that the cross-over point might be reached, as the number of casualties was sapping their people's confidence. A prolonged war might lead to Communist collapse, in line with US aspirations. They committed their forces to a major scale offensive, hoping to spark a full-scale uprising in the South which might win them a decisive battle, or just keep them in the war. This was a desperate gamble by a leadership faced with imminent defeat.

 A **The head of the pacification program in South Vietnam recalls the impact of the Tet Offensive in Saigon and Washington.**

'I always felt the Tet Offensive was a desperate gamble on the part of Hanoi. They saw the American presence going up and up, they saw us beginning to get a pacification program going, and they decided they had better go for broke. And they did dislocate us. It cost them enormously. They had snuffed out the best of the southern cadre by sending them into the cities. We had a startling success after the Tet Offensive because the enemy had sacrificed the core of his guerrilla movement. Westmoreland reported confidently to the President 'Boss finally it is beginning to pay off and we look forward to 1968 as a big year of success for us.'

Robert Komer, memoirs, 1987

The Hanoi interpretation

The idea of a general offensive had been part of the strategy of the North Vietnamese since the early 1960s. The leadership in Hanoi knew that the war of attrition had achieved little success for the USA and were convinced that victory was within their grasp. The offensive was based on the hope that it would consolidate their existing gains and free South Vietnam.

B **The Commander of the Viet Cong at the time of the Tet offensive recalls the circumstances.**

We were winning in 1967 and we held the initiative despite difficulties and weaknesses such as:

- replenishing our forces
- building our political strength and conducting mass movements in urban areas
- ensuring material and technical supplies

These were within the context of a favourable situation.

President Johnson had to make an important decision:

either: to yield to the military and escalate the war, expanding it to all of Indochina, including an invasion of North Vietnam

or: to listen to McNamara, de-escalate the war and negotiate with Hanoi.

The anti-war movement in America and the world's condemnation forced an extremely cautious stand on Johnson. This was further frustrated by his very gloomy prospects for the 1968 presidential election. The Political Bureau of the Vietnam Worker's Party Central Committee noted 'the situation allows us to shift our revolution to a new stage, that of decisive victory.

From: General Tran Van Tra, memoirs, published 1993

The Viet Cong interpretation

The government and forces of South Vietnam had feared a general uprising in favour of communist forces in the South, but this aspect of the Tet Offensive had totally failed.

C **Southern communists acknowledged political as well as a military defeat, as there had been no uprising in the South. Their assessment of Tet in March 1968 stated:**

- In military terms, we have not been able to annihilate much of the enemy's live force. Our forces have not created favourable conditions for motivating the masses to rise up in towns and cities.

- In political terms, organised popular forces were not broad enough and strong enough. We had not had specific plans for motivating the masses for violent uprisings co-ordinated with military offensives.

- The implementation of our policies had not been closely controlled. Our plans were simple, our co-ordination poor, requests for instructions delayed.

These weaknesses have limited our successes and must be overcome.

From: Vietnam Workers' Party report on the Tet Offensive, 1968

The impact of the Tet Offensive

General Westmoreland accurately judged Tet as a communist defeat, but that was not how the cameras and reporters had portrayed events (Figure 5.2), nor how the American people perceived it. They saw it as a deep humiliation for the USA that a small Third World nation could mount such a forceful attack on territory heavily defended by US forces. Of the village of Ben Tre, a US officer said 'It became necessary to destroy the town to save it.' The Marine base at Khe Sanh was abandoned for a more secure location only weeks after US forces had relieved the siege there. Giap said of the Americans,

'Until Tet, they thought they could win the war, but now they knew that they could not.'

Figure 5.2 The US media covered events graphically, and the images were beamed to televisions in every home in America. Day by day the slaughter was witnessed by ordinary Americans, who watched as the bloody fighting entered Saigon and Vietnamese General Nguyen Ngoc Loan executed a Viet Cong prisoner. The General later claimed the guerilla had killed a member of his family.

The Tet Offensive had not been a success for the North either. Their attack had not been well co-ordinated in some areas, and went off too soon in others, enabling the US forces to reinforce weak areas. The ARVN fought better than expected and local people did not offer as much help as the Viet Cong had hoped. PLAF and PAVN forces suffered heavy losses, 5000 of them in the city of Hue alone, where the communists executed nearly 3000 civilians and the bombing was so severe that 100,000 refugees were forced to flee.

US Secretary of Defence Clark Clifford recalled in 1969 addressing the Council on Foreign Affairs, stating that the enemy's Tet offensive had been beaten back at great cost, and that the confidence of the American people was badly shaken. The Council questioned whether the South Vietnamese government could restore order, morale and army discipline. Clifford stated:

'President Johnson forbade the invasion of North Vietnam because this could trigger their mutual assistance pact with China. He forbade the mining of the principal port through which the North received military supplies, because a Soviet ship might be sunk. He forbade our forces pursuing the enemy into Laos and Cambodia, for this would spread the war.'

Clifford asked 'Given these circumstances, how could we win?'

The 'revolt' of the 'wise men'.

In March 1968, Westmoreland's judgement was that the communists were on the political and military defensive. He requested 206,000 extra US troops to take advantage of this opportunity to bring the war to an end. Johnson's immediate reaction was to support this demand, even though it would run against the swell of US public opinion. Clifford advised against the action, along with several of the 'wise men' who had previously advised escalation. They decided that McGeorge Bundy, Johnson's special adviser on National Security, should be the spokesman for the group. George Ball, who felt US objectives were unobtainable, recorded their conversation. Cabot Lodge advised a shift from 'search and destroy' strategy to one of using US military power as a shield. This might allow South Vietnam to develop a stable society like that in North Vietnam. They agreed that time was short and the USA must begin to take steps to disengage, as they were unable to build an independent South Vietnam. The only troops required should be in support of those already there. He added:

> 'We presented our strong advice to the President, "Look, this thing is hopeless, you'd better begin to de-escalate and get out." This was the first time he'd heard anything of this kind, and he could hardly believe his ears. I think he was very shocked, and he kept asking very probing questions. He really couldn't believe it.'

"For the sake of our health, perhaps we ought to go on a diet."

Figure 5.3 A Kenneth Mahood cartoon, *The Times* (22 November 1967) after US bombing raids of Vietnam result in the killing of an International Control Commission member in Hanoi. It shows, from the right, LBJ, Dean Rusk, Robert McNamara, Vice-President Hubert Humphrey and Westmoreland considering that they had been too greedy in escalating troops in Vietnam and should cut back.

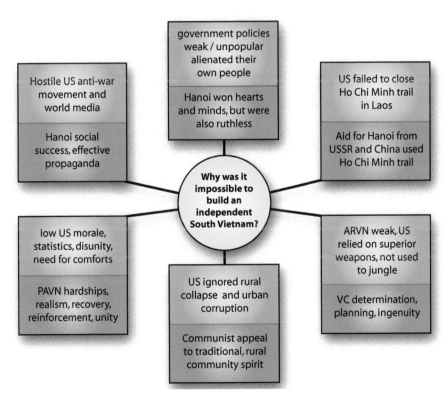

Figure 5.4 The US and North Vietnamese factors that prevented the building of an independent South Vietnam.

ACTIVITY

How far do you accept the view, in the centre of the Mind Map (Figure 5.4), that it was an impossible task to build an independent South Vietnam?

Text in blue boxes represents US factors, text in red boxes represents North Vietnamese factors.

1 Can you think of any other reasons?

2 Use the Mind Map as a basis for a debate on whether it was the Communists of the Americans themselves who made the task impossible.

What part did opposition to the war within the US play?

The public gave the troops an uncomfortable homecoming when on leave. Whether they were spat on by anti-war protesters or not, veterans *felt* they had been spat upon, stigmatised, contaminated. In television drama they were portrayed as psychotic killers; crazy people with automatic weapons. Johnson closely watched the public opinion polls. His goal was not to adjust his policies to follow public opinion, but rather to adjust public opinion to support his policies. Until the Tet Offensive, he systematically downplayed the war, making few speeches, no rallies, parades or advertising campaigns about it. He feared that publicity would encourage the 'hawks' who wanted total victory, and weaken both his containment policy and his priority of domestic social welfare. But increasingly, the Vietnam War came to be seen as 'Johnson's War'. The US media made the public aware of what was happening in Vietnam each day. By 1968, the anti-war protesters were chanting slogans like, 'Hey, hey, LBJ, how many kids did you kill today?' and one particular event, the **My Lai Massacre**, especially brought home the immorality of the war.

Case study

The My Lai Massacre

On 16 March 1968 there occurred one of the most significant incidents in influencing US public opinion against the War. The Army succeeded in covering up the incident at the time, and it was not revealed to the public until reported in the *New York Times* in November 1969.

Men of 'C' Company, 1st battalion, 11th Infantry Brigade were part of a major US 'search and destroy' offensive to hunt down remnants of the 48th NLF battalion in Quang Ngai province. The village of My Lai was suspected of harbouring them. US orders were to burn the houses, kill the livestock, destroy foodstuffs and close the wells. They entered the hamlet at a time when the villagers were expected to have left for market, so those remaining would be expected to be NLF or NLF sympathisers. They went in shooting. One eyewitness, and Army photographer, said 'Some of the people were trying to get up and run. They couldn't and fell down. One woman, I remember, tried to run with a small child in her arms, but she didn't make it.' Those remaining alive were shot in a ditch. In all more than 200 innocent Vietnamese villagers were massacred.

The My Lai massacre, 16 March 1968.

On 29 March 1971, a Court Martial convicted Lieutenant William Calley of multiple murders, causing a split in public opinion. Some felt he was a scapegoat and higher ranks had avoided their responsibility. Though he was given a life sentence, Calley appealed, his sentence was reduced and he was released on parole after only three years.

Sources

A 'What the hell is going on? I thought we were winning the war.' The shocked reaction of an influential TV journalist to the Tet Offensive. He went on to announce that the US ought to seek a way to get out of Vietnam.

We need to realise that any negotiations must not be an attempt to dictate terms. For it seems now more certain than ever that the bloody experience of Vietnam is to end in a stalemate. If we escalate, the enemy can match us. That applies to the invasion of the North, the use of nuclear weapons or the mere commitment to 300,000 more American troops to the battle. And with each escalation, the world comes closer to the brink of cosmic disaster. It is increasingly clear to this reporter that the only rational way out will be to negotiate, not as victors but as an honourable people who lived up to their pledge to defend democracy and did the best they could.

From: Walter Cronkite, CBS evening TV news broadcast, 27 February 1968

B The brother of the late President Kennedy, who had served as Attorney-General, speaks at Kansas State University about a turning point in the Vietnam War. Robert F. Kennedy launched his presidential campaign with this speech.

Our control over the rural population has evaporated. The Saigon government is now less of an ally. Our victories come at the cost of destroying Vietnam. Its people are disintegrating under the blows of war. The war is weakening our position in Asia and the world, and eroding international cooperation that has directly supported our security for the past three decades. The war is costing us a quarter of our federal budget and tens of thousands of our young men's lives. Higher yet is the price we pay in our own innermost lives, and in the spirit of America.

Robert F. Kennedy, Landon Lecture, 18 March 1968

Johnson's withdrawal from the presidential election

By March 1968, the President was an extremely disillusioned and broken man. The rapid escalation of US military commitments had weakened the dollar in the international money markets, and in March 1968, the USA had suffered a severe economic crisis. Treasury gold reserves were sold off and Johnson was forced by Congress to completely shelve his 'Great Society' welfare programme. He decided not to stand for re-election in the coming presidential election and met the Soviet Ambassador to inform him of change in US policy in Vietnam. Troops along the DMZ would still be protected, but there would be no further bombing above the 20th parallel. He felt that, the USSR, as co-chairman of the Geneva Conference and a major supplier of arms to Hanoi, should use its influence for a conference to make peace. At 9 o'clock that evening he gave a televised address to the nation which sent shockwaves throughout America (see Activity overleaf).

ACTIVITY

Make a comparative evaluation of the views expressed in Sources A and B for their power in influencing the US public.

Johnson had lost the support of the American public. Eugene McCarthy now ran for the Democrat presidential nomination supported by the 'hawks', and Bobby Kennedy was enticed to stand on an anti-war ticket. Johnson backed his Vice President, Hubert Humphrey, but he was defeated by the Republican candidate, Richard Nixon, who promised to bring the Vietnam War to an honourable end. The voting showed that the US public was as divided as ever over whether to continue the Vietnam War. The Paris Peace talks, which began in May, soon stalled. During that month, 1800 US soldiers were killed in Vietnam and 18,000 seriously wounded. On 3 July, General Westmoreland was replaced as Military War Commander by General Creighton Abrams.

Sources

 A BBC News report on the My Lai massacre.

Soldiers went berserk, gunning down unarmed men, women, children and babies. Families which huddled together for safety in huts or bunkers were shown no mercy. Those who emerged with hands held high were murdered. Elsewhere in the village, other atrocities were in progress. Women were gang raped; Vietnamese who had bowed to greet the Americans were beaten with fists and tortured, clubbed with rifle butts and stabbed with bayonets. Some victims were mutilated with the signature 'C Company' carved into the chest. By late morning word had got back to higher authorities and a cease-fire was ordered. My Lai was in a state of carnage. Bodies were strewn through the village.

BBC News, 1969

Overview of policy change

The 1968 election was a turning point in policy. Media coverage of the Tet Offensive, the rising death toll among US troops and the anti-war movement destroyed Johnson's confidence, and he decided not to stand for the presidency. Though Nixon was strongly anti-communist, he realised the USA must disentangle itself from Vietnam. Nixon was tricky and underhanded, as Johnson discovered when wire taps revealed Nixon had persuaded South Vietnamese leaders not to attend peace talks aimed to secure a Democrat election victory. Nixon, who hated the anti-war movement and claimed to represent the silent majority of conservative Americans, scraped into power on a ticket of 'peace with honour'.

Sources

(B) **A US soldier, who fought in Vietnam in 1965, later reflects on reasons why American soldiers committed what others saw as war crimes.**

'There has been a good deal of exaggeration about US atrocities in Vietnam. The most popularly held explanations for outrages like My Lai have been the racist theory, that the American soldier found it easy to slaughter Asians because he did not regard them as human beings, and the frontier-heritage theory, which claims that he was inherently violent and needed only the excuse of war to vent his homicidal instincts. Yet both ignore the barbarous treatment the Viet Cong and ARVN inflicted on their own people and by the French during the first Indochina War. Retribution for the deaths of friends, greed for survival and the lack of mercy he could expect if taken prisoner all help explain such actions. General Westmoreland's strategy of attrition also had an important effect on our behaviour. Our mission was not to win terrain or seize positions, but simply to kill. Victory was a high body count; defeat a low-kill ratio, war a matter of arithmetic. It is not surprising that some men acquired a contempt for human life. In hostile country with a relentless enemy, we sank into a brutish state.'

Philip Caputo, *A Rumor of War*, 1977

(C) **The commander of C Company troops who committed the atrocity at My Lai on 16 March 1968 explains his feelings about why it occurred.**

'When my troops were getting massacred and mauled by an enemy I couldn't see, I couldn't feel and I couldn't touch, it seemed that nobody in the military system ever described them as anything other than Communism. They didn't give it a race, they didn't give it a sex, they didn't give it an age. They never let me believe it was just a philosophy in a man's mind. That was the enemy out there.'

Lieutenant William Calley, comments made after his trial, 1971

The Nixon administration: the impact of the Draft, and renewed bombing campaigns

Nixon stated privately: 'I'm not going to end up like LBJ. I'm going to stop that war. Fast!'; and in his inaugural address: 'The greatest honour history can bestow is the title of peacemaker.' Nixon had campaigned on a promise to end the draft, as an effective way to undermine the anti-Vietnam war movement. He believed well-off young men would stop protesting against the war once the possibility of their having to fight in it was removed. But Congress and the Defence Department opposed a volunteer army, so the process of withdrawal of the draft was to happen only after a further four years of war. Furthermore, when Richard Nixon left office, his reputation was more tarnished than any other President in history, and it was Vietnam which had begun his slippery slope to disrepute.

The Anti-War Movement became more outspoken after Nixon's lifting of the exemption of students from the draft in 1968. This resulted in the Kent State University protest of 4 May 1970, when four people were killed by National Guardsmen who fired into a crowd of student protesters. Polls suggested many of the US public agreed with the invasion of Cambodia, but there was a general unwillingness to see expansion of a war that was being scaled down.

News of atrocities such as the My Lai Massacre encouraged the US Anti-War movement to escalate their activities during Nixon's presidency, to the lyrics of 'I Feel Like I'm Fixin' To Die Rag' by Country Joe McDonald, and John Lennon's 'Give Peace a Chance'. To win over the public opinion, Nixon appealed to the 'silent majority' stating:

'North Vietnam cannot defeat or humiliate the United States. Only Americans can do that.'

Vice President Spiro Agnew's efforts brought more negative media coverage of mass rallies, such as the *36-hour March Against Death* by half a million people in November 1969.

ACTIVITY

How far do Sources A–C explain why the My Lai Massacre took place

(See also pages 146 and 147.)

Source

John Kerry addresses the Senate Committee of Foreign Relations as the spokesman for Vietnam veterans. Later, as the Democrat nominee, he was defeated by 34 votes in the 2004 presidential election by the Republican President George W. Bush.

We found most people didn't even know the difference between communism and democracy. They only wanted to work in rice paddies without helicopters strafing them and bombs with napalm burning their villages and tearing their country apart. They wanted America to leave them alone in peace. They survived by siding with whichever military force was present at a particular time, be it Viet Cong, North Vietnamese or American. We saw first-hand how American taxes supported a corrupt dictatorial regime. We saw America lose its sense of morality as it accepted My Lai very coolly.

John Kerry, 'Vietnam Veterans Against the War Statement', 23 April 1971

ACTIVITY

Analyse and evaluate John Kerry's views on the impact of the Vietnam War.

BIOGRAPHY
Henry Kissinger

Born in 1923, Kissinger came to the USA as a German-Jewish refugee in 1938. He studied at Harvard, became a National Security Adviser in 1969 and Secretary of State in 1973. A believer in old fashioned realpolitik based on pursuing national self interest, he spotted the possibilities of the Sino Soviet split in the 1960s for bringing pressure on the North Vietnamese to make concessions, although some argue that the Moscow/Beijing influence over the North Vietnamese has been exaggerated. He was linked to the bombing of Cambodia and Laos to exert pressure on the North Vietnamese and controversially awarded the Nobel Peace Prize for the final peace.

Anti-War protests gained momentum when Vietnam Veterans Against the War (VVAW) mounted a series of springtime demonstrations in 1972. In June, *The Pentagon Papers* were published, despite Nixon's attempt to suppress them in the Supreme Court. They revealed how American administrations had lied to the public, ignored international agreements, manipulated Saigon regimes and misled Congress. Nixon now lost any semblance of a public mandate to continue the Vietnam War. His only option would be to gain a negotiated settlement.

Nixon was bound by his promise to end the war honourably, so his task was extremely difficult. He could not win an honourable military victory due to the nature of the guerrilla war his troops had to fight. He could not invade the North for fear of Chinese or Soviet involvement and a global nuclear war. He could not carry out an honourable US withdrawal, as the USA had a moral responsibility to Thieu after US complicity in the assassination of Diem. The only way was to achieve a limited victory similar to that in Korea, by creating two separate independent states. Nixon remembered Eisenhower's success in pressurising and coaxing China and the USSR to sign a Korean armistice in 1953. Nixon and Henry Kissinger, his National Security Adviser, decided to use similar strategies. They would coax China and the USSR with trade and arms agreements. To achieve this, the USA would have to exchange ambassadors, meaning recognition of the PRC, after 20 years of denial. Pressure would be applied by allowing Hanoi to believe Nixon was capable of resorting to the use of nuclear weapons if angered, frightening them into coming to the bargaining table. This was known as the **Madman Theory**.

Strategy 1: Military Pressure 1969–71 with hints of the 'Madman' Strategic Bombing

In February 1969, the North Vietnamese launched another spring offensive. Nixon began a new strategy of bombing communist camps across Cambodia, in an attempt to wipe out the Ho Chi Minh Trail. He hoped this would bring a breathing space from insurgency for the ARVN, allowing Washington to 'Vietnamise' the War, meaning building up South Vietnam so it could play a much larger part in its own defence. The main target of US bombing was COSVN (Central Office for South Vietnam), the Communist headquarters thought to exist in Cambodia. When few results had been achieved by April 1970, Nixon escalated the bombing but kept this change of policy secret from the US public (more than 31,000 Americans had already died in Vietnam). Kissinger was in favour of blockading Haiphong and invading North Vietnam, in line with 'Madman theory'. The USSR was looking for a *détente* with the West, so Nixon hoped to coax Moscow into pressurising Hanoi to scale down their military strategy.

Nixon met with Thieu on Midway Island on 8 June 1969 to inform him of the **Vietnamisation policy**. Thieu thought the US were evacuating, and requested time to build up his military strength with US aid. Nixon agreed that the US presence would remain until a negotiated settlement had been reached, but during that same month 25,000 US troops returned home. Meanwhile, Nixon applied 'Madman theory' by secretly warning Ho that if negotiations did not make progress, he would take 'measures of great consequence and force'. The impression of escalation had to continue, to reassure Thieu and to frighten Hanoi, even though Nixon publicly stated that 150,000 troops would be withdrawn in the spring of 1970.

So, despite General Abrams' disapproval, US troops were reduced to 475,000 by the autumn of 1970 and 335,000 by summer 1971. Casualty figures amongst American forces also began to drop, deafening the US public to the anti-war protests. At the same time, South Vietnamese troop numbers increased to one million by 1970, but ARVN efficiency, leadership and courage failed to improve, so Vietnamisation had only a superficial effect. It had, anyway, blurred the purpose of the War. Nixon's **Accelerated Pacification Campaign** increased the security of the rural South and encouraged political and social reforms, such as education. Rural development teams handed over local control to rural councils, offered amnesties and land reform. But security depended on US forces rather than Thieu's regime, which did not gain popularity and remained corrupt.

Accelerated Pacification Campaign

On 1 November 1968, the US launched the Accelerated Pacification Campaign, with an objective of expanding government control over 1,200 villages currently controlled by the Viet Cong. The Campaign was controlled by William Colby. It was given a ninety-day time frame and was basically a 'clear and hold' strategy using Regional Forces (RF) and Popular Forces (PF). Operating in or near their home villages, the RF and PF were familiar with the countryside as well as the people, knew how to recognise Viet Cong and non-political families, and built some confidence because villagers knew they would remain in the area. After destroying the Viet Cong infrastructure, the Campaign encouraged economic development. This included clearing roads, repairing bridges, building schools, and increasing farm production. The Americans also tried to train villagers in free elections and then trained elected officials in village administration. Finally, the Campaign tried to redistribute land to peasant farmers. The results were mixed at best. By March 1970 more than one million hectares of land had been redistributed, and 500,000 of RF and PF forces were engaged in pacification. They were armed and trained with M-16 rifles. But destruction of the Viet Cong infrastructure was never achieved, nor did Accelerated Pacification really change the way most South Vietnamese looked upon the government of Nguyen Van Thieu. Ultimately, Accelerated Pacification could not really survive the withdrawal of American troops which began in the summer of 1969, and it didn't.

The invasion of Cambodia 1970

To reassure Saigon, Nixon ordered the Ho Chi Minh Trail to be heavily bombed in January 1970, provoking the North Vietnamese to launch an offensive in Laos. Nixon widened the war and speeded up Vietnamisation by moving 30,000 troops into south-west Cambodia, to seize large quantities of war equipment. The pro-American faction there had seized power under Lon Nol, who demanded the withdrawal of all North Vietnamese troops from his country. Nixon had secretly channelled US aid to his faction. All these actions were to put more pressure on the North to negotiate, and on Congress to continue to fund the war.

Madman Theory

Applying pressure at the negotiating table by allowing your opponent to believe that you will resort to the use of nuclear weapons if they don't agree to terms.

Détente

De-escalation of Cold War tensions through diplomacy and confidence-building measures, from the late 1960s until the start of the 1980s.

Vietnamisation policy

The policy of shifting responsibility for the conduct of the war onto South Vietnam.

Source

In a televised speech on 30 April 1970, Nixon explains the US and South Vietnamese invasion of Cambodia.

I have concluded that the actions of the enemy in the last ten days clearly endanger the lives of Americans who are in Vietnam now and would constitute an unacceptable risk to those who will be there after withdrawal of another 150,000. We have not previously moved against these enemy sanctuaries because we did not wish to violate the territory of a neutral nation. We counselled patience to our South Vietnamese allies and imposed restraints on our own commanders. Tonight, American and South Vietnamese units will attack the headquarters for the entire Communist military operation in South Vietnam. This is not an invasion of Cambodia. The areas in which these attacks will be launched are completely occupied and controlled by North Vietnamese forces. If, when the chips are down, the world's most powerful nation, the United States of America, acts like a pitiful, helpless giant, the forces of totalitarianism and anarchy will threaten free nations throughout the world. It is not our power, but our will and character that is being tested tonight.

ACTIVITY

Use this Source to draw a mind map of Nixon's justifications for US actions in Cambodia. Has he left out any reasons?

Prioritise the reasons for US actions.

Hundreds of acres of jungle were levelled, by the 30,000 US and 50,000 ARVN troops who invaded Cambodia. PAVN supplies were temporarily cut off and vast quantities of weapons and supplies were seized, giving the ARVN the hoped for breathing space. 1592 Americans and 3553 ARVN died in Cambodia. The expected COSVN proved nothing but 'a scattering of empty huts' and no concessions were made at the peace talks as a result. The North Vietnamese were pushed deeper into Cambodia and US troop withdrawal was disrupted.

By late June, US troops had pulled out of Cambodia and the North Vietnamese quickly returned to their bases. Enemy insurgency had increased by the end of 1970, but only 175,000 US troops remained in Vietnam by the end of 1971.

The invasion of Laos 1971

On 30 January 1971, US forces supported an ARVN invasion of Laos, the *Lam Son Offensive*, to disrupt North Vietnamese supply lines and forestall a communist offensive expected in 1972. ARVN forces, withdrawing six weeks later, were routed in a bloody battle with 36,000 PAVN soldiers supported by Russian made tanks. Half the ARVN forces were killed or wounded, and their tanks, artillery and equipment were left behind as they fled. Kissinger said angrily 'Those sons of bitches. It's their country and we can't save it for them if they don't want to.' Abrams' view was that the ARVN could not 'sustain large-scale major cross-border operations without external support.' After three years, Vietnamisation was having little success in terms of military security.

Figure 5.5 An horrific memory from the Vietnam war in 1972. This little girl was amongst the crying children running along Route One, Trang Bang, after she had just been severely burned following a napalm attack.

Strategy 2: The Paris peace talks 1968–73 backed by hints of the 'Madman'

Talks began in Paris on May 1968.

America demanded:

- that North Vietnam withdraw from South Vietnam;
- that Saigon be freed of communists.

Hanoi demanded:

- that the USA withdraw from South Vietnam;
- that Communists participate in the Saigon government.

Therefore no progress was made at first. Nixon soon began to realise the improbability of a military victory, so as early as April 1969 he suggested secret negotiations between Washington and Hanoi.

Nixon's main objective in negotiating was to obtain conditions on which the USA could withdraw from Vietnam with honour. In May 1971, Kissinger offered American withdrawal within seven months of a cease-fire in return for:

- the acceptance of the Thieu regime;
- the return of American POWs (prisoners of war), and
- the end of infiltration from the North, though no longer US insistence on the withdrawal of North Vietnamese troops from the South.

These offers resulted in deadlock. Le Duc Tho offered to release prisoners of war if the USA dropped the demand to recognise the Thieu regime. This Kissinger refused to do. Hanoi

would not cease fighting, as this was their main bargaining ploy and they felt there was still a chance of military victory. On the other hand, Nixon was unwilling to make terms until his planned Summit meetings with China and the USSR had failed.

The American 'opening to China' 1971–72

On 9 July, while on a visit to Pakistan, Kissinger pretended to be ill in his room, when in fact he flew to Beijing for secret talks with Zhou Enlai, the Chinese Prime Minister. The secrecy reflected international tensions. Not only had the Americans persistently refused to acknowledge the PRC, but since 1966 and the Cultural Revolution, all Chinese ambassadors had been withdrawn from other countries except Egypt. Sino-US links had been conducted through occasional communications between their ambassadors in Warsaw.

So there were a number of obstacles in the path of Sino-American rapprochement:

- Ideologies – Communist China saw the USA as aggressively imperialist and capitalist while Washington saw Chinese communism as even more absolute than that of the USSR.
- The USA's part in the Chinese Civil War had caused deep wounds on both sides, left to fester by continued US recognition of Taiwan's permanent seat on the UN Security Council, while the Communist People's Republic of China regarded Taiwan as part of China.
- The Chinese mistrusted American *détente* with the USSR, with whom Communist China had severed its links.

The objectives and terms of Kissinger's mission to China

Kissinger wanted to:

- persuade the Chinese, who had supplied substantial aid to North Vietnam, to use its influence in making Hanoi agree to peace terms;
- use an agreement with China as a lever in persuading the USSR to co-operate, fearing the impact of its opponents forming a united front;
- win over US public opinion, giving Nixon an advantage in the coming presidential election, though equally, a rapprochement might offend the anti-China lobby in the USA.

He was empowered to offer terms:

- The USA offered to make a public statement that they would withdraw all US forces from Taiwan.
- In return, the PRC would invite Nixon to a Summit meeting in Beijing early in 1972, and use their influence to end the War in Vietnam.

It was seemingly unthinkable for the USA to offer the hand of friendship to the Chinese for many reasons, and in fact Zhou Enlai asked Kissinger whether he was 'one of those Americans who refuse to shake hands with Chinese leaders', referring to John Foster Dulles' refusal to shake hands with him at the Geneva Conference. It shocked the world when Nixon announced, on 15 July 1971, that he was to visit China the next year. On stepping down from the aircraft in Beijing, on 17 February 1972, Nixon made sure to shake hands with Zhou Enlai in full view of the television cameras and photographers. It was a very theatrical moment, as was his meeting with Mao, where again they shook hands for the

cameras. Nixon wished to impress US public opinion and raise America's international prestige.

The US Agreement with China

Only two points were presented jointly:

- Neither country should seek total dominance of the Asia-Pacific region.
- Each country is opposed to efforts by any other country or group of countries to seek to establish such dominance.

The second of these points was clearly understood to refer to the USSR.

Other terms were presented separately by the two governments, with those on Vietnam and Korea showing that Mao was also aware of his global audience.

- The USA declares that it seeks peace in Vietnam.
- The PRC declares that it firmly supports the Vietnamese people and all oppressed peoples struggling for liberation.
- The USA reiterates its support for South Korea.
- The PRC backs the demands of North Korea for Korean unification.

The other Chinese terms were:

- The People's Republic of China is the sole legitimate government of China, and Taiwan is part of China.
- The liberation of Taiwan is an internal Chinese affair.
- All US forces should be withdrawn from the island of Taiwan.

The other American terms were:

- The USA recognises that all Chinese (in China and Taiwan) maintain that there is only one China, of which Taiwan is a part.
- The USA affirms its interest in a peaceful settlement of the Taiwan question by the Chinese themselves.
- The ultimate objective of the USA is the withdrawal of its troops from Taiwan.
- The US affirms its intention to progressively reduce the number of its forces in the area.

This final statement was to reassure the Chinese that the USA intended to withdraw from Vietnam.

The impact of this agreement did not alienate the USSR, but had the contrary effect. Nixon was invited to Moscow for the first of four Summit meetings between 1972 and 1974. Nixon had successfully opened up diplomacy with the Communist powers, but he had not solved the nagging dilemma of how to withdraw from Vietnam with honour and keep the reputation of the USA intact.

The impact of US army morale on negotiations and escalated bombing

The American bargaining position was weakened by a crisis in morale amongst its forces. In 1970, Defense Department research showed that 60 per cent of US soldiers used drugs, including heroin and opium. In 1971, an estimated 40,000 were using heroin. Insubordination, racial tensions and '**fragging**' had reached a dangerous level. In 1970, there were 350 courts martial for the murder or attempted murder of officers by their own

Fragging

Attacks on unpopular officers.

troops. Over the decade from 1963 to 1973 half a million US soldiers deserted, 20 per cent of them for more than a month. 570,000 of the ARVN also deserted from 1967 to 1971. In contrast, the North Vietnamese were resolute in their strategies, ruthless fighters and intransigent negotiators. They were willing to suffer casualties four times those of their opponents without flinching.

Early in 1972, Hanoi began its *Spring Offensive*, hoping to take advantage of Nixon's need to withdraw troops in the period leading up to the November presidential election. The Communist North was cautious, due to the deterioration in relations between China and the USSR, and because of the cool reception they received in Geneva in 1954. Their moderate aim was to inflict a blow on the ARVN to undermine Vietnamisation. Full victory would only be measured by the fall of Thieu and the total withdrawal of US forces.

American troops were unprepared for the three pronged attack by 120,000 PAVN troops in March 1972 which saw them sweep southwards across the demilitarised zone. Thieu sent most of his reserves to defend the communist targets of Hue and Kontum as they advanced, so the PLAF diverted a second attack to the Mekong delta and the area around Saigon. A US air response called *Operation Linebacker* knocked out military targets in the Hanoi-Haiphong area. Kissinger unsuccessfully attempted to persuade the USSR to restrain the Communists with the threat that no agreement would be acceptable while northern forces remained in the South. The 'Mad bomber' ordered a massive escalation in bombing, the mining of Haiphong harbour and a naval blockade of the North, despite contrary advice in Washington. The Cabinet feared damage would be done to *détente* with the USSR, but in fact, though both China and the USSR protested, they pushed Hanoi to make peace terms. Hue was held by the ARVN and the Operation prevented the Saigon regime from collapsing. Even the US public remained quiet. The North sustained 100,000 deaths, the South one quarter of that figure.

Source

A South Vietnamese ARVN Lieutenant Colonel explains the impact of the Spring Offensive 1972.

In retrospect, Hanoi's conventional invasion of the South did not help it attain the major objectives desired. Although always the defender of an extremely disadvantageous strategic position, South Vietnam emerged stronger than ever. Hanoi's effort had been thwarted by US and RVN determination. The American response during the enemy offensive was timely, forceful and decisive. This staunch resolve of the US to stand behind its ally stunned the enemy. Additionally, it brought about a strong feeling of self-assurance among the armed forces and population of South Vietnam.

From Ngo Quang Truong, Report on the Easter Offensive, 1972

ACTIVITY

Use the Source to argue a case that US co-operation with South Vietnam helped the bargaining process.

Ngo and Thieu were anxious that US withdrawals and *détente* would leave South Vietnam in a vulnerable position and wished to hold up the progress of a negotiated settlement. Hanoi suffered troop losses in the Offensive and received less support from China and the USSR, so were willing to return to the negotiating table, assuming Nixon were re-elected. Nixon needed his 'peace with honour' in order to get friendlier relations with China and the USSR. So talks between Kissinger and Le Duc Tho resumed in secret. Kissinger, who had already dropped his demand that northern troops withdraw from the South, began to offer more flexibility regarding US support for Thieu. Hanoi suggested a coalition government with NLF presence to be known as the People's Revolutionary Government (PRG).

In October 1972, a preliminary agreement was reached on these terms:

■ a cease-fire with armies retaining their areas of control;

■ US troop withdrawal within 60 days;

■ exchange of prisoners of war;

■ shared control by the Saigon government, the PRG and a neutral faction in reaching a negotiated political settlement which would implement;

  • democratic elections in the South;

  • peaceful unification of Vietnam, and

  • reconstruction including American funding.

Figure 5.6 'Sorry, this is for the folks at home - why don't you try to conjure up one yourself?'
Cartoon by Leslie Gibbard, first published by the *Guardian* on 25 January 1973.

However, Thieu was furious and refused to sign. As the November 1972 presidential election loomed, fearing the moment might be lost, Kissinger unadvisedly let slip that peace was 'at hand'. Hanoi refused the 69 changes to the terms that Thieu had put forward, and talks broke down.

Nixon was re-elected with 60.7 per cent of the popular vote against the Democrat candidate's 37.5 per cent. He won the support of every state bar Massachusetts. He now felt he had a mandate to intensify the pressure on North Vietnam. Nixon resorted to *Operation Enhance Plus* to strengthen Thieu's regime with military equipment, aircraft and armoured vehicles. He secretly reassured Thieu that the USA would give his regime military support should the North break the terms of the agreement and invade the South. He hoped Thieu would finally be willing to sign the agreement.

On 24 January 1973, Nixon announced the agreement of a ceasefire in Vietnam. He said it would bring 'peace with honour'. All US prisoners-of-war would be released within 60 days and the withdrawal of US troops from Vietnam would be completed in the same period. That same day *The Times* wrote:

> 'The war might be over for the United States but as millions of Americans welcomed the end of their involvement in Indo-China it became obvious that the ceasefire agreement did not look optimistic for a durable and lasting peace.'

Strategy 3: 'Madman Strategy' as a final push towards peace

A US air attack known as the 'Christmas bombing' then began, which was intended to push Hanoi into final concessions. So intensive was the bombing of Northern cities by American B52s that there was international outrage. Nixon's popularity rating fell sharply. However, though the USA suffered heavier losses of aircraft than ever before, Hanoi re-opened talks 12 days after the start of the air offensive, and on 27 January 1973, the Paris Agreement was finally signed between the USA, North Vietnam, South Vietnam and the PRG.

Thieu had given in and signed terms very similar to those agreed in October, but at least his government remained, though weakened. Nixon had not achieved his 'peace with honour', as he had not managed to secure the future of a democratic South Vietnam. North Vietnam could lick its wounds in the assurance that it would achieve its goal of a unified Vietnam.

Sources

(A) The Chinese leader shows his support for North Vietnam as part of the East Asian revolutionary movement which he led, on condition that Hanoi conforms to his views.

Mao Zedong: The Americans do not have enough man power to distribute in the world, since they have already been overextended. When their people were killed, their hearts were broken. It is inevitable for some of you Vietnamese also to be killed.

Le Duan: Our ways of fighting cause low casualties, otherwise we could not persist long. We rely on your support.

Mao Zedong: China has a large population, which makes the Americans fearful. We do not fear. The Americans are afraid of being beaten, and they have no guts. I am not saying that you should not negotiate, but your main energy should be put into fighting.

Mao Zedong, conversation with Le Duan, 1970 (abridged)

(B) The Soviet Foreign Minister and the US National Security Adviser discuss the American terms for a Vietnamese peace settlement.

Gromyko: As the President and yourself said, you would like to end the war and withdraw American troops, but you oppose a settlement by the Vietnamese themselves and insist it must be under the presence of American troops. You wish to preserve Thieu for an indefinite period of time. Why should every effort be made to preserve the Thieu regime? Official American statements show the main US preoccupation is to do everything they can in order to prevent the possibility of a government not liked by the United States.

Kissinger: It is absurd to pretend we would prefer it if Communists would not win in South Vietnam.

Andrei Gromyko and Henry Kissinger, talks, May 1972 (abridged)

(C) The Chinese Premier and the US National Security Adviser discuss the American terms for a Vietnamese peace settlement.

Zhou: the Vietnamese want both a military and political settlement. If the question of government is not settled, peace will not be possible in the southern part of Vietnam. If you withdrew, hostilities between the two Vietnamese sides would break out again. A political agreement should settle the issue. The government would be more friendly to the USA. This is one of the steps needed to normalise relations between the USA and China.

Kissinger: We will withdraw our remaining troops, if the North Vietnamese accept a ceasefire and return our prisoners. We believe that China is a factor for peace in the Pacific. Why should we build barriers in Indochina? We want to leave.

Zhou Enlai and Henry Kissinger, talks, June 1972 (abridged)

D **The US President renews his promise to the President of South Vietnam to persuade him to agree to the Paris Peace Accords to end the Vietnam War.**

The gravest consequences would ensue if your government chose to reject the agreement and split off from the United States. You refusal to join us would be an invitation to disaster, to the loss of everything we together have fought for over the past decade. It would be inexcusable above all because we have lost a just and honourable alternative. The actions of our Congress have clearly borne out the many warnings we have made. You have my assurance of continued assistance in the post-settlement period and that we will respond with full force should the settlement be violated by North Vietnam.

Richard Nixon, letter to President Thieu, 5 January 1973

E **The US National Security Adviser returns to Hanoi to meet with North Vietnam leaders a few weeks after the signing of the Paris Peace Accords. Their discussion focuses on the possibility of American economic aid for Vietnam.**

Pham Van Dong: We would like the free use of this money to buy goods from the United States to reconstruct and develop the very important branches of our destroyed economy. These are: communications and transport, industrial factories and enterprises or agricultural works and public utilities, accommodation and housing. The Joint Economic Commission will list them.

Kissinger: If the Economic Commission can be free to use the funds without ties to any political condition, then we agree. Within agreed programs you are free to dispose of the funds. You should never talk of 'reparation'. The committee this money goes through finds 'moral obligation' and 'honour' difficult words to understand.

Pham Van Dong: But we stick by what we have said.

Kissinger: If you stick to the understanding you had with us, we will stick to the understanding we have with you.

Henry Kissinger and Pham Van Dong, 12 February 1973 (abridged)

Northern victory and the fall of Saigon 1975

Most of the agreement turned out not to be worth the paper it was written on. A Joint Military Commission of the four parties was to supervise the implementation of the agreement, and an International Control Commission of eight outside powers solemnly acknowledged, approved and supported the agreements for ending the War, but played no further part.

Nixon had transferred the military bases and large amounts of supplies to Thieu's regime before the peace agreement was signed. He also failed to keep his promises to 'react strongly' if the North attacked and to provide $75 billion of reconstruction aid to Thieu over five years. Congress assumed control, removing Nixon's flexibility of action. 159 US Marines were left to guard the American Embassy in Saigon, and 10,000 discharged military men became officials to maintain the impression of US support. By the time the last American troops had left Vietnam on 29 March 1973, fulfilling a key North Vietnamese requirement, 591 American POWS had been released. However, the South freed only 27,000 of the 42,000 prisoners the North claimed they held.

Thieu maintained a policy known as the 'Four Nos':

1. no negotiations with communists
2. no coalitions
3. no loss of land
4. no communism in South Vietnam.

ACTIVITY

1 Compare Sources B and D as evidence for US attitudes towards President Thieu of South Vietnam.

2 Using your own knowledge, assess how Sources A–E support the interpretation that defence of America's reputation was the main reason why negotiations to end the Vietnam War took so long.

The ceasefire was not observed. Fighting continued between South, North and supporters of the Provisional Revolutionary Government. The Saigon government retained nearly a million troops, and used them to recover most of the hamlets taken in the weeks before the Paris agreement. Nixon's 'honourable peace' and 'national reconciliation' seemed to be mere mockery. The war-weary North found neither China nor the USSR would help them, as they were more interested in *détente* with the USA. The North Vietnamese cautiously infiltrated tens of thousands of additional troops into the South via the Ho Chi Minh trail. They then launched another general offensive towards the end of 1973, gaining control of the Mekong delta and central Vietnam during 1974, overrunning the whole of Vietnam. Meanwhile, the South Vietnamese economy had been hit by a bad harvest, withdrawal of the spending power of US forces and a global oil crisis.

In 1974, the new US President, Gerald Ford, was unable to gain support for substantial aid for the South, and settled for $700 million. Corruption and low morale in the South led to swift Communist advances, and Saigon fell to the Communists on 21 April 1975. The remaining US Marines had to be airlifted by helicopter from the roof of the US Embassy. The city now became known as Ho Chi Minh City after the greatest hero of the national struggle, who had died in 1969. General Duong Van Minh replaced Thieu. The North Vietnamese had finally achieved their uncompromising objective, total victory. An ex-colonel of the North Vietnamese army reports the fall of Saigon 1975 for the Party Nhan Dan newspaper.

'They had waited at the independence Palace for an officer of sufficient rank before entering the building. I was asked to go in and talk to the president because I held the rank of colonel. I was only a journalist now, but I agreed. To reduce tension, I asked two young soldiers to leave their AK-47s outside. A cease-fire had already been announced over the radio, so I said that it was time to stop the war and avoid further sacrifice on both sides. At that time, I believed our policy was to achieve reconciliation between all Vietnamese. Seeing a lot of anxious and tense faces around me, I went on to say that all Vietnamese should consider this a happy day because our victory belonged to the whole people and only the American foreign invaders had been defeated. Thieu had resigned and left the country two weeks earlier. Some, including the prime-minster designate, Vu Van Mao, began to smile when suddenly there was a burst of gunfire outside which broke one of the window panes. Everybody ducked, but I told them not to worry. Our soldiers were firing into the air to celebrate. One had raised the National Liberation flag over the Independence Palace.'

Bui Tin, memoirs, 1995

Pathet Lao

The Communist movement in Laos

The Khmer Rouge

The Communist ruling political party of Cambodia from 1975 to 1979

Cambodia and Laos also became communist states, after Congress condemned Nixon's bombing of Cambodia and prevented further funding for air attacks. The **Pathet Lao** regime seized control of Laos by December 1975. The Khmer Rouge took control of Cambodia, aided by the USSR and China. Its capital, Phnom Penh, fell under their control on 17 April 1975. **Pol Pot**, the **Khmer Rouge** leader, began a reign of terror against domestic and foreign opponents. An estimated two million people were systematically starved to death or executed in Cambodia during the following four years.

What was the impact of the War?

General estimate of casualties, where figures are available:

	Killed	Wounded	Missing
USA	57,685	152,303	695
South Vietnam armed forces	183,528	500,000	
South Vietnamese civilians	415,000		
South Korea	4407		
Australia and New Zealand	492 + 35		
Thailand	350		
North Vietnam armed forces, plus Viet Cong	950,000 + 1,100,000		
North Vietnamese civilians	2,000,000		
Total Vietnamese	4,648,528		
Total non-Vietnamese	58,685		

Despite their high profile in the US media, American casualties represented a tiny proportion of its population of 200 million. On the other hand, Vietnamese casualties represented nearly 12 per cent of its population of an estimated 37 million.

Unlike previous conflicts, the War had led to deep divisions within the American public that cut across political affiliations owing to the involvement of four presidents, two from each party. Supporters disagreed with opponents of the War; veterans who had served there were disgusted with draft-dodgers and were alienated from those who took no part for other reasons. One section of a whole generation of young men were traumatised or physically damaged by their experiences. Suicide, divorce, drug addiction and alcoholism often came earlier than the psychological symptoms of rage, panic, anxiety, depression and emotional emptiness years later. President Jimmy Carter later granted a blanket pardon rather than an **amnesty** to draft-dodgers, excluding deserters.

It is estimated that the War cost the USA $167 billion, stimulating domestic inflation. Government institutions and fundamental national values suffered severe criticism from the US public. The strongest global superpower had been defeated and humiliated in the eyes of the world. It had been accustomed to achieving total military victory. The morale of the US Army took a long time to recover, its reputation tarnished by high-profile reports of massacres and brutality. America's very public crisis of national reputation coincided with the weakening of President Nixon's influence due to the Watergate scandal.

However, for the USA not all the effects of the war were negative. Washington realised the need to listen to the opinions of its own people, and consider the weaknesses of its Army. It realised the limits of its power and was forced to adopt a more realistic approach to intervention overseas. Congress overrode Nixon's veto of a bill to end all military operations immediately. It passed the *War Powers Act* (1973) to gain more influence over future deployment of US military forces. This attitude later developed into the **Weinberger Doctrine**. However, recent wars in the Middle East have eroded this attitude, and the present Iraq War has been portrayed as a 'second Vietnam'.

BIOGRAPHY

Pol Pot: Saloth Sar, (1928–1998)

Saloth Sar, widely known as Pol Pot, was the leader of the Cambodian Communist movement known as the Khmer Rouge, and was Prime Minister of Democratic Kampuchea from 1976–1979. Pol Pot became the de facto leader of Cambodia in mid-1975.

Amnesty

Restores those who may have been guilty of an offence to the positions of innocent persons. It includes more than a pardon, in as much as it obliterates all legal remembrance of the offence, whereas a pardon merely forgives the offence.

The Weinberger Doctrine

This developed in the light of the Vietnam War, and was first publicly disclosed in 1984 by the then Secretary of State, Caspar Weinberger, in a speech to the National Press Club. It said that:

- The USA should not commit forces to combat unless the vital national interests of the United States or its allies are involved.

- US troops should only be committed wholeheartedly and with the clear intention of winning. Otherwise, troops should not be committed.

- US combat troops should be committed only with clearly defined political and military objectives and with the capacity to accomplish those objectives.

- The relationship between the objectives and the size and composition of the forces committed should be continually reassessed and adjusted if necessary.

- US troops should not be committed to battle without a 'reasonable assurance' of the support of US public opinion and Congress.

- The commitment of US troops should be considered only as a last resort.

The Summit meeting with Mao had shown the Communist bloc to have divisions that could be exploited. Now Nixon and Kissinger set out to develop détente with the USSR to see what advantages it might bring. Above all, the 'domino theory' had proved to be flawed. Though Vietnam, Cambodia and Laos fell to communism, the other 'dominoes' in South-East Asia, such as Malaya, Singapore and Thailand, did not fall. In that respect, the whole Vietnam War seemed rather futile.

Vietnam had many hideously deformed victims of napalm and Agent Orange. The higher than average occurrence of cancers and other toxin-related diseases continues there today. Arable land and jungle was rendered uncultivable and land mines often kill farmers ploughing their fields. The Communists failed to convert their success in war to peacetime achievements. The collectivised economy could not support a rapidly growing population, and, as in Stalinist Russia, peasants preferred to sell their rice on the black market than hand it over to the government requisition officials.

Fish became scarce because of the numbers of 'Boat People' escaping Vietnam in fishing boats. In all, more than 1 million Boat People fled from Vietnam, many of them to the USA. For years, many of them lived in squalid refugee camps in the countries of South-East Asia. The mixed race children of US soldiers were outcasts from Vietnamese society and often turned to begging or prostitution. Supporters of the old regime of the South were persecuted or brain-washed in concentration camps.

Against the odds, Vietnam emerged as a strong and successful state within its region. It invaded Cambodia (Kampuchea) and set up its own puppet government there, known as the People's Republic of Kampuchea (PRK) in 1978. Vietnam successfully resisted a Chinese invasion of its own territory in 1979, proving that for them the Vietnam War had been a nationalist struggle rather than just a communist one. Communist states were shown to be willing to embark on war against each other.

ANALYSIS

Why was it so difficult to disengage from the Vietnam War?

Political factors

- Successive American governments failed to differentiate between local national movements and what they saw as the aggressive expansion of Soviet communism.

- Communist North Vietnam was unflinching in its demands for a free and unified Vietnam, as it received backing from China and the USSR.

- The USA was locked into a containment policy based on Eisenhower's 'domino theory'.

Military factors

- The US army was trained and equipped to fight conventional battles similar to those of the Second World War, rather than jungle guerrilla warfare, but had to appear to take strong action.

- US statistical data and intelligence was seriously flawed, leading the JCS and State Department to overestimate the progress and success of the war.

- The North Vietnamese and Viet Cong remained determined to hold out for victory, despite huge casualties in comparison to those of the USA. This reflected Ho's comment to the French in 1946 'You will kill ten of our men, and we will kill one of yours. Yet, in the end, it is you who will tire.' Such was the strength of Vietnamese national feeling.

- Both North and South Vietnam wished to bargain from a position of strength, so Thieu held out against accepting the demands of Hanoi, making Washington choose between support for his regime or allowing it to collapse.

Economic factors

- If the USA allowed communist control of the trade and economy of South East Asia, the resources of Japan and the Western democracies would be seriously undermined.

- The USA fell into a 'quagmire' of escalating amounts of men and money poured into a seemingly 'black hole' of corruption, defeat and inefficiency in Saigon.

Reputation and prestige

- Containment also involved the international reputation of the USA, which had been seriously damaged by the fall of China.

- Washington had a moral obligation to the Saigon government after admitting complicity in the coup which had led to the assassination of Diem, but the South was not strong enough to stand alone.

- The USA lost the moral high ground by failing to insist military governments in South Vietnam fulfilled their demands for democratic reform and reconstruction, while the North presented themselves as freedom fighters.

- Successive administrations did not wish to be seen as appeasers. They therefore worked on the assumption of a worst-case scenario, similar to that of the Second World War but nuclear-based.

- The USA fell into the 'commitment trap': after pouring vast resources of men and money into Vietnam, they could not afford to lose face by withdrawing quickly.

Media and the electorate

- US public opinion and electoral votes played an important part in undermining US military morale and in directing presidential policies at times of election campaigns.

- The media portrayed the Tet Offensive as a military failure when in fact it was a defeat for the North

ACTIVITY

Draw a mind map to prioritise the relative importance of political, military, economic, reputation and media factors.

Conclusion

At the start of 1945, the USA was the dominant superpower, proudly confident of its values of liberty, democracy and capitalism. The American public paid little attention to foreign policy, regarded Third World countries as weak and their cultures as alien. By 1975, some traditional American values had been shaken to the core of its society; people gained an insight into the problems and plights of Asian peoples, and were willing to hold out the hand of friendship to their erstwhile Cold War enemies to reach *détente*. During the intervening years, approximately 8 million people were killed in the Korean and Vietnam Wars, and a generation of US veterans had their lives shattered. Though the repercussions of the Cold War continue to this day, the recent Iraq War shows that the lessons of Vietnam have not been learned.

Skills practised

In this chapter you have:

- learned and practised the skills of source analysis, comparison and evaluation
- had to link sources to a question in order to answer it
- studied the contextual information to understand these sources and their provenance
- practised using sources and knowledge to evaluate an historical interpretation
- gained knowledge of continuity and change in US Cold War strategies in Asia, and have formed judgements on the extent of the success or failure of US policy in different Asian countries.

Bibliography

(see also Chapter 4 bibliography)

Isaacs, A. R. (1998). *Without Honor: defeat in Vietnam and Cambodia*. Baltimore: John Hopkins University Press.

Sheehan, N. (1990). *A Bright Shining Lie: John Paul Vann and America in Vietnam*. New York: Picador Press.

Walton, D. (2002). *The Myth of Inevitable US Defeat in Vietnam*. New York: Routledge.

Articles

Bickerton, I. J. 'The US and the Unintended Consequences of War', *History Today* January 2008 Volume: 58 Issue: 1

Jenkins, G. 'From Kennedy's Cold War to the War on Terror', *History Today* June 2006 Volume: 56 Issue: 6

Paris, M. l. 'The American Film Industry & Vietnam', *History Today* April 1987 Volume: 37 Issue: 4

Sanders, V. 'Turning Points in the Vietnam War', *History Review* September 2008 Issue: 61

Videos/DVDs

CNN video: *Vietnam* Ch. 11

Battlefield Vietnam video series

20th Century Battlefields series (the Tet Offensive), Dan and Peter Snow

Fog of War (2003) based on the career of Robert McNamara

Now we proceed to the final skill of synthesis.

SYNTHESIS

How far had American foreign policy in Asia changed between 1945 and 1975?

Continuity and change in the politics of American foreign policy

At the start of 1945, the USA was part of the wartime Grand Alliance alongside Great Britain and the USSR. In successive wartime conferences, Roosevelt had conciliated Stalin by underplaying his demands and glossing over his lack of commitment to democratic liberties. Towards the end of the year, it became apparent that, although Truman had kept Roosevelt's promises at Potsdam, he was not prepared to be labelled an 'appeaser.' The Truman Doctrine of 1947 marked the change to a hard-line policy of 'containment' of the Soviet-backed communist expansion so apparent in Eastern Europe. This change was partly brought about by George Kennan's 'Long Telegram' and Churchill's 'Iron Curtain' speech. At this point, the political climate changed to one of a 'Cold War'.

However, when 'containment' was applied to Asia, the Truman administration made the mistake of assuming all local nationalist movements for independence to be communist and Soviet-inspired.

Perhaps the fall of China to communism was partly the result of Roosevelt's conciliation of Stalin in allowing the USSR to liberate Manchuria at the end of the Second World War. However, its half-hearted defence of the corrupt Nationalist regime in China led to a communist perception of American weakness in Asia. Furthermore, its stubborn insistence on recognising Taiwan as the only legitimate Chinese state in the face of international acceptance of the PRC further undermined the US position in Asia. This did not prevent harsh accusations from the Republican right, and sections of the public, that the Truman administration had been infiltrated by communists. Successive presidents were aware of McCarthyism and its effects in shaping a more aggressive anti-communist foreign policy. Mao was thrown into the arms of Stalin, and, though Acheson perceived the friendship would inevitably sour, in the intervening period Sino-Soviet support for emerging communist movements gave them confidence in challenging the American presence in the region.

'Domino theory' extended containment into a new political commitment: to prop up states bordering on those with a potential to fall to communism. With little understanding of Asian cultures and the impact of generations of imperial domination, successive US administrations attempted to impose democratic and capitalist values on rural Third World

ACTIVITY

Group

a) successive US Presidents

b) US advisors

c) US 'puppets' (Chiang, Roxas, Rhee, Diem and Thieu)

by their similarity and difference in:

- policies, e.g. aggressive or defensive; military, ideological, diplomatic, economic

- attitudes, e.g. cautious or rash, independent or co-operative

- aims and achievements – balance successes with failures in pursuing their aims.

Use linked factual examples to support evaluation of continuity and change 1945–75. Use the index to help you find relevant information.

countries. In the case of Japan and the Philippines, democracy was imposed and constitutions established. However, although the USA successfully contained the spread of communism to North Korea, the South remained a corrupt and undemocratic satellite regime, which continues to this day. In Vietnam, a deeper and more determined national movement had evolved over generations of imperial domination, and successive US Presidents failed to grasp the forceful nature of their communist opposition. The perception of Orientals as an alien form of life led American officials and military forces into serious policy errors.

The complicity of the Kennedy administration in the assassination of Diem's South Korean regime was a fatal mistake. It led Johnson into the 'commitment trap', with the USA having to support successive undemocratic and corrupt military regimes. Throughout this whole period, US administrations made the fundamental error of *'going for the man rather than the movement'*, and their choice of man proved consistently flawed. It seemed that the very existence of American support gave corrupt regimes a sense of invincibility, which led them into policies of self-interest rather than democracy. Communist perceptions of these rulers, as 'running dogs' of American imperialism, weakened their local influence and gave support to their opponents.

Before long, support for corrupt local regimes had drawn the Johnson and Nixon administrations into a 'quagmire' of commitment, where escalating military and economic aid was the only way to attempt a rapid victory. Presidents realised the need for public support in order to obtain the Congress funding necessary for a policy of escalation. This drew them into justifying their policies to the US public and using the media to gain support. However, the presence of television cameras covering the Vietnam War made it impossible to hide unpalatable truths from their American and international audiences.

The 'doctrine of credibility' and 'psychological domino theory' placed the international reputation of the USA at the forefront of strategic planning under Kennedy. A shift away from Defence Department influence over foreign policy, and toward domination by the Joint Chiefs of Staff (JCS), under Kennedy, led to a more aggressive stance by Johnson, who became obsessed with Vietnam at the expense of his 'Great Society' welfare programme. Public opinion became deeply divided in 1968 when the draft was extended to students, who had previously been exempt. Foreign policy offensives were often designed to gain public support, especially at times of presidential elections. Nixon prolonged the American presence in Vietnam in the hope that the USA could establish an 'honourable' peace where South Vietnam would remain outside communist control for at least a reasonable period.

Diplomacy became secretive and manipulative during this period. CIA intelligence was often flawed, as in the case of MacArthur's assurance that there were no Chinese troops in North Korea as UN troops advanced to the Yalu River in November 1950. The USSR and China gave secret military aid to local communist regimes, and Mao's forces intervened as 'Chinese volunteers' in the Korean War. Kim Il Sung played Stalin off against Mao in order to get the support he needed to invade South Korea in June 1950. Kennedy had to balance the views of the State Department and the JCS to keep his options open, but made the mistake of publicly admitting he knew of the Generals' coup that overthrew Diem. Johnson made many public gaffes and was surrounded with conflicting advice, to the extent that he was shocked by the shift to de-escalation by the 'Wise Men' of his administration.

The reputations of individual advisers rose and fell as Congress increased its grip on foreign policy, resulting in an element of straitjacketing of Nixon. Nixon was, however, able to act secretly to take advantage of divisions between China and the USSR to eventually end the

Vietnam War. Kissinger flew secretly to Beijing to deal with Zhou and Mao to gain maximum propaganda impact when the news was beamed around the world. Nixon was to pay the price of his duplicity and corruption by his disgrace in the Watergate scandal.

Continuity and change in 'Defensive Perimeter' Strategy

At the start of 1945, the focus of American policy was on removing the threat to peace posed by Germany in Europe and Japan in Asia. Of the two, Europe was the area of concentration of American forces because of its long-standing commitment to democratic values and the special relationship between the USA and Great Britain. Though it was not the main US priority, South-East Asia's natural resources, which included petrol, tin and rubber in the Philippines, Malaya and Burma, were vital to the capitalist economies of the Western democracies. American neo-colonialism in the Philippines gave US policy makers the experience of setting up a 'model state' at the centre of a free trade area there. The reconstruction of Japan at the centre of a defensive perimeter, a chain of offshore Pacific islands, protected the free trade area in South-East Asia. The Philippines, Japan, Okinawa, the Ryukus and the Aleutians became the springboards for the limited American military forces committed to the Pacific Rim.

The unexpectedly swift collapse of Japan due to the successful development of the US atomic bomb made unnecessary the earlier agreements with Stalin, which allowed the USSR to occupy Manchuria, North Korea and some Pacific ports. Although the US monopoly of nuclear weapons held Stalin back from encroachment on Japan itself, Soviet occupation of the Kuril Islands brought its presence close to the demilitarised Japan, and threatened the island chain. The USA continued its policy of maintaining its limited Pacific forces in Japan and the offshore defensive perimeter.

The fall of China to communism in October 1949 reinforced this policy. Truman and the State Department realised that support for the CCP amongst the huge population of China had made its fall inevitable, and vowed not to commit forces to mainland Asia. The US presence in Korea was therefore one of civilian officials supported only by military advisers. Taiwan became another link in the offshore defensive perimeter, recognised by the USA as the only legitimate state of China.

A change in the geographical location of policy came when South Korea suffered a communist invasion from the North in June 1950. The USA had to turn its attention to the Asian mainland due to its commitment to contain communism. Successful maintenance of the status quo as a result of the Korean War led to the public declaration of 'domino theory' by Eisenhower in 1954. From this point onwards, the USA became committed to intervene in mainland Indochina to support any state threatened by communist encroachment. This could also be seen in some ways as a continuation of the 'Defensive Perimeter Strategy', as Indochina stood at the corner of the South-East Asian 'free trade' area and its fall to communism would build a barrier between the American-dominated offshore chain and the resources of Malaya, Burma, and Singapore.

A policy of supporting the old colonial powers in reinforcing democracy in their Asian colonies limited the geographical area of American military commitment and shared the costs of reconstruction. However, the failure of the French to control national movements in Indochina forced the USA to step in and support South Vietnam in 1954. Though the intention was to limit the area of concern to South Vietnam, the USA found itself drawn into Cambodia and Laos. South-East Asia began to affect the foreign policies of successive Presidents from Kennedy to Nixon, though the State Department continued its concern with Europe and it was the Joint Chiefs of Staff who took a dominant role in Asian policy. When the USA finally withdrew from Vietnam, Laos and Cambodia, its presence remained within the chain of military bases along the defensive perimeter.

Continuity and change in US military strategies

In August 1945, the USA held a global monopoly of nuclear weaponry and by 1949 had stockpiled 50 nuclear weapons. This underpinned a policy of military cutbacks after the end of the Second World War, when US forces were reduced to approximately one-tenth of their wartime capability. When the Truman Doctrine was announced, it appeared to some, such as George Kennan, that this would cause 'overstretch' of US forces in the fulfilment of their declared duty to contain communism. Scanty US forces had been allocated to Asia during the period up to 1949 as the priority for US attention was in Europe. Small military bases formed the front line of 'Defensive Perimeter Strategy' and Japan was de-militarised by 1949, leaving it unprotected at the outbreak of the Korean War when its remaining occupation forces left to fight in Korea.

By August 1949, the military situation had taken an unexpected turn for the worse for American policy makers. Their nuclear monopoly had been lost when the USSR successfully tested its own nuclear device at the end of August 1949 and the alliance between Communist China and the USSR had severely upset the balance of power in Asia. Even before that, in August 1946, Mao had commented that the USA was a 'paper tiger', and American forces showed their weakness in dealing with Nationalist movements in Asia. However, the development of a new generation of hydrogen and thermo-nuclear bombs escalated the Cold War and added the spectre of Mutually Assured Destruction.

It was against this intensification of the nuclear threat that the wars in South-East Asia was played out. The advance of the Communist North Koreans into the American-backed South in June 1950 made the Truman administration remilitarise Japan and issue NSC 68, to triple its defence spending. From this point onwards, both Congress and the JCS gained more influence over the conduct of foreign policy and the US troop presence in Asia increased. This could not, however, happen overnight, and in the meantime, the USA appealed to the United Nations to contribute troops to fight in the Korean War. Though the Korean War is now seen as predominantly a local war of independence, at the time it was presented as a Soviet-backed threat to the 'free world'. The USA portrayed the War as one of 'collective security', though this was a cloak for US strategies and command. The 15 countries that fought alongside US troops in Korea fought and gave their lives for democratic values and peace.

For US forces fighting within the UNC, the experience of warfare in Korea was a shock, after the comfortable lifestyle they had experienced in the period of Japanese reconstruction. The requirement to try to pursue a 'comfortable war' to keep up American troop morale and placate the general public was a consistent feature of the rest of the period. However, the Korean War was the first 'limited war' fought by American forces, and many of them, MacArthur a case in point, were unwilling to pursue limited aims. A turning point in attitude was forced onto Truman as MacArthur approached the Yalu River and confronted the Chinese: whether or not to pursue total victory, invade and liberate Communist China. Truman restrained and sacked his Supreme Commander, grasping how unrealistic this objective was, but, more importantly, recoiling from the spectre of global confrontation with the USSR.

From this point, total victory was never an option for US administrations. They found it more difficult to sell the idea of a 'limited war' to their electorate, who shunned Korean veterans on their return home. However, the national humiliation suffered at the time was a mere shadow of the deep damage to the national psyche caused by the later Vietnam War.

For the first time, US forces found themselves under-prepared for warfare against an enemy who used Mao's tactics of guerrilla warfare, the support and indoctrination of the local rural community, who were used to the terrain and climate and used both to their advantage. From this time onwards, warfare in Asia would depend less on technology than on determination and local support. Of course, secret Soviet military assistance underpinned the success of the north alongside Chinese 'volunteers'. The US fleet defended Taiwan and the increased use of airpower, especially helicopters, marked a change in methods of warfare. Militarily, the 1953 Korean demarcation line remains an area of increasing tension as the South did not sign the Peace Agreement and North Korea now has its own nuclear capability. However, the Korean War represents success in two ways. Communism was contained in North Korea, and global nuclear **Armageddon** was avoided.

Kennedy's use of the Green Berets in Vietnam represents a change in military tactics, where conventional forces tried to adapt to jungle guerrilla warfare. However, young conscripts drafted to serve in Vietnam found themselves involved in unproductive rural policies such as the Strategic Hamlets strategy, 'search and destroy' missions and the use of chemical warfare with napalm and Agent Orange. The Viet Cong proved a totally new type of foe, determined never to surrender, willing to suffer massive casualties so that 'crossover point' was never reached and replacement forces could always be raised. Strategically, the Ho Chi Minh Trail, which skirted Vietnam through Cambodia and Laos, was literally a lifeline as well as a military and economic supply route.

Successive US administrations were hampered by the views of a negative section of the public, and the fear of Chinese intervention. This held them back from waging full scale war against North Vietnam and made the Communists there not only more confident in their Offensives, but unwilling to accept any bargain which did not give them total victory. They were willing to end the fighting for nothing less than total independence for a unified Vietnam. Instead, US administrations followed a 'limited war' strategy that involved them in relentlessly bombing South Vietnam and destroying the jungle with herbicides. This was hardly an effective way to establish an independent, democratic model state that could contain the advance of communism.

Escalation of US troop numbers in Vietnam to more than half a million by 1968 reflected the 'quagmire' of pouring in more and more troops without any possibility of victory. The average US foot soldier, or 'grunt', in Vietnam, was only nineteen years old and on a year-long tour of duty. He found himself dropped by helicopter in jungle terrain, seeking an elusive enemy where there were no observable front lines. He was encouraged to kill as many Viet Cong (VC) as possible for promotion, but there was no way in which he could identify the VC enemy from the innocent civilian. It is no wonder that frustration caused a brutalisation among a generation of US foot soldiers. That they blamed their commanders is also unsurprising, as officially sanctioned battle strategies involved torture, poisoning of wells, burning of peasant homes and brutally slaughtering 'enemies'. After battles had taken place, and pitched battles were few, troops were airlifted out of the area and the VC moved back in, so success could never be judged by land gained, only by body count. Flawed statistics kept Washington pursuing the impossible goal of victory. Little attempt was made at pacification of Vietnam, and Vietnamisation of the war failed because of the weakness of the ARVN and of Thieu's regime.

Armageddon

In the Bible (Revelation 16:16.), the battle between the forces of good and evil that is predicted to mark the end of the world and precede the Day of Judgment.

Bombing of Hanoi and North Vietnamese ports had little effect on the morale of the North, which was fighting for national unity and independence and had a well-regulated regime. However, US media claims that the Tet Offensive was a defeat of US forces misled the public into demanding withdrawal when victory might have been achieved militarily. The Cold war backdrop, fear of the USSR and China prevented a more decisive war strategy, and this was only overcome by Nixon's efforts to gain *détente* with China and the USSR. Even then, it was the withdrawal of Congress funding which forced his hand.

Changes in the economics of US foreign policy

ACTIVITY

Use the following section to help you reach a supported judgement on how far US economic strategies had changed between 1945 and 1975.

In 1947 the Marshall Plan laid out the strategy of supporting democratic regimes with economic, rather than military aid. The economic aim of keeping control of the resources of South-East Asia was a fundamental basis of US policy. This policy worked well in the reconstruction of Japan and the establishment of a US satellite in the Philippines. It worked less well in relation to Nationalist China, South Korea and South Vietnam, where corrupt, undemocratic regimes pocketed the money in order to prop themselves up. They stashed much of it away in Swiss bank accounts rather than investing it to develop their Third World economies for the benefit of the local people. In contrast, their communist neighbours often made land reforms and gave communities control over local administration. Their propaganda assured the people of their economic successes and played down subsequent brutal purges. Though the fundamental idea behind US economic aid was to increase local prosperity as a bulwark against communist expansion, Japan was the only resounding success, and this was at the expense of free trade, running counter to US ideology.

Neither Korea nor Vietnam had any economic resources of interest for the USA. The hypocrisy of US support for corrupt undemocratic regimes in Taiwan, South Korea and South Vietnam played into the hands of their communist enemies in the glare of the global media. 'Dollar imperialism' was the ideological charge, but in practical terms, huge sums of money were wasted without any gain in return. There was a significant turning point when it became apparent that containment would have to involve a military commitment and NSC 68 tripled military spending. In May 1965, Congress voted $700 million for military operations in Vietnam. This became the thin end of the wedge, and overall the escalation policy in Vietnam cost the USA a total of $167 billion. Manipulation of statistics, concerning bombs dropped, offensives launched and bodies counted, maintained Congress funding by assuring Washington the War was about to be won. Only after the media portrayal of the Tet Offensive did Congress begin to refuse funding, causing de-escalation of troop numbers and eventual withdrawal from Vietnam.

Effects of its foreign policy on the international reputation of the USA

ACTIVITY

Use the following section to help you reach a supported judgement on how far US global prestige had changed between 1945 and 1975.

In 1947, Marshall Aid brought support for the USA from European democracies such as Britain and France. The United Nations attempted to implement a 'trusteeship' for Korea at the request of the USA, though this failed. In 1949 the formation of NATO laid down a framework for the consolidation of European support, and the Korean War gave this organisation a formal military structure. European countries were therefore locked into supporting the USA, for fear of losing US protection in Europe and US economic aid. This allowed the special relationship with Britain to continue despite their difference of opinion over recognition of Communist China on the UN Security Council. When military support was required, as in the case of the UN intervention in the Korean War, these countries and their allies or Commonwealth partners joined US forces in the period up to 1953.

The Geneva Accords marked a turning point in America's international recognition, as Eisenhower's administration refused to sign the agreement and Dulles refused to shake hands with Zhou Enlai. When it came to the Vietnam War, America felt the full condemnation of the international community for its escalation of the war and the brutality of its methods.

Changes in US domestic public opinion concerning foreign policy

At the start of 1945, the American public were unwilling to pay taxes for military forces in peacetime, contributing to military cutbacks and overstretch in the US role of global policeman under the Truman Doctrine. Businessmen watched the progress of foreign policy with an eye to economic profit, supporting the development of trade in South-East Asia by the 'Defensive Perimeter Strategy'. They also supported the reconstruction of the Japanese, Taiwanese and Philippines economies with preferential US trade arrangements.

The 'domino theory' was accepted by the American public, who, after 1949 had been softened up by the 'Red Scare' of McCarthyism. After harsh criticism of Truman's administration for the fall of China to Communism in 1949, the charge of 'appeaser' led successive presidents to adopt a forward policy. After the assassination of Diem in 1963, the USA had a moral obligation to support the South Vietnamese regime after the shock of Kennedy's assassination. Johnson's appeal for support in aiding Vietnam, followed by his re-election with a landslide majority in November 1963, appeared to give him a clear mandate for escalating the American presence in Vietnam. This 'commitment trap' led him down a slippery slope to the deployment of more than half a million US troops in Vietnam by 1968. By then, 46 per cent of Americans felt that the commitment in Vietnam was a mistake. This loss of support was partly caused by the shelving of the 'Great Society' welfare programme so close to his heart.

The American media played a major part in dividing the US public into supporters and opponents of the Vietnam War. Journalists and broadcasters, such as Walter Cronkite and David Halberstam reported on the live television pictures that flooded into living rooms across America. Until the time of the Tet Offensive, much of the coverage accepted the government line that the war was being won and the troops would soon be home. However, the Tet Offensive, early in 1968, was a turning point in the coverage of the War, revealing a Third World enemy seemingly effective in humiliating and defeating a global superpower. Walter Cronkite's report on the CBS News broadcast shook the confidence of Americans.

Student protests followed, coinciding with the extension of the draft to those who had previously been exempt. The cameras now portrayed brutal repression of domestic student protests on university campuses in various parts of America. Mass peace rallies undermined the unity of American Society, as Martin Luther King Jnr. linked the Civil Rights Movement to the conduct of the Vietnam War, focusing the world's attention also on the plight of black soldiers in the US forces in Vietnam. Courts martial, such as that of Calley in 1971 over the My Lai Massacre, destroyed the morale of troops and public alike and the army desertion rate soared. Finally, public pressure caused Johnson to turn down the nomination for the 1968 presidential election.

Nixon was more careful and secretive about his policies, and tried to keep his actions out of the public eye. Public criticism of his Vietnam policy played a part in his paranoia, which led to wire-tapping, dirty tricks and the Watergate scandal that finally led to his resignation to escape impeachment. We will never know if he might have prevented the fall of Saigon had he stayed in office.

ACTIVITY
Use the following section to help you reach a supported judgement on how far the influence of US public opinion had changed between 1945 and 1975.

Why did US foreign policy fail in China and Vietnam, yet have more success in Japan and South Korea?

The extent of US failure in China and Vietnam

In China and Vietnam the extent of US failure differed. There was harsh criticism of the Truman administration's weakness in preventing the fall of China, but this was of much less consequence than the deep humiliation of the withdrawal from Vietnam after 20 years of involvement. At a cost of $167 billion dollars and the deaths of approximately 4 million people, the failure in Vietnam had profound repercussions at home and abroad.

Figure 5.7   Cartoon by Bruce Shanks; first published in the *Buffalo Evening News* on 30 September 1965.

Reasons – similarities and differences

In China and Vietnam there were some similar reasons for the failure of US policy:

- Both countries had a strong and determined national movement, which the USA mistakenly saw as Soviet inspired.
- The USA failed to win over the local population, by associating themselves with tyranny rather than democracy.
- Both national movements had a charismatic and heroic leader, Mao Zedong and Ho Chi Minh.
- Neither movement was dependent on Soviet support, but both received it, when requested.
- The USA had little interest in either country other than as part of overall containment strategy.
- In both cases the corrupt local regime was weak and lacked popular support.

There were also some differences in the reasons:

- The USA failed to give adequate military aid to the Chinese Nationalists, similarly to South Korea, showing themselves to be weak and encouraging the communists. This is similar to Truman's policy in Korea, where he felt that substantial military support for Rhee might have led him to attack the North, so causing a civil war and a communist victory.
- On the other hand, in Vietnam, Johnson poured in half a million US troops and millions of dollars in aid, but still alienated the local population and encouraged the communists.
- The Truman administration recognised that the sheer size and population of China made its recovery a near impossible task, in the light of Mao's support among the peasant population. In contrast, in Vietnam, Johnson's forces failed to distinguish between neutral local peasants and Viet Cong enemies so alienating the people.

- The USA was caught up in jungle warfare against the guerrilla tactics of a ruthless and skilful enemy who could disappear across the long border with Laos and Cambodia. In China, Jiang's tactics were flawed and the US did little to help him.

The extent of US success in Japan and South Korea

In Japan and South Korea the extent of success differed. Japan is seen as a total success, with the reconstruction of a western-style society, a prosperous capitalist economy and a strong democratic constitution. In South Korea, there was no total victory, merely a restoration of the status quo at the end of the war. However, though communism was contained to the North of the DMZ, the country remained divided and unstable.

Reasons – similarities and differences

In Japan and South Korea there were some similar reasons for the success of US policy:

- Unlike Vietnam, US policy makers were prepared to make some compromises, regarding the Emperor in Japan and in relation to war strategy in the Korean War.
- The American public took little notice of US policy in either country, unlike Vietnam.
- The international community was supportive of US action in both countries, unlike Vietnam. The UN was supportive of US policy in Korea, and Truman listened to Atlee's advice in sacking MacArthur.
- Neither country tied down large numbers of US troops, unlike Vietnam.

In Japan and South Korea there were also some different reasons for the success of US policy:

- The Japanese played a much more significant role in the reform and reconstruction of their country. A truly democratic government was established, unlike that of South Korea.
- The USA built upon existing Japanese institutions and expertise to build up a prosperous economy, whereas in South Korea Rhee's corrupt regime refused democracy as support for communism was strong. In Japan, there was less popular support for communism and US purges took place successfully.
- Korea was of little interest to the USA, as part of mainland Asia, and, like China, US policy there was half-hearted until 1950. In contrast, Japan lay at the heart of US Pacific strategy within the defensive perimeter. The success of the Japanese model state influenced policy in Korea and Vietnam. The USA could not afford to allow Japan to fall to communism, or its trading partners in South-East Asia to fall to Communism like dominoes.

Now you have integrated your skills of analysis, use of knowledge and evaluation of Source content and provenance into a synthesis. You should have gained the confidence to reach your own balanced and supported judgements.

Exam Café Exam café (pages 174–190). At this point, it would be useful to undertake an audit to see what skills you are comfortable with and what you need more support in developing. Go to pages 179 and 184–185 of the Exam café and complete the activities there.

Bibliography

Adler, B (2004). *Letter from Vietnam*. Random House.

Dinh, B. (1994). *The Sorrow of War*. London: Vintage.

Exam Café
Relax, refresh, result!

Relax and prepare

Siân

I wasn't relaxed when I started the AS course because **I had a lot of problems with the sources**. The ones at GCSE were a lot easier and I couldn't see what the new ones were getting at. They didn't always start to talk about what was in the question and I used to just write down what they said. So my advice to anyone starting is not to get upset if you can't do it right away. I got the idea after a couple of weeks.

Tom

I couldn't really see what to write about the evidence bit. I would do what I did at GCSE and say they were biased (see I spelt it right this time, Mr. Davis!) or say they were from the time. But **you have to do more than this and try and link them to what you know about the time they were written and why they were written**. But how do you prepare for this? Luckily my teacher gave me a list of the sort of things to look for and kept saying that this was the skills bit. It must have worked because I got an A.

Jonny

I wasn't looking forward to revision – I'd had enough for the GCSE when I had to really shut myself away for hours. For this Sources paper I decided that I would test myself a bit more than I did at GCSE. Looking back, I think I wasted quite a bit of time then and I didn't want to do that this time, so I made sure that whatever I learnt I really knew. It was like when I was in the school play and had a lot of lines to learn, I had to make sure I knew them so I got someone to test me. **I knew that I had to make sure that I knew about the issues and where there were different views**, so I made sure that I learnt about these and when I was sure that I understood them, I tested myself.

Student tips

Maria

My teacher hadn't given us a lot of notes and I got a bit upset when I came to revise and wasn't sure what to do. I tried making notes on my notes, but got fed up with this. I talked to the others and we talked to Miss Carter. She told us to **revise round the key themes rather than just learn a lot of facts**. This was hard because we had to think quite a bit, but in the end it was better and I made sure that I covered all the 'key issues'. I was happier that I was making progress.

Susannah

When I looked back at my first work in September I realised that I had come quite a long way. My teacher warned me not to rely too much on work I'd done at the start of the course, so I went through the earlier topics quite carefully to make sure they were at the same level as what I was doing by March. I really cringed when I read my first answers again, but it was useful to think how much better I might be able to do now.

Ashleigh

I found it hard to remember all those islands of the defensive perimeter. So I tried something which worked when I was learning French last year. I stuck sticky notes up round the house and went from one island to another in order through the different rooms. My boyfriend Jake really gave me a hard time about this but I don't care – it worked for me.

Enquiry studio – Cold War in Asia

Type (a) questions – comparing two sources

There are two types of questions to prepare for – type '(a)' and type '(b)'. **Type '(a)'** needs a **comparison** of what the sources say about a given issue and also a comparison of their 'provenance'. You need to make sure that you use the relevant aspects of provenance, i.e. the authorship, audience, purpose or tone of the source. But remember, adopting a formulaic approach mentioning all aspects of provenance may lead you into irrelevance.

So it's a good idea to have a check list in your mind about the range of aspects you might compare. Remember that not all sources lend themselves to all the possible comparisons that could be made. Sometimes the date will be the key thing to look for; at others it may be the possible audience that the writer is aiming at.

None of this is new to you, but you have to bear in mind that it's easy under pressure of time to focus on what the source is saying and not give enough attention to the source *as evidence* for a key issue in the question

Have a check list

When you revise go back over your previous answers and see how many points in the list you covered, and if necessary do a better version. In the examination, remember the list and don't forget to compare each point across both the sources.

- **Date:** When were the sources written? Is there anything important to say about this? If one source were written in 1948 and another in 1950, is this significant in terms of what might have happened to change the views of the authors? Is there anything significant in the timing of the source? If sources on Korea, for instance, are being studied, would it help to know whether they were *before* or *after* the USSR tested their own atom bomb?

- **Nature:** What are they? This may be obvious, but is the source a speech, or an extract from a diary, or a memoir, or a letter. This will make a big difference to its value as evidence.

- **Audience, purpose, tone:** To whom was the source addressed? What reaction was it intended to achieve? A speech in Congress or to the Joint Chiefs of Staff may have a very different style and tone to a speech delivered on TV, addressing the nation.

- **Is the source typical?** This is sometimes the key question. LBJ has a very blunt tone in many of his private discussions with his advisers. Is his use of slang and directness typical of the man, or are his cautious words untypical, expressed when he feared high American casualties or wanted to do everything possible to win an election? Then again, if a Senator criticises Truman – is he typical of public opinion?

- **Is the source reliable?** Is this person in a position to know? Is he writing for a particular purpose which might make his view questionable? Remember that 'reliable' is not the same as 'useful'. It might be very useful to know why a source is exaggerating or distorting an event.

- **How useful is the source as evidence?** Don't forget to assess this and make a judgement about which of the sources could be more useful – they may be equally useful, but you need to discuss their pros and cons and have supporting evidence for your judgement.

Some students use the anagram 'DNA.TRU' to sum up the list. However, do be sure that this is not a mechanical process or a 'formula' as it does depend on what type of sources you are considering as to which of these aspects are more relevant.

Type (b) questions – evaluating several sources

Type (b) questions also need an evaluation of the sources, but in answering a different kind of question – assessing and judging how convincing an interpretation is. Revision should mean that you have considered the major issues beforehand. For instance, it is not a good idea to be thinking how effective American policy in Korea was for the first time in the exam. The whole revision process should have been built round thinking about major issues. For example, did Acheson underestimate what effects his National Press Club speech would have in 1950? Why did US policy makers help the Chinese Nationalists but fail to view the Viet Minh as a national movement? Was Nixon justified in claiming an 'honourable peace' at the Paris peace talks? And so on.

Your views on the major issues might have changed during the course, but you will have thought about them well in advance of the examination.

Interpreting and grouping sources

This will help you INTERPRET the sources. Make sure you are clear about what each is saying about the key issue.

In turn this will help you to GROUP the sources. It is likely some will support the interpretation in the title (let's say, that 'Domino theory' was the main reason for US military intervention in Vietnam) and some will support different interpretations, such as the need to protect the reputation of an individual President or that of the USA itself. It is much easier to comment on sources if they are grouped.

So if, say, Sources C and E generally take the view that US support for Diem was due to the fear that South Vietnam would fall to Communism without it, you have not only to explain what the sources say, but how convincing this view is. To do this you have to look at their use and reliability as evidence AND use your own knowledge of their provenance and historical context. If you know that a majority of the US public were in favour of military escalation after the Gulf of Tonkin incident, then you could say that Johnson was justified in escalating the role of the USA in the Vietnam War. If you know that Johnson had already decided to step up the war and exaggerated the incident as an excuse to intervene, then you might find the Gulf of Tonkin Resolution an unconvincing piece of evidence. Having studied the topic, it is extremely unlikely that you will have no knowledge to use, but if you cannot remember the details you must make a conscious effort to use whatever you know appropriately to answer a question.

Don't give up because you don't know very detailed facts – use what you do know.

Using your interpretation and grouping of sources to answer the question

Remember to offer a clear and supported judgement on the key issue in the title of the question. It should be an issue you've thought about before, and you need to justify your judgement by referring to the use and reliability of the sources as well as your knowledge about what they say. There is no correct answer and the judgement should follow logically from what you've said about the sources and their context throughout your answer.

So to sum up

- Don't be taken by surprise by the issue in the question – you should be prepared for it by having thought through the key issues of the topic.

- Make sure that the answer is SOURCE-led. Don't write an essay on the issue with a few references to the sources. The main task is to look at what the sources say and evaluate this by considering the nature of the sources and your own knowledge.

- Don't illustrate your own views by references to the sources. Use the views in the sources to argue, and test their validity by applying your own knowledge to them.

- Group the views in the sources – don't assume each source has only one view.

- Synthesis – offer a clear, logical judgement supported by evidence and sources. Try to control the argument and build in judgement throughout.

Show you have focused on the heart of the issue, group the sources, use their views in argument, evaluate how convincing their views are (referring to their provenance and using your knowledge) and come to a supported judgement in your synthesis (see pages 165 – 73).

Revision checklist

Refresh your memory

Key Issue One

How was the US policy of containment applied to Asia?

- How successful was US containment policy in achieving its aims in the Philippines?

- What lessons might the USA have learned from the experience of creating a 'model state' in the Philippines?

- What part did the USA play in the reconstruction of Japan 1945-50? Which strategies guided US reconstruction?

- To what extent did the US policy of Japanese reconstruction succeed in its objectives?

- Why did the USA fail to prevent a Communist victory in China in 1949?

- How justified were Truman's critics in blaming him for the fall of China?

- What was the 'defensive perimeter strategy' and why did the USA adopt it?

- How did differing expectations of this strategy contribute to conflict in Asia?

- Why and how did the USA support South Korea 1945–50?

- How did NSC 68 mark a turning point in US foreign policy?

Key Issue Two

How far did the Korean War and its origins (1950–53) change the US conduct of the Cold War in Asia?

- What were the origins of the Korean War?
- What part did Korean nationalism play in the origins of the War?
- What was US policy towards Korean nationalism up to 1945?
- Was Truman to blame for the failure to discuss Korean independence at Potsdam in 1945?
- Who was responsible for the division of Korea?
- How did the US military help Rhee to power in the south?
- How did the Soviet forces help Kim to power in the north?
- What was the role of the UN, US, USSR and China in the War?
- How did the Korean War cause disagreements between Truman and MacArthur?
- What were the military, strategic and financial consequences of the Korean War?

Key Issue Three

Why and with what results did the USA become involved in Vietnam to 1968?

- What were the reasons for the rise of the Viet Minh?
- Why was there controversy over the Geneva Agreement?
- What policy did Eisenhower follow concerning the end of French control in Indochina in 1954?
- Why and how did the NLF emerge in 1960?
- What policy did the US follow in the lead up to the fall of Diem's regime?
- What effects did Kennedy's policies have (1961–63)?
- Was Johnson's policy concerning the Gulf of Tonkin incident a miscalculation?
- What were the results of intervention to 1968?

Key Issue Four

Why did the USA fail to win the Vietnam War?

- What part did the US military play in Johnson's failure to win the war?
- What part did the Vietcong and guerrilla warfare play?
- What part did the Tet Offensive play in the US failure to win the War?
- What part did opposition to the war within the USA play in the failure to win?
- What was the impact of the Draft, Nixon and the bombing campaign?

Synthesis

- How far had US foreign policy in Asia changed between 1945 and 1975?
- Why did US foreign policy fail in China and Vietnam, yet have more success in Japan, South Korea and the Philippines?

Get the result!

The following sample questions and answers focus on Korea.

(a) Study Sources A and B.

Compare these Sources as evidence for North Korean attitudes towards civil war in Korea.

Source

(A) **The commander of the emerging North Korean revolutionary army training in China comments on plans for a Korean war of independence.**

Korea will soon be ours. At present there is not a single unit in the communist united forces now driving the Nationalists from Manchuria that does not have my forces in it. At the end of the Manchurian campaign these troops will be seasoned, trained veterans. When the Americans and Russians withdraw, we will be able to liberate Korea immediately. We will use our friends in the South to aid us. We will start a civil war we can win. We have many sympathisers and supporters in the South, ready to rise up, support and help us overthrow their hated rulers.

Choe Yong-Gon, Intelligence Report, May 1947

Source

(B) **The North Korean Foreign Minister protests at United Nations intervention in the Korean conflict.**

The civil war was started by American imperialists and their running dogs headed by Syngman Rhee. The US government is solely responsible for the tremendous calamities and hardships inflicted upon the Korean people. They supplied the traitorous bandits of Rhee with political, economic and military aid, built and trained his army. They worked out the aggressive plan for the invasion of North Korea, encouraging Rhee to start a civil war.

Pak Hon Yong, 28 September 1950

Examiner's advice

First read ALL the passages through. Don't start planning (a) before you've done this – your brain cannot work on more than one thing at a time and you should give it at least five minutes to digest all the passages. This way you get an overall feel for the paper and the ideas behind it.

Remember how much time you have for a type (a) question – not more than 20–25 minutes once you've read all five Sources.

Highlight the key issue in question (a) – North Korean attitudes towards civil war in Korea – and keep it firmly in the front of your mind when you are comparing Sources.

Make a brief plan to help you link the key similarities and differences of the Sources.

Start with relevant 'provenance'. This might be one or more of the following:

Authorship   date   nature   purpose
audience   tone

Think about:

- Who the author is.

- The nature, and date of the two Sources.

- Think why they were written and to whom.

Then look at the detail of what they say, remembering who wrote them and why.

Highlight and link key phrases of three or four words to quote and comment upon – never quote full sentences. Show how the quotes cross-reference to help you answer the question.

Remember to make a point-by-point comparison linking your ideas across both the Sources – don't write too much about any one Source but try to balance comments on both. Never write everything about each Source one after the other.

Remember that 16 out of a total of 30 marks are given for linking, comparing and contrasting the provenance and content of the Sources (A02a). There are 14 marks for showing understanding by using relevant historical context for analysis, explanation, structure and reaching a supported judgement (A01b).

Your judgement is about which of the two Sources provides the better evidence – 'better' might be judged by the completeness of a Source's content or aspects it has deliberately ignored, and the reliability or use of its content and provenance in answering the specific question.

Ahmed's answer

Both these Sources are from North Korean officials, the author of Source D is a Foreign Minister and the author of Source A later becomes the Defence Minister. However, the author of A is in command of soldiers at the time, 1947, whereas D is written three years later. They have very different views about a civil war. Source A is very much in support of starting one, while Source D seems against it because the USA have started the civil war and caused 'tremendous calamities and hardships'. **1**

So in Source D the Americans are to blame for the civil war, but in Source A the North Koreans themselves wish to do it, after the Americans and Russians have left. Source A doesn't mention Syngman Rhee but talks about the North Koreans having friends in the South who will support them. **2**

The tone of Source D is a bit extreme – America's friends are called 'their running dogs'; whereas in Source A, North Korea's friends in the South are ready to support the North and are looked upon in a much more friendly way, and the tone is much more positive. So civil war may have begun because the North and South had fallen out because of the Americans. **3**

Both Sources refer to troops. In Source A these are troops of the 'emerging North Korean revolutionary army training in China' who are involved in the Manchurian campaign, whereas in Source D the troops are Rhee's, and have been trained by the USA. It is the USA who has worked out 'the aggressive plan for the invasion of North Korea'.

Both Sources talk about 'Korea' as a country, as though it should be united. This is because of the division of the country along the 38th parallel after World War II. Both the North and South Korean governments wished to unite the divided country under their own ruler, and this is what led to civil war breaking out. In Source A, the North Koreans want Korea to be theirs, but in Source D they think the Americans want to own it, and are behind Rhee, who has started the civil war.

In conclusion, Source A is better evidence, because it doesn't use such extreme language and has more information because it was written later, after the war had started.

This is a bad error. Though Ahmed's points are fair, his comments on the differences between the natures of the two Sources as evidence for this particular question need to be developed. The overall judgement isn't convincing and is based on the date, without clear knowledge of the changed context.

Ahmed has been thinking along the right lines, by cross-referencing the Sources but could develop his ideas about their provenance and show how context links to the two Sources – without necessarily inserting factual information for its own

1 Examiner says:

This is a good start, because Emily has linked the provenance of the Sources. She has not listed points from each Source separately, but has adopted a point-by-point approach. However, his ideas could have been developed further, especially in light of the changed historical context.

2 Examiner says:

Ahmed has some perceptive ideas about civil war here, but he doesn't show clear understanding of the context of either Source. The reference to Syngman Rhee has not been explained clearly, and has not been linked to the mention of him in Source D, so the comparison fails on this point

3 Examiner says:

It is a good idea to talk about tone, but the comments on provenance aren't very well developed here, and there is little understanding shown about the significance of these comments for the question. 'May have begun' implies uncertainty. However, Ahmed does try to link to the question at the end.

sake. The mark scheme will give him credit for using some ideas on provenance as well as content; it will give some credit for analysis and understanding, but his marks for contextual knowledge will not be high. He is on his way to a good answer, so let's see an improved version

Ahmed's improved answer

Both these Sources are from North Korean officials; the author of Source D is a Foreign Minister and the author of Source A later becomes the Defence Minister. However, the author of A is in command of soldiers at the time he writes, 1947, whereas D is written three years later after the outbreak of the Korean War. Choe Yong-Gon, in A, has been gaining experience in fighting in the Chinese Civil war, hoping to be able to use his army to unite Korea in a civil war against the South when the troops of the USA and USSR have left Korea. Therefore he supports the idea of starting a civil war at the time he is writing, because he thinks the North will win. In Source D, Pak Hon Yong is protesting about the USA and the United Nations, whom he is addressing, having got involved in the Korean Civil War which had been started in June 1950 by the North, as planned in A. This evidence is missing from Source D, so it is incomplete and selective in its view.

Pak Hon Yong, in D, is unreliable when he says that the civil war was started by the Americans, as North Korea had started it with Soviet and Chinese support, by crossing the 38th parallel in June. In September, when he is writing, it looks as though the North may lose, so he is no longer in favour of the war, as it is no longer a civil war, but has become an international one. Source A is very much in support of starting a civil war, while Source D is against it and blames the USA for starting it and causing 'tremendous calamities and hardships'. ①

The tone of Pak Hon Yong, in Source D, is emotive, with the intention of making you feel angry about US actions, unlike the optimistic style of Choe Yong-Gon in Source A. In D, America's friends are called 'their running dogs' and 'traitorous bandits' and are blamed for aggression, whereas in Source A, it is the North and their 'many sympathisers and supporters' in the South who are going to liberate Korea. They do not seem to consider planning a civil war to be an act of aggression but of liberation. The difference in tone is partly because Source A is an internal Intelligence report, whereas Source D is propaganda for a United Nations audience, with the purpose of trying to persuade the UN to end its support for the USA in fighting against North Korea. The arguments against the USA lack balance and accuracy. Source A suggests that many South Koreans hate their rulers and will support the North in a civil war to unite the country, but there is no mention of whether they have done so in Source D. ②

Both Sources refer to troops. In Source A these are troops of the 'emerging North Korean revolutionary army training in China' who are involved in the Manchurian campaign during

① Examiner says:

This has kept the good point-by-point comparison, but has extended the analysis using solid knowledge of historical context to help analyse, explain and link to the question. The reliability of Source D has been discussed and linked to the question.

② Examiner says:

Now there is clear understanding and development of the tone, nature and purpose of the Sources, integrated with comments on the content of the Sources. Ideas have been developed well, using historical context.

the Chinese Civil War, gaining the experience to help them start a civil war in Korea, whereas in Source D the troops are Rhee's, and have been trained by the USA, who have started the civil war. It is the USA who have worked out 'the aggressive plan for the invasion of North Korea', and the civil war has developed into a broader conflict which will be difficult for the North to win, so they are angry enough to appeal to the UN to try and stop support for the US position. There are things left out – for example they ignore support given to the North by China and the USSR. Both Sources talk about 'Korea' as a country, as though it should be united. This is because of the division of the country along the 38th parallel after World War II. **3** Both the North and South Korean governments wished to unite the divided country under their own ruler, and the only way to do this seems to be by starting a civil war, so the North welcomes this as they think they will win in Source A. In Source A, the North Koreans want Korea to be theirs, but in Source D they think the Americans want to own it, and are behind Rhee, who has started the civil war. This is unreliable, as the North Koreans were the ones who started the civil war, because they did not think the USA would intervene and they would quickly win.

In conclusion, Source A is better evidence for views on civil war in Korea, because in Source D, though civil war is mentioned, the war has become much broader due to UN intervention. Source D is unreliable propaganda which misrepresents what has happened, whereas Source A is confidential and more reliable about plans for a civil war.

There is a more solid judgement here about the relative usefulness and reliability of the two Sources.

In conclusion

The second answer has developed analysis, clear focus and explanation. It is consistently comparative and uses both provenance and content. Contextual knowledge has been integrated and used to help in answering the question. It would gain Level I marks for AO1, use of historical context, explanation, analysis and judgement, as it adopts a point-by-point approach and reaches a reasoned judgement. The comparison of Source content is by cross-reference of similarity and difference. The comparison of provenance is integrated, and includes the nature of the sources, their intention, their date and their audience; their completeness, reliability and usefulness. This would be a Band I answer when assessed for AO2.

Note: It is not necessary to know who Choe Yong-Gon and Pak Hon Yong are – the key point is that one is a military commander, the other a Defence Minister. More important is that the nature, audience and purpose of the Sources are different and the context has changed their perspective.

3 Examiner says:

This is now a much better section with developed comments on audience and purpose, and clear use of context.

(b) Study all the Sources.

Use your own knowledge to assess how far the Sources support the interpretation that the USSR was mainly to blame for the outbreak of the Korean War in June 1953.

Sources

(A) **The commander of the emerging North Korean revolutionary army, training in China, comments on plans for a Korean war of independence. He became North Korea's first Minister of National Defence.**

Korea will soon be ours. At present there is not a single unit in the communist united forces now driving the Nationalists from Manchuria that does not have my forces in it. At the end of the Manchurian campaign these troops will be seasoned, trained veterans. When the Americans and Russians withdraw, we will be able to liberate Korea immediately. We will use our friends in the South to aid us. We will start a civil war we can win. We have many sympathisers and supporters in the South, ready to rise up, support and help us overthrow their hated rulers.

Choe Yong-Gon, Intelligence Report, May 1947

(B) **A Russian journal records a conversation between Stalin and Kim Il Sung, where he explains the reasons why he has decided to support Kim's invasion of South Korea.**

Firstly, the victory of the Chinese revolution, the alliance signed between the USSR and the PRC and the USSR's own atomic bomb.

Secondly, the obvious weakness of the reactionaries. The shameful defeat of America's intervention into Chinese affairs and Western troubles in south-east Asia. The inability of the South Korean regime and its American masters to improve the social, economic, and political situation in South Korea.

Thirdly, the dishonest, untrustworthy and arrogant behaviour of the United States in Europe, the Balkans, the Middle East. Its decision to form NATO reveals that America is no longer a partner, but an enemy. The Soviet Union cannot bind itself any longer to such an enemy.

Fourthly, the aggressive designs of the South Korean regime. It is determined to launch an attack on the North, sooner or later. It is important to forestall this aggression.

Russian journal, Moscow, April 1950

(C) **A Soviet General reports a conversation between Mao, Zhou Enlai and the North Korean ambassador to China, Li Chou-yuan, about Kim Il Sung's intentions.**

Mao turned toward Li as if asking when Kim intended to begin the unification of Korea. Without waiting for an answer, he said that if Kim intended to begin military operations against the south in the near future, a meeting between Kim and Mao should be unofficial. He saw the unification of Korea by peaceful means as impossible, only military means would work. There was no need to be afraid of the Americans. They would not enter a third world war for such a small territory. Kim reported to me that he wishes to begin the operation in June.

Shtykov, telegram to Moscow, 12 May 1950

Sources

D The North Korean Foreign Minister protests at United Nations intervention in the Korean conflict.

The civil war was started by American imperialists and their running dogs headed by Syngman Rhee. The US government is solely responsible for the tremendous calamities and hardships inflicted upon the Korean people. They supplied the traitorous bandits of Rhee with political, economic and military aid, built and trained his army. They worked out the aggressive plan for the invasion of North Korea, encouraging Rhee to start a civil war.

Pak Hon Yong, 28 September 1950

E The US Secretary of State recalls the reasons for the North Korean attack on South Korea in June 1950.

It seemed the North Korean attack had been mounted, supplied and instigated by the Soviet Union, and that it would not be stopped by anything short of force. If South Korean forces proved unequal to the job, only American military intervention could do it. This was clearly an open challenge to our internationally accepted position as the protector of South Korea, an area of great importance to the security of American-occupied Japan. Therefore, we could not accept the conquest of this important area by a Soviet puppet.

Dean Acheson, *Present at the Creation: My Years in the State Department*, 1969

Examiner's advice

1. Group these sources and look carefully at the brief introductions – this will give you a starting point.

2. Make sure you really deal with the different views and reach your own clear judgement.

3. Make sure you use ALL the Sources.

4. Source E is different as it is written with hindsight and may wish to enhance the author's reputation or justify his actions.

5. Don't worry if you feel you don't have enough specialist knowledge – say you don't know anything about Japanese or Korean geography – this doesn't matter, but try to use the relevant contextual knowledge you do have and apply it to the sources. You might question whether D is exaggerating for instance about Rhee being a puppet. You might question, in B, given the nationalist nature of Mao's revolution, whether the alliance between China and the USSR is strong or weak. You might know quite a bit to comment on the views in E, but don't worry if you can't comment on everything.

Sara's answer

Source E suggests that the USSR was to blame for the Korean War. The source is written by the US Secretary of State and he believes that the war was provoked by the Soviets. 'Supplied and instigated by the Soviet Union.' The Soviets supplied North Korea with everything that it would need for a war, tanks, troops and military advisors. The Source suggests that by supplying the North, it made Kim confident that they could invade the south as the Americans hadn't supplied the South for a war. **①**

Sources B and D however, suggest that it was the USA's fault that the Korean War arose. Source B is written by Stalin, telling Kim Il Sung why he decided to support him in invading the South. Stalin says that America had become an enemy because of its own actions. 'Its decision to form NATO reveals that America is no longer a partner, but an enemy.' The Soviets felt like the Americans were leaving them out and weren't invited. NATO was a military alliance, however it wasn't a threat to the Soviets as they defended not attacked and so this reason that Stalin has given isn't very convincing. **②**

The Soviets realise that the Americans are struggling for popularity as they aren't managing to improve the situation in the South: 'inability of the South Korean Regime and its American masters to improve social, economic and political situations in South Korea.' The Americans kept the Japanese ways of running the country which was a bad plan as the Japanese were an enemy of the Koreans due to the way that they treated them. **③**

Source D is written by the North Korean Foreign minister who is protesting at the UN intervention in the Korean conflict. The source says that the Americans were 'solely responsible' for the war. The source suggests that the Americans were trying to encourage and help Rhee to start a civil war, 'supplied the traitorous bandits of Rhee with political, economic and military aid, built and trained his army.' The Source uses emotive language such as 'running dogs' as the minister is trying to persuade the UN not to support the USA and intervene. Therefore this source is quite biased. **④**

It is also possible that it was Kim and Mao that was to blame for the Korean War. Kim had played Mao and Stalin against each other in order to be supported in invading the south. Mao wanted an unofficial meeting with Kim to talk about the invasion before it went through. Mao can be seen as encouraging Kim 'no need to be afraid of the Americans.' Mao didn't think that the Americans would bother to enter the war just for Korea. **⑤** Mao thought that the only way to unite it was to fight – 'unification of Korea by peaceful means as impossible, only military means would work.' Rhee could be seen as being to blame for the Korean War as he was very keen on making the whole of Korea united under 'democracy'. In source B Stalin says that the reason he decided to support Kim was because he thought that the South was going to launch an attack on

---

1 **Examiner says:**

It's good to start with a brief introduction grouping Sources according to their view, for or against. Sara has grasped the key view in Source E and linked it to the question, using knowledge to extend her explanation.

2 **Examiner says:**

Here is an attempt to evaluate the reliability of content of Source B, but it isn't linked to the question.

3 **Examiner says:**

This is a valid use of knowledge in relation to Source content, but the reference to Source D is implicit rather than explicit, and the link to the question has not been made.

4 **Examiner says:**

The content of the Source is used for reference, and Sara has explained what it shows rather than evaluating its view. There is comment on provenance and reliability but it is not used to answer the question.

5 **Examiner says:**

This uses Source C without explicitly mentioning it. There is only a hint of evaluation but there is use of relevant historical context.

the South very soon: 'Aggressive designs of the South Korean regime. It is determined to launch an attack on the North, sooner or later.' In source D Rhee is described as a 'traitorous bandit'. Hodge and Rhee introduced rice quotas and crushed People's Committees which made the public dislike the government they were being ruled under. Rhee also had US economic and political aid, which made the South more of a threat. **6**

Overall I think that the USSR was to blame for the Korean War as they supplied the North with everything it would need to invade the South, whereas the Americans only gave economic and political aid. **7**

The conclusion does not focus clearly on 'blame'. The content and context of the Sources has been used, but the only provenance mentioned is that of Source D, and its unreliability is not taken into account in the conclusion. The answer scores low Level III for AO2, with a limited attempt to evaluate the Sources, but some analysis and use of them. There is limited coherence or integration of the Sources into an overall argument to assess the view. Though rather mechanical, it does more than merely reference the Sources one after the other. The answer would achieve low Level II for AO1, for use of contextual knowledge and understanding and for considering different views. It does create a sense of different views, but the attempt at a judgement is weak, so only just above Level III.

Kate's answer

1 To some extent, the sources support the view that the USSR was mainly to blame for the outbreak of the Korean War. Source E completely blames the USSR, suggesting that 'the North Korean attack had been mounted, supplied and instigated by the Soviet Union', talking of it as an extension of the Cold War, and of Stalin's expansionist policies — 'that was clearly an open challenge'. However, this is an extract from Dean Acheson's memoirs, the Secretary of State at the time of the Korean War. The defensive perimeter strategy was Acheson's policy; he wouldn't have wanted to admit that it had been a mistake, or that America was in any way to blame for the Korean War. Acheson, speaking from the later date of 1969, is almost justifying his actions, wanting history to blame the Soviets. This means the source is possibly biased, and we cannot completely trust its blame of the USSR. **2**

B and A do not so openly blame the USSR, but obviously implicate them, especially B. Source B reveals that Stalin 'decided to support Kim's invasion of South Korea', and contains Stalin firmly portraying America as an enemy 'dishonest, untrustworthy and arrogant' that the USSR could not 'bind itself any longer to'. This confirms the suspicions in E that the USSR wished to bring down America, and saw them as a threat, not an ally as they had previously. Stalin speaks from a position of power, implying that America is weak, using examples such as 'the victory of the Chinese revolution' — China's newly Communist status in 1949. Stalin knew at this time that America did not want to

6 Examiner says:

The ideas here are focused and relevant, but could do with more development and evaluation. Overall, the paragraphs tend to stand alone rather than create a coherent answer to the question. The Soviets' reasoning for why they supported Kim is very poor. NATO was not a threat to the Soviets as NATO defended not attacked.

7 Examiner says:

US aid to whom?

1 Examiner says:

It would be a good idea to start with a brief introduction grouping the Sources by view.

2 Examiner says:

This is an excellent start. Kate has integrated her comments on the content and provenance of Source E, using it clearly to support the interpretation in the question. She has chosen the most pertinent aspects of provenance. The reliability and use of the Source has been evaluated.

4 **Examiner says:**

A developed analysis of provenance has been achieved, with clear evaluation of the use and reliability of the Sources in answering the question. A foundation has been laid to link with a later comment on Kim Il Sung for an alternative view. A range of ideas on provenance have been developed and there is good balance. Kate shows sophisticated attention to detail.

5 **Examiner says:**

This is an excellent paragraph. The Sources have been accurately grouped for argument and contrasted with E. The provenance of the Sources has been evaluated - their authorship, tone and purpose. Well-chosen factual knowledge has been used to evaluate the reliability of the content of the grouped Sources, and the evaluative comments have been balanced.

become involved in mainland Asia, preferring to maintain the defensive perimeter in the Pacific, and seems to be using this knowledge against them to expand communist influence. 3

However, as with E, there are problems with the sources' reliability, mainly because of the Cold War context. Both sides wish to appear best, and the leaders of both sides are obviously going to be the most biased. We also know that Kim Il Sung played off Mao and Stalin against each other in an attempt to get support for the invasion (something that puts some of the blame on him, as will be discussed later) meaning that Stalin is even more likely to want to seem powerful, especially if talking to Kim, and could be lying, making the source less reliable. On the other hand, this is an objective report of a conversation — those things were said, so even if Stalin was lying, he still agreed to support Kim, and can therefore be blamed. Source A implicates the USSR is to blame also, in a way: 'when the Americans and Russians withdraw, we will be able to liberate Korea immediately'. This line from an Intelligence Report obviously puts more blame on Kim, but also suggests that if occupying forces had not withdrawn from Korea so soon, in 1949, or had handled the handover better, then there would not have been an invasion. 4

5 However, this means that A also implies that America was to blame for the outbreak of the Korean War, as do other sources. B and D both openly blame America. Stalin talks about America's 'obvious weakness' in defending and improving South Korea, and D speaks strongly — 'the civil war started by American imperialists and their running dogs'. This is a completely opposite view to Acheson's, as is to be expected from the authorship. However, these sources have different tones to the others — they are more impassioned and emotive, which could lead the reader to doubt their objectivity. D is a protesting speech, given in front of the UN, attempting to persuade the members to side with North Korea, using emotive language such as 'dogs' and 'bandits'. Pak Hon Yong would never suggest that North Korea, or the USSR were to blame for the war, even if they were, so we cannot entirely trust Source D. To back this up, D is also factually unconvincing in some respects. For example, Yong says that the US government 'built and trained his [Rhee's] army', when in actual fact the only army being trained in Korea was in North Korea — as mentioned in Source A, America, keen to prevent a civil war and its inevitable costs, left no military power behind when it left South Korea. These factual inaccuracies are also present in Source B. Stalin blames the US for forcing an invasion, talking about 'the aggressive designs of the South Korean regime'. Furthermore, Stalin uses the formation of NATO in 1949 as a reason to be an enemy of the USA — 'its decision to form NATO reveals that America is no longer a partner, but an enemy', illustrating that he felt betrayed and threatened by America, leading to him attempting to fight back. However, this is unconvincing. For one thing, NATO was a defence treaty concerning Europe, and Stalin using it in a point about Asia seems to be merely a way for him to justify his actions

and make himself look good, as he needed to in the Cold War period when this was written.

Although Source A does implicate America and Russia in the outbreak of civil war in Korea, the person who seems most to blame for it is, of course, Kim Il Sung, leader of North Korea, and the person in charge of this 'North Korean revolutionary army training in China'. The very fact that he has commissioned this army suggests that he planned an attack on South Korea – the report even says 'Korea will soon be ours'. This is very incriminating evidence against Kim, as is C, reporting that Kim 'wishes the operation to begin in June'. This 'unofficial meeting' between Kim and Mao is also evidence of Kim's craftiness, executed in almost playing off Mao and Stalin, two powerful Communist leaders, against each other, in order to obtain support for an invasion. All these things indicate that Kim was very eager for an invasion. **6**

Source C could also be said to implicate Mao, and China, as could Source A. Mao wishes to be involved in Kim's invasion, and says that he 'saw the unification of Korea by peaceful means as impossible', so obviously supported it, also evident in the fact that he let the army train in China – revealed in Source A. It would be in the interests of China to have influence in a united, communist Korea – Korea is on the border of Manchuria, which was in the control of the USSR, and Mao wished to gain more control in Asia. Therefore, it is safe to say that China may be partly to blame for the outbreak of the Korean War, at least because they gave support to the movement. **7**

Finally, Rhee is also blamed by some Sources for the Korean War – B and D. In both he is blamed for incompetent and corrupt leadership, B mentions 'the inability of the South Korean regime', and D calls Rhee's government 'traitorous bandits', as well as implying that Rhee was aggressive, and 'encouraged to start a civil war'. Both sources have their problems, and bias, as I have mentioned before, so they cannot be taken as completely accurate, but their points about the 'social, economic and political situation in South Korea' are partly valid. Rhee's government did not improve the state of the country, keeping Japanese systems of government, and worsening the economics by introducing rice rationing. This could have led to people being more likely to welcome communism, however these changes were influenced by the USA military advisers in Korea, and can therefore also be blamed on them. **8**

In conclusion, it is difficult to attribute blame completely to the USSR from the sources, although they do illustrate Kim's seeming determination to invade, and the support that the USSR gave. They support this interpretation, and things that could incriminate the USA are not mentioned, for example the division of Korea at the 38th parallel.

The judgement is a little uneven, and ends with an unfinished note. If taken further, it might have concluded that there is a case for the USA being equally or more to blame than the USSR.

6 Examiner says:

Here Sources A and C have been linked to provide a clear argument attributing blame to the North Korean leader, Kim Il Sung. Contextual knowledge has been integrated and used well to extend the argument and evaluate the Sources. The question has been kept very sharply in mind throughout and a mini-judgement reached.

7 Examiner says:

This paragraph links Sources A and C to argue a case for China bearing some of the blame. Knowledge has been used to qualify and validate the Sources, and a mini-judgement reached.

8 Examiner says:

This paragraph links Sources B and D to argue a case for Syngman Rhee being to blame. Provenance is again used very effectively to evaluate the reliability and use of the sources in argument. The coherence of the answer is strengthened and balanced by referring back to the argument that the USA was to blame in supporting Rhee.

Kate's answer in terms of the Assessment Objectives

A01 Use of historical knowledge, explanation, analysis and judgement. Kate's answer reaches Level I. It has excellent use of pertinent contextual knowledge. Note that knowledge is not comprehensive, but it is extremely well used, and there is a high level of understanding. The writing is clear, fluent and well-organised, with good balanced structure and control of the material. The issues are clearly understood and views are solidly analysed and evaluated. However, the overall judgement is a little open.

A02 Analysis and evaluation of Sources; integration of the Sources with knowledge in evaluating an interpretation. There is a sophisticated understanding of the way to criticise evidence. There is a sustained analysis and evaluation of the grouped Sources with cross-reference of both their provenance and content. They are consistently linked to the question. There is very sharp focus on the key issue and the interpretation in the question. Knowledge and Sources have been integrated to evaluate and balance a range of arguments. There is sustained cross-reference and coherence throughout. Level I.

Index

Index is in alphabetical order, except for subheadings, which are in chronological order. Page numbers in bold show material of major significance. Page numbers in italics denote illustrations. Headings in italics show documents, unless otherwise stated.